GLUED TO GAMES

How Video Games Draw Us In and Hold Us Spellbound

Scott Rigby and Richard M. Ryan

New Directions in Media
Robin Andersen, Series Editor

 PRAEGER

AN IMPRINT OF ABC-CLIO, LLC
Santa Barbara, California • Denver, Colorado • Oxford, England

Library of Congress Cataloging-in-Publication Data

Rigby, Scott.
   Glued to games : how video games draw us in and hold us spellbound / Scott Rigby and Richard M. Ryan.
      p. cm.—(New directions in media)
   Includes bibliographical references and index.
   ISBN 978-0-313-36224-8 (hard copy : alk. paper)—ISBN 978-0-313-36225-5 (ebook)
1. Video games—Psychological aspects. 2. Video games—Social aspects. I. Ryan, Richard M. II. Title.
   GV1469.3.R55   2011
   794.8—dc22   2010040752

ISBN: 978-0-313-36224-8
EISBN: 978-0-313-36225-5

15   14   13   12   11   2   3   4   5

This book is also available on the World Wide Web as an eBook.
Visit www.abc-clio.com for details.

Praeger
An Imprint of ABC-CLIO, LLC

ABC-CLIO, LLC
130 Cremona Drive, P.O. Box 1911
Santa Barbara, California 93116-1911

This book is printed on acid-free paper (∞)

Manufactured in the United States of America

To our wives Jasmine and Miriam, who at least pretend to believe that the many hours we spend playing video games are for the purpose of research.

CONTENTS

ACKNOWLEDGMENTS

This work was a collective effort, and we are very appreciative to all who helped in its completion. In particular, we would like to thank Andy Przybylski, Nicholas Murray, and Edward Deci for their important and ongoing contributions to our research on the psychology of video games. We also wish to acknowledge Shannon Hoefen, the members of the Motivation Research Group at the University of Rochester, and Drew Hanson, along with the other crack staff members at Immersyve, all of whom provided support and feedback that helped us hone our views on video games. We also offer a sincere thanks to Will Ryan for his help in reviewing and preparing this manuscript. Finally, we have especially appreciated and benefitted from the many players who have participated in our studies and given us an open look into the direct experience of games and virtual worlds.

INTRODUCTION

Chances are, either you play video games or someone close to you does. In the United States alone, more than 100 million people play video games regularly, many opting to spend time gaming over other forms of leisure entertainment such as TV and movies. And unlike those watching a rerun of Seinfeld, video game players are often yelling, jumping, sweating, or otherwise so engrossed in what they are doing they wouldn't notice if the roof collapsed (unless it unplugged the game in the process). It's not just that the video game industry has, in just a couple of decades, become a dominant form of entertainment—it's that it has done so in such a loud, entrancing, and often violent way. Games have ascended to a position of cultural prominence with much sound and fury.

The spectacular audiovisuals games present, and their strong ability to draw and hold our attention, have fueled passionate positions about the psychological impact of gaming. It is a controversial subject that sparks small skirmishes on a daily basis between parents and children, husbands and wives, and in millions of homes as the allure of games competes with life's other requests (and demands) for our time. And as the industry grows, it's hard to keep track of all of the experiences that games offer us. Thirty years ago, there were only a few types of games and ways to play them. Now there are many different platforms—consoles like the Xbox and PlayStation, handheld devices such as the Nintendo DS, personal computers, and even mobile phones.

On a broader level, because many of the most popular games contain very violent content and are so powerful in occupying our time, battles are playing out between social scientists, politicians, parents, and the video game industry over the possible negative influence of video games, actively leading to regulation and legislation in countries around the world. Simultaneously, proponents of games make the case that the powerful motivational pull of games can have meaningful positive effects on players and can be harnessed to enhance education, training, and the development of social and leadership skills. In short, there are lots of perspectives to evaluate when trying to come to an understanding of the psychology of games.

Compounding this challenge is the industry's relative youth: The video game phenomenon is only a few decades old, and despite its dominance, we just haven't had time to get our heads around the psychology of gaming. Simply put, we don't yet fully understand games. As such, the arguments being wielded on all sides of "game psychology" are usually speculative attempts to hit a moving target—detractors and proponents alike focus only on narrow aspects of games to make their points, fortifying isolated islands of knowledge but leaving us with little terra firma in understanding games' basic appeal and impact. One month we'll read about a new study of shoot- 'em-up games that demonstrates that "violent games make players feel violent," and the next we'll hear about a study of arcade style games demonstrating that "games increase visual-motor skills." Proponents and detractors of video games selectively point to these data to make their case, while most game players just want to enjoy their games in peace. Overall, there is little meaningful dialogue about what *everyone* can agree on: Games have an incredible motivational pull.

Over the years that we've watched the growth of gaming, we've increasingly felt an understanding of its motivational power was important. The palpable love people have for video games is clearly not going to change. If we want to understand the deeper psychology of games, there is no better place to begin than the strong motivations they provide.

As motivational psychologists who ourselves play and enjoy video games, we also think that it's important to note that we don't carry a torch either way for gaming as good or bad. Debating all sides of the issue ourselves in our conversations and research has given us a respect for the complexity of gaming and its potential for experiences that are both good *and* bad. More importantly, we believe that the strength of participation in games and virtual worlds by so many—young and old, male and female, rich and poor—demonstrates that gaming deserves to be understood through psychological models that can help discern both its promise and its peril. Having a clearer sense of games' emotional appeal and motivational pull will provide a better vantage point for exploring how the fundamental dynamics of games can manifest both positively and negatively.

This book is the result of years of research that focuses on the satisfactions and consequences of video games. Deeper still, it is rooted in a broad theory of human motivation, *self-determination theory*, that is the basis for hundreds of research projects worldwide focusing on people's motivation and well-being across many arenas of life. On this foundation, we outline a basic motivational language for gaming psychology that we hope will be useful for both experts and laypersons alike: for parents who are deciding how to regulate gaming, for researchers who are working to understand it, for the developers who are creating tomorrow's games, and for the policy makers who are wrestling with issues such as game violence and addiction. This aspiration to speak to such varied audiences has encouraged us to make the language of this book accessible to nonexperts, while at the same time presenting ideas of value to those engaged with gaming professionally (such as developers and researchers). Because we illustrate points through individual stories, some of which are ours personally, we will sometimes adopt the first person in the discussion. That first-person account may be from the experience of either author, but because it's the story itself that matters, we focus there rather than on tracking whose story it is.

Throughout this book, we also use examples from current games to illustrate our ideas and make them accessible to the reader. We do this with full certainty that before the ink is dry, there will be new blockbuster games on the market that didn't exist as we wrote this book. We also see the area of game psychology to be developing very quickly, with lots of interesting new work coming out each year that is relevant to the question of what keeps us glued to games. In order to provide an ongoing resource, we have a companion Web site, http://www.gluedtogames.com, which provides additional examples of the principles discussed, along with supplemental material. Our goal for the site is to provide new game examples and research that, as of the writing of this book, do not yet exist.

Nonetheless, even though the examples in the pages ahead will become quaint with time, we believe the principles of game psychology we describe will persist in their value and applicability. Already we have seen this across the years we've been studying games directly, as well as in our general work in human motivation over several decades. As game design and technology inevitably evolve, we expect the fundamental principles of motivation will remain sharp and relevant.

Our hope is that the chapters ahead will give all readers a greater appreciation for this motivational power of games and a clearer understanding of their strong appeal both today and long into the future.

Chapter 1

THE EMOTIONAL EXPERIENCE OF GAMES TODAY

The other day while out walking in the forest, the opportunity to be a hero was thrust upon me. As I was looking skyward, admiring the pattern of sunlight streaming through the trees, I heard sounds of distress nearby: A fellow hiker and a wild animal had surprised each other and their first meeting was not going well. I ran over to where he was flailing at the beast, and together we managed to fight it off. There was palpable gratitude from the hiker, and I had a deep sense of success and altruistic pride. I mean, we all daydream about whether we will take action if the circumstances call for it, but how often does day-to-day life give us the opportunity to do so?

Who knows how long I could have savored that moment of victory if the doorbell had not rung. Exhilaration was eclipsed by my worry that I didn't have enough singles to properly tip the pizza guy.

Yes, as you may have guessed, my story actually took place in a digital forest, and not a molecular one—I was in the "virtual world" of an online video game. Were you witness to my feat of courage, you would have seen me sitting on a desk chair, slightly hungry, staring intently at my computer screen. There was no real forest, no real wild animal, and ultimately no real danger. The game was merely a harmless distraction until dinner arrived, presumably no more psychologically meaningful than watching a rerun of *Gilligan's Island*. Many people (particularly my family) might even say that I'd show more *real* courage if I had spent the time finally taking out the garbage. It has been sitting there a frighteningly long time.

But hold on a second. The place I had my little adventure may not have been real, but what about my experiences? Walking in the virtual forest, I did appreciate the sunlight through the trees. I can conjure an image of it now in a way that is quite satisfying to remember. The virtual person that I saved was also "real" in the sense that it was controlled by another person, a fellow player sitting at his computer somewhere in the world. His expression of gratitude was certainly real (his virtual death would not have been without some consequence), as was the feeling of altruism I had at coming to his rescue. So if such a variety of experiences can feel quite genuine, perhaps it's premature to dismiss video games as merely distractions. Maybe respecting how today's games provide such experiences can help explain why gaming is such a growing global phenomenon.

Simply put, video games seem to have the ability to not just *tell* us a story, but to let us actively *live* it, making opportunities for bravery, heroism, and gratitude not the exception, but the norm. That's pretty powerful stuff.

Of course, I suspect many are already bristling at the idea that this book will romanticize games in such a way. After all, most video games available today aren't about altruism, but about shooting people, blowing things up, or usually both. Games are filled with violent content that require gamers to act violently (and often selfishly). Sometimes players are rewarded for behaving in a downright antisocial manner through assault, extortion, and theft. More troubling is that the industry wouldn't keep building these games if they weren't appealing to so many people. Why are otherwise kind, successful folks (kids and adults) gleefully running around virtual worlds with a sawed-off shotgun? Is it really the violence that is motivating them to play or are there deeper things they are enjoying about these games (perhaps less insidious things) that draw them in?

These are the sorts of questions that face the millions of people today trying to understand the ascendency of games and the psychology of gaming. Whether you picked this book up because you are a parent or teacher of a gamer, the spouse of a gamer, or a gamer yourself, getting a better understanding of what draws us to games and how they satisfy us is a necessary first step in identifying when they are providing meaningful experiences, as well as when gaming is interfering with health and happiness.

GROWING PAINS IN THE GAMING REVOLUTION

Regardless of your feelings about video games, they have come of age. Daily, tens of millions of video game players worldwide come together from opposite ends of the Earth to collaborate and compete in online games. Despite its young age, revenue from the game industry is running neck and neck with the film industry, with some suggesting it has already passed Hollywood in size. Already more than one in three people in the United States play video games, with similar statistics in countries around the world. Gaming is on a roll.

Because it's so prevalent, more and more questions are being asked about gaming. Is it addicting? Can it be a learning tool? Is it just harmless fun? Never before has there been such a strong interest in understanding the motivational pull of games, their potential ills and benefits, and the psychological and health-related outcomes of playing them. To reach accurate conclusions on all of these issues, we need to have a handle on the basic psychological appeal video games clearly possess.

The need to understand games grows stronger as we see the boundaries between virtual worlds and the real world starting to blur. Consider the following:

• The distinction between virtual money and real money is starting to fade. Hundreds of millions of real transactions between the two are taking place worldwide, including the ability to exchange virtual currency for real legal tender. In some cases, the money you earn within the virtual world can be directly withdrawn as cold, hard cash from a nearby ATM. Simply put, it is now the case that designing and selling your own line of digital furniture for someone's digital house can help pay for the real sofa in your living room.

• Some corporate recruiters are now seeking out the leaders of multiplayer games on the assumption that leadership skills in virtual worlds might translate to work environments. In addition, there are consulting and software firms popping up that focus on translating the principles of games into real-world businesses, on the strong belief that games can drive stronger relationships with customers and better productivity.

That's pretty remarkable considering that the industry itself is half the age of television, going public in the 1970s with small blips of light on a black-and-white screen. And the game craze has grown so fast, we've had little time on the science side of things to figure out the psychological meaning and impact of games that now immerse us for hours on end. Across the globe, parents and spouses of gamers struggle with the deep immersion games can induce, often for extended periods of time, in those whom they love. Is this time engrossed in games corrupting our brains? Will my child grow up to be a hardened criminal if I let him play too much *Grand Theft Auto*? Aren't there healthier things we can be doing?

Even at the level of national politics, lawmakers are trying to make sense of video games and are feeling pressure to set policy without a lot of good information. In the United States and other nations worldwide, politicians are holding hearings on the negative effects of video games. But the research on topics such as violence and addiction has yet to fundamentally address this: *What makes games so compelling in the first place?* Without clear data on this question, fear understandably creeps in. Do games bring out some deep-seated attraction to violence that will increase crime? Do they trigger brain responses that mean they should be classified as an addictive substance?

The good news for now is that the vast majority of those who play and love games—violent or otherwise—remain law-abiding citizens who by many accounts are very high functioning. Nonetheless, the lack of research on games' powerful motivational pull allows some very extreme positions to rush in, such as those expressed by UK politician Boris Johnson:

[Video game players] become like blinking lizards, motionless, absorbed, only the twitching of their hands showing they are still conscious. These machines teach them nothing. They stimulate no ratiocination, discovery, or feat of memory . . .[1]

Other than needing to look up *ratiocination* ("the process of logical reasoning"), what jumped out at us in this quote is how games take these beatings based on very little . . . ratiocination. Video game paranoia is driving tangible political agendas, with games readily connected to ills ranging from addiction to the shootings at Columbine High School in Colorado. We were recently doing radio interviews on our game research around the time a nine-year-old boy had gone on a car-stealing spree, eluding the police and leading them on not one, but several high-speed car chases. When asked about the episode, his mother off handedly suggested he may have learned to drive from a video game. Now there's no data we know of that yet demonstrates that a driving game can teach you how to outrun the police, let alone do so repeatedly. Maybe it can, maybe it can't—but as of this writing, there is zero research on the topic. Nonetheless, the media jumped on this story as another treacherous consequence of games. For us, these kinds of reactions highlight how much magical (and sometimes paranoid) thinking we have about games, stemming from a poor understanding of their psychology and impact.

On the other hand, even though these issues grab most headlines, the press on games isn't always bad. Regularly, there are articles that describe the positive potential of games, alongside growing movements—such as the "serious game" movement we'll discuss in a later chapter—that are committed to using games to achieve positive outcomes. For example, video games such as *Sim City* have been used in classroom settings for years as a teaching tool. In our work with the University of Rochester, we've found that games can have at least short-term effects on well-being. Increasingly, we are also being asked to help optimize motivation for games not just as entertainment, but in areas of education and health care.

One thing is clear—games are here to stay. So it would be a good idea to understand them better, regardless of how we may feel about them now. Our goal in the chapters ahead is to provide a new way of thinking about the impact of video games and to provide a very practical explanation of the strong motivational dynamics that draw so many people to them on a daily basis. In tandem with this, we will explore the impact of games on the well-being of gamers, both young and old.

To get started, we're going to ask you to do two things as you read the chapters that follow that may not seem intuitive:

1. Stop thinking *primarily* about the content of video games (things like the guns, explosions, spaceships, and magic swords) when evaluating a game experience, and
2. Stop thinking "people play games because they are fun."

That second item may seem particularly odd. Of course we know that games are fun, and we'll discuss in detail what makes games so enjoyable. We'll also talk about the content of video games, particularly violent content. But we ask you to set aside the usual ways you think about games because we want to deepen your understanding of the psychological experience of gameplay itself. Because most of the writing and hubbub about games in the public discourse focuses on game content, or implicitly categorizes games as superficial entertainment (i.e., fun), we've missed the opportunity to see the *really* interesting psychological aspects of gameplay. By looking at things differently, putting aside the usual explanations, we'll begin to see game motivation much more clearly. This, in turn, will empower our understanding and relationship to games.

Games certainly are not the first media revolution that required a paradigm shift. Until television went mainstream in the 1950s, the only media people experienced at home were print and radio. So when television arrived, nobody really knew what to do with its new, rich, visual media. Take a look at the earliest television shows: Essentially they are cameras pointed at people standing in front of *radio* microphones. Television production started with what we knew (radio shows) and tried to figure it out from there.

In the late 1940s and early 1950s, shows began to emerge that better captured television's potential. Early classic shows like *Howdy Doody* used visuals to engage an audience more deeply, drawing them in to its content and stories. The golden age of television began during this time and brought with it a remarkable creative surge with programs such as *I Love Lucy*, *The Twilight Zone*, *The Jack Benny Show*, and many others. In short, television needed to find its own voice. And that voice is now pervasive. Who could have foreseen that today the average American would spend four to five hours a day in front of their TV screen, and that television would become perhaps the central source of our culture?

Video games may ultimately represent an even bigger shift over previous forms of media because unlike film, TV, and radio, games are fundamentally interactive. All other media forms, while they may engage us emotionally and spark our imagination, are unaffected by their audience. They are fundamentally about *their* content, *their* story, and *their* actors. Games are about *our* stories and *our* actions. Compared to earlier media theory, this requires us to shift our thinking about games in very important ways.

IN GAME PSYCHOLOGY, PERHAPS CONTENT ISN'T KING

It's quite natural when trying to make sense of something new to first apply old rules that have served us well. With respect to media and psychology, one of these rules is that the psychological appeal and impact of media lies in its content. Like TV cameras pointed at radio microphones, we continue to apply this rule—developed in response to decades of passive media—even though we are now looking at something fundamentally different. Even within the game development industry, professionals will talk about the virtual worlds they are building using language borrowed from film, television, and even theater (e.g., words like *stage* and *sets* are used to describe the design of game environments). Across the board, we just haven't had time to build a vocabulary for games that captures their unique qualities and potentials.

As a result, society is almost exclusively focused on the content of games, particularly the violence, because this is a kind of analysis with which we are familiar. Content is the cornerstone of all previous forms of media, after all. In traditional media, there is a setting, a story, images, and perhaps sound—creative elements that are combined together by the author or filmmaker and presented as a finished piece that, like the *Mona Lisa*, never changes. The psychological impact lies solely in the ability of this product to have an emotional impact on the audience, because in traditional media, there is no other interface with the audience except for this content.

While this content focus makes sense for traditional media, it weighs down our understanding of the psychology of gaming. Time and again our research shows that the content of games simply isn't the most important factor in explaining either the appeal of games or their psychological impact. For example, violent content isn't really what matters most to the players of shoot-'em-ups. While the industry struggles against political groups crying out against violence, our research suggests that in most cases, you can turn the violence way down and players still find the game just as enjoyable (and often more enjoyable). The much more compelling psychological dimension is the *interactivity* between the game and the player, and how the "action/reaction" between player and game satisfies some very specific psychological needs. So the first point to emphasize is that to really understand the psychology and motivation of games, we have to distinguish between the *content* of games and the *interactive experience* of the player, and the interactivity is much more important.

As a simple example of the content/interactivity distinction, think about your DVD player. You can put any kind of movie you want into the machine—documentary, drama, comedy—but no matter what kind of content is on the screen, you control them all with your remote (i.e., stop, pause, fast forward, etc.). In other words, there is the content of your DVD experience (e.g., *Die Hard* or *Casablanca*) and there is the interactive experience you have with your DVD player that is independent of the content (the functions on your remote). The buttons on your remote don't care whether you're playing *Bambi* or *Death Wish 3*. In other words, your ability to interact with your DVD has nothing to do with its content.

Of course, you don't really have the opportunity to interact with a movie's story. You can fast-forward through the boring parts, but yelling at Janet Leigh to turn off the shower and look behind her isn't going to change what happens at the Bates Motel, no matter how hard you try. In fact, every time we go to the movies, a booming disembodied voice tells us to sit quietly and keep our mouths shut (unless it's to eat more snacks, which, in case you forgot, are on sale now in the lobby).

This is where video games are different. Games want you to express yourself, and in fact, they require it. They continuously offer you *opportunities for action*. You make choices, and those choices in turn impact the game itself. It is this kind of active experience with games—taking action and seeing it have a meaningful impact—that affects us psychologically regardless of whether we are skipping through a virtual gumdrop forest or unleashing hell with a rocket launcher.

In this sense, games really represent personal potential. If you doze off while watching the movie *Star Wars*, the Death Star still gets blown up. Luke Skywalker and Han Solo don't need your help or even your attention. Not true if you're playing the game version, where dozing off will likely result in an unhappy ending for Luke and friends. This is a huge difference: In video games, the *agency* for how things unfold shifts from *author* to *audience*. Agency in this case refers to the "the capacity or state of acting, or of exerting power,"[2] or more simply, it identifies *who* is responsible for the action taking place. In the movies, Superman melts cars with *his* heat vision; in video games, you can melt cars with *your* heat vision. The agency for what happens in film and books belongs to the characters, or more fundamentally to the author or writer. You're just along for the ride. But in a well-developed video game, agency shifts to you as the primary actor, and the action is brought directly under your control. That shift is what increases the psychological impact games can have compared to other media.

This personal agency is something we all intrinsically value, thus making the dynamics of games immediately appealing. Consider that for decades, countless young boys have tucked a red bath towel into the back of their shirt collar and raced around the house using their superpowers on the family dog (reluctantly cast in the role of the villain). They have always wanted to be Superman, and video games now give them the chance to do so in a way that the little boys of yesteryear could only dream of. Historically, kids at play regularly shoot each other with water pistols or perhaps just "pow pow" at each other with their fingers. So the idea of "combat as play" didn't start with video games, even if they made the action more spectacular. As we progress through the chapters ahead, we'll talk specifically about why the desire to be at center stage in our own lives and to take action is a deeply seated intrinsic need, which we call the need for autonomy, and we'll see how this need is powerfully satisfied through many games.

The opportunities for action that games open up for players bring a lot of psychological complexity to games and to understanding them. Compared to traditional media, games put players in the pilot seat rather than merely having them sit quietly as a passenger. Thus, we have to understand what motivates players to fly here versus there, or whether they choose to take off at all. All of the complex interactivity in games must ultimately boil down to one simple psychological goal: The game experience, the way it offers us opportunities for taking action and then responds to our choices, must satisfy something in us in order to engage us and keep us airborne. In other words, it has to be fun, right?

THE PROBLEM WITH "FUN"

For years, most have assumed that the answer to "why we play games" is self-evident: We play games because they are fun. Listening in on industry conferences on game design would confirm this; phrases like "finding the fun" within the game being built, or on increasing the "fun factor" are used liberally. After all, fun is to games what water is to pools—the defining ingredient.

Given this, we were surprised when we first began looking at this area that there was remarkably little psychological research or solid theory into what "fun" actually means in the context of games. Virtually all designers in the gaming industry have a personal theory of what makes their games fun, but little has been done to pull ideas together or to test them in any structured way. Admittedly, it isn't an easy task. "Fun," after all, is a pretty broad concept. We use it all the time not only to describe a pleasant afternoon playing video games, but also going to a good movie, playing with the dog, or even for experiences that normally we'd consider boring or tedious (e.g., waiting in a long line, but with that crazy friend who always keeps you laughing).

And that's the problem: Broad concepts like "fun" have multiple meanings and typically aren't easy to nail down when you are trying to understand things clearly. What do we mean when we say we are having fun playing a video game versus having fun at a dinner party? Probably we are talking about different things even though we use the same word; it's the context of the situation that helps us understand what "fun" means. Therefore, we need to understand the underlying experiences that bring about "fun" specifically within the context of video games because they have a particularly strong power. After all, even a great dinner party gets long in the tooth by the fifth or sixth hour. But a single good game is capable of holding a gamer's interest for scores, even hundreds of hours. It seems important, therefore, that we zero in on this "video game fun" with more precision.

Before we get to that, there are the other signs that "fun" is not sufficient for explaining the powerful draw of video games. Namely, for many players, games are a serious and very involved business. Gamers will spend hours studying and preparing to play games to maximum effectiveness. They will undergo significant suffering in order to play, skipping meals and bringing their bladders to the breaking point. In understanding game motivation, are we really satisfied that all this is "fun?" Perhaps this intensity is why many game enthusiasts prefer the term *gamer* rather than *player*, as "play" seems to unfairly diminish the experience. Consider this answer to a question one gamer asked another about how certain special items in the fantasy game *World of Warcraft* increase or decrease their spell and healing power in the game. Mind you, unless you are a die-hard player of this game, you probably won't want to waste too much time trying to understand this (or even reading it in detail)—but just let it wash over you for a second in terms of how "fun" it sounds:

> Time cast divided by 3.5 will yield how much + heal or + spell will happen.
>   For example, if u have +150 to spell damage and cast a 2 second spell, to calculate + spell damage you would take 2/3.5 and then that would be the proportion of the 150+ damage that would be added.

2/3.5*150 = 86 damage added.

Note for any spell longer than 3.5 it gets full damage or healing no matter the link.

So for some of the more common times,

1.5 second cast = 3/7th of + damage or healing = 43% of number given

2.0 second cast = 4/7th of + damage or healing = 57% of number given

2.5 second cast = 5/7th of + damage or healing = 71% of number given

3.0 second cast = 6/7th of + damage or healing = 86% of number given

3.5 second cast or longer = normal total given

Hope this helps![3]

Sure makes you want to rush right out and buy the game, right? We play *World of Warcraft and* research games for a living, and many of these kinds of analyses never even occur to us. And there are hundreds, if not thousands of these kinds of conversations going on with regard to games—players who are spending many hours of statistical, logical, and strategic analysis outside of actually playing the game. They are writing formulas, building spreadsheets, authoring fan fiction, and constantly sharing information.

The important thing to emphasize is that *World of Warcraft* is, to the outside observer looking at its content, a cartoon-like fantasy world that involves running around with your friends and killing make-believe monsters. It's not, as the previous exchange might indicate, a training session for the SATs. Given the popularity of the game, we get the sense when we read the previous example that if someone were to author a math textbook using *World of Warcraft* for example, it's got a good shot at becoming the first math textbook ever to achieve best-seller status.

The point is that "fun" feels a bit thin to describe what is going on here. We think that if he were being fair, even Boris Johnson would have to admit the possibility that there is a teensy bit of ratiocination happening in explaining this behavior. How fascinating that this level of effort is invested without the extrinsic inducements (e.g., salary) that accompany similar "real-world" work.

Clearly something powerful is going on motivationally that words like *fun* do not adequately capture. There is something deeply satisfying when we are engaged by a game, and until we understand what that's about, we'll never really understand game psychology.

THE SHIFT FROM FUN TO NEED SATISFACTION

Our theory and research on player motivation lies in understanding the deeper satisfactions that provide games' powerful pull: knowing both what specific psychological needs games satisfy and how those needs are fulfilled by games of all shapes and sizes. Building a fundamental model of these needs acts as a motivational Hubble telescope, enabling us to explore a vast array of games more clearly. It has given us a better understanding of both the positive experiences games provide, as well as when gaming behavior can turn negative. More importantly, it's a detailed model of fun for games that better explains their power to engage.

The model we'll be reviewing and using as a foundation for the upcoming chapters is called the Player Experience of Need Satisfaction (PENS). Its roots lie in more than 30 years of research into human motivation and psychological health, and nearly seven years of research on games specifically. Having looked at more than 20,000 gamers across all types of games, we consistently see that video games are most successful, engaging, and fun when they are satisfying specific intrinsic needs: those of competence, autonomy, and relatedness. We'll be devoting a full chapter to each of these needs and how games fulfill them, but let's review them briefly here.

Competence refers to our innate desire to grow our abilities and gain mastery of new situations and challenges. Even watching infants at the earliest stages of development, we can clearly see the innate energy for competence at work as the child learns to master movement, language, and problem solving. Hundreds of research studies have validated that this innate mastery motive operates in each of us and influences us in our personal and professional lives.

Autonomy needs reflect our innate desire to take actions out of personal volition, and not because we are "controlled" by circumstances or by others. Experiencing a sense of choice and opportunity in our lives, and acting in ways that truly reflect our wishes, result in a satisfaction of this intrinsic autonomy need.

Relatedness refers to our need to have meaningful connections to others. As with competence and autonomy, we see time and again that people seek out quality relationships simply for the intrinsic reward that comes from having a mutually supportive connection with others. Feelings of camaraderie, belonging, and the experience that you matter to others are all part of feeling relatedness.

A broad program of research on these intrinsic needs and their relationship to sustained motivation and general well-being has been underway for several decades through a network of colleagues and scholars worldwide. This work is consistently demonstrating that a focus on these intrinsic needs creates optimal environments for learning, work performance, sports, and personal health. In other words, competence, autonomy, and relatedness have each shown remarkable value as a framework for understanding the core motivational dynamics that operate across multiple domains of life. Simply put, when these needs are satisfied, we experience positive feelings and are more motivated to engage in those activities that satisfied us. When these needs are thwarted, we feel our energy and motivation wane.

What our research is showing is that it is precisely because games and virtual worlds are so good at satisfying these needs that they evoke such deep engagement in those who play them. In particular, compared to many other activities in life, games are remarkably good candidates for need satisfaction, largely because of the *immediacy, consistency,* and *density* of intrinsic satisfactions they provide. What do we mean by these terms?

By *immediacy,* we mean the ready availability of video games to offer highly engaging experiences. My wife once came into my office on a rainy weekend day and glancing at my computer screen said, "Wow . . . you have such a beautiful castle in that other world. How cool that you can go to a place like that so easily." Video games have that ability to transport us to rich worlds filled with opportunity and challenge almost instantaneously. Think about how quickly you can go from sitting on your couch, yawning as you flip through a back issue of *Time,* to instead being immersed in a race through an exotic jungle or as the leader of an empire, strategizing epic solutions to manage the happiness of your citizens. Even participating in other exhilarating activities such as sports requires coordinating schedules with others, gearing up, and travelling to the field—none of which video games require. On the same computer where we're writing this is an instantaneous portal into game worlds with opponents ready to offer challenging battles on 10 seconds notice. That immediacy in being able to satisfy motivational needs such as competence/mastery (and others) is a key component of games' psychological appeal and powerful draw.

Consistency refers to the high likelihood that games will deliver on their promise of engagement and need satisfaction. We all know that there are no guarantees in life—particularly when it comes to things going as planned! The softball game you were looking forward to all week gets rained out in the second inning. The bonus you were counting on at work after a very successful year gets delayed because of budget issues. Good video games rarely let us down in these ways: Once we know their rules and conventions, we can be confident that the outcomes will consistently reflect our actions and expectations. This is one of the many ways in which the ambiguity of real-life activity—particularly the unreliable connection between effort and result that is so important to the satisfaction of competence needs and to our sense of autonomy—is often not as compelling as the more reliable connection between action and result in games.

Put differently, video games give us the "just world" in which we instinctively wish to live. They establish very clear links between actions, consequences, and rewards. There is never any doubt when playing a game that if you work hard toward a goal that the goal will be achieved; in virtual worlds the ambiguity and haphazard connection between effort and reward that exists in the real world is replaced by a consistent and dependable system that all but ensures that you will get what you work toward and deserve. In virtual worlds, you are never passed over for promotion or unfairly misunderstood by the game. Because games ultimately boil down to the math of computer programming, the connection between action and result is as dependable as $2 + 2 = 4$.

Finally, *density* refers to games' ability to deliver competence and other satisfactions with a high rate of frequency. Good games are almost always built around a constant stream of mastery feedback, giving players information about their success and rewarding that success meaningfully by increasing their abilities and strength to conquer the even greater challenges ahead. In addition, many games provide players with multiple opportunities that they can pursue freely, instilling a sense of choice and volition that satisfies autonomy. In this way, games weave a tapestry of stimulation, opportunity, and well-balanced challenges for players that keep a constant stream of engaging and enjoyable experiences going from start to finish. And this tapestry of engagement is increasingly strong as games take advantage of the raw technological horsepower available to them to create rich and deep virtual worlds for players.

In other areas of life, the landscape of opportunity and the path to success is often less clear and more drawn out. As one player put it when reflecting on our research on the motivational satisfaction of games, "this helps explain why I like games—in real life I've been grinding [away] at my job for 20 years, and still haven't leveled up." Games rarely let us down in these ways.

With these concepts of immediacy, consistency, and density in mind, consider now the average person coming home from a day at school or work who is looking for some "down time" to enjoy themselves. While we all hold romantic notions of being adventurers in our lives—planning that trip to climb Kilimanjaro or walk the stony shores of the Galapagos Islands—on a day-to-day basis, these things just aren't practical. Our most immediate choices are much more mundane, and for most of the modern world probably include a trip to the mall, some time in front of the television or at a movie, or perhaps a night bowling with friends.

Now consider what any of these activities entails. Going to the mall means driving some distance, stopping at multiple traffic lights with our blinkers on, flipping around the radio to find a song to listen to, and finally finding a parking spot. We then browse around looking at many things that perhaps we can't afford, probably waiting in a line or two. Bowling means similar driving and other logistical hassles (waiting for people to arrive, wearing uncomfortable shoes), plus expense. It's not that there aren't moments of fun and enjoyment in these activities—sometimes very significant amounts of fun—but the point is that in real life, there is a lot of time spent in getting to those moments, and often many frustrations as well.

Let's expand that sphere a bit and think about what happens in our day-to-day job or school experiences. There is a lot of work involved (by definition) as we strive to meet our responsibilities. We have a sense for the rewards that will result from this activity—good grades, a raise, our weekly paycheck—but each and every day has a lot of ambiguity about such things. A raise may be months away at best, and even then not a guarantee. We could get hit with a pop quiz for which we aren't prepared. We might get passed over for a promotion because the boss gave the job to his daughter-in-law. "Tough luck" our co-workers tell us as they pat us on the shoulder with a look of sympathy. "That wasn't fair . . . but that's life, right?"

Yes, that certainly is life, except for life in video games. In these virtual worlds, life is fairer, more rule bound, more predictable (despite the built-in surprises), and thus more reliably satisfying. And while this may sound like we are framing games as a utopian "escape" from reality, our goal here is to identify the source of their motivational power so we can then explore both their positive and negative dynamics more clearly.

The first layer of foundation in understanding the strong motivational draw of games is to outline the intrinsic needs in the PENS model and how games are so good at meeting them. In the chapters ahead, we'll then explore the implications of all that for gaming's promise as well as its controversy.

THE PLAYER EXPERIENCE OF NEED SATISFACTION

Already we hope you've started to think a bit differently about what makes games so compelling. Notice that the previous discussion wasn't about any particular type of game or game content. In fact, the principles described herein can really be applied to understanding the motivational pull of any video game, because the needs we are describing are fundamental. In our research on PENS, we've studied a broad spectrum of games, exploring how the needs for competence, autonomy, and relatedness predict not just fun, but vitality, well-being, social functioning, and many other variables. As we go through each of the PENS needs in more detail, we'll describe how different types of games excel at satisfying certain needs over others, and how some of the most compelling (and successful) games satisfy multiple needs simultaneously.

Ultimately, the PENS model details the satisfactions gluing us to games. We hope it will help you understand why you can't seem to turn off *World of Warcraft*, even though it's 3 A.M. and you have to get up for work in four hours. Or why your kids seem to have so much joy in blowing through the violent and stressful world of *Halo*. In fact, with some more detailed explanation of the motivational dynamics of gaming, we'll understand our relationship with games based on some good solid psychological facts, rather than mere speculation. Or, to put it into the language of our intrinsic needs: Together we'll gain a greater mastery of game psychology that will give us more confidence, freedom, and choice in how we engage games, both now and in the future.

NOTES

1. Boris Johnson, "The Writing Is on the Wall—Computer Games Rot the Brain," *Telegraph*, December 28, 2006, http://www.telegraph.co.uk/comment/personal-view/ 3635699/The-writing-is-on-the-wall-computer-games-rot-the-brain.html.

2. *Merriam-Webster's Collegiate Dictionary*, 11th ed., Springfield, MA: Merriam-Webster, 2003. Also available at http://www.merriam-webster.com/.

3. *World of Warcraft* Forum Page at http://forums.worldofwar.net/showthread. php?t=392495.

Chapter 2

GAMES AND THE NEED FOR COMPETENCE

We've established in a basic way that what games ultimately do is satisfy basic psychological needs extremely well, motivating sustained engagement and enthusiastic fans. But to really understand the power of games, we need to dive into each of the needs in the PENS model (competence, autonomy, and relatedness) and see how they operate in games to create this enthusiasm. The evolution of video games over the last 30-plus years helps us tell that story because the game industry itself has developed along a specific motivational path: Games largely began with a focus on competence satisfactions and evolved to satisfy additional needs for autonomy and relatedness over time. As we'll see, it is precisely because today's games have developed the ability to satisfy multiple needs so well (and are continuing to get better at it) that they engage us so compellingly.

OUR INTRINSIC NEED FOR MASTERY

Often when we are climbing into bed at the end of what we would consider to be a "good day" we feel this way because we've had some experience of success. Perhaps we finished a large assignment at work or school, finally ran four continuous miles without stopping for a doughnut, or successfully bluffed our best friend during poker night for a big win. It's no surprise that accomplishment is something that makes us all feel good and is something that we pursue in big and small ways each day.

Underlying these pursuits and the satisfactions that accompany them is what we call the *need for competence* or *mastery*. We include competence as a basic "intrinsic" need because it happens spontaneously for all of us throughout our lives. From the moment we're born, we naturally seek to gain mastery over ourselves and our environment, learning how things work by observing, exploring, and manipulating them—first through play and later through work, hobbies, sports, and a variety of activities. We see this intrinsic need energizing us from the very earliest ages, motivating children to stretch their abilities as they learn to crawl, stand, and walk. The truth is, there is a sheer joy that comes from mastering new challenges that is an inherent part of who we are, from birth straight into adulthood. Seeking out and mastering challenges is inherently enjoyable and energizing.[1] Indeed, it is in those activities that we experience mastery and competence that we tend to enjoy ourselves and stay engaged.

To be truly satisfying, however, our successes often need to occur in the context of a real challenge. It simply isn't that satisfying to slam dunk a basketball through a hoop three feet off the ground. Perhaps we'd find it fun once or twice, but certainly not as satisfying as dunking it at a more challenging height against a talented opponent. This is because a three-foot hoop doesn't really represent mastery of a challenge—the situation is not stretching us to reach new levels of ability and experience. In intrinsic terms, we are unlikely to feel that a three-foot dunk reflects competence in a meaningful way. A truly challenging dunk, however, could be a significant moment of mastery, one greatly satisfying and long remembered.

This same dynamic is operating in our work lives. Having a job that rarely changes or does not present us with new responsibilities inevitably grows old. So we look for new challenges. We want "room to grow." When we go to our bosses and seek promotions, it is often not just about the money, it is a desire for more responsibility, novelty, and challenge. Even in jobs that by their nature are repetitive, we intrinsically look for ways to create mastery opportunities. For example, psychologist Carol Sansone and her colleagues reported that workers in repetitive jobs invent all sorts of challenges and games related to work just to stay interested and awake during the day![2]

One summer, I worked in a railroad office. Conductors would sell tickets on the train and had to turn in that money to me with a report of each train they worked, the number of tickets sold, and so forth. There was a rather mind-numbing process of collecting and counting money, inputting totals into a register, reconciling the conductor's report with my count, and issuing a receipt. It's boring just taking two sentences to describe it, isn't it? Often I would do this for 16 hours straight.

To keep the job somewhat motivating, I was consistently challenging myself to improve the processing time between taking the money from the conductor (step one) and delivering the receipt back through the window (the last step). I timed myself and would continually try to beat my best time while maintaining accuracy. A process that initially took three to four minutes to complete was pared down to under a minute by the end of the summer. When I was working alongside a coworker, I would playfully see if I could handle my customers' reports faster than they could. In other words, I made a game out of it on as many levels as I could.

Chances are, you can relate to this account. We all have stories of the "minigames" that we spontaneously create to satisfy our competence needs, particularly when life throws us something mundane. The energy for all those paper clip and business card sculptures that materialize during the boring moments of our lives must come from somewhere within us; they are just one example of how we are intrinsically motivated to seek out and master challenges and constantly experience a satisfaction of our need for competence.

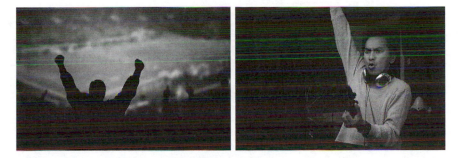

Figure 2.1 Like sports, video games can evoke strong feelings of excitement, achievement, and mastery. (© 2007 quavondo/iStockphoto (gamer image) / © 2009 Adam Kazmierski/iStockphoto.)

VIDEO GAMES AND SPORTS

In sports, we also see the need for competence satisfactions strongly fulfilled. When players are intrinsically engaged in sports, most are striving to overcome challenges for the pure satisfaction of doing so. They will push through pain and fatigue, stretching to improve their performance and overcome greater challenges (e.g., a more difficult opponent or obstacle).

So is it true with video games. When games provide us with challenges, they are inviting us to stretch ourselves to new levels of mastery, which, once achieved, satisfy our intrinsic need for competence. As with sports, gamers will often push through the pain of a tired hand or a full bladder to reach their goals for no other reward than the feelings of mastery and achievement. In many cases, they need no other incentive to play.

A large part of the emotional engagement and satisfaction intrinsic to both sports and video games is our intrinsic need for competence. The fundamental design of these activities is to create challenges and competition as a test of skill and ability. Squaring off against a new opponent—whether real or computer generated—gives us the opportunity to extend our abilities and gain greater mastery. During the disco days of the 1970s, arcade games first captured the hearts of players through their amazing ability to satisfy this need for competence clearly and compellingly (see Figure 2.1).

THE ARCADE REVOLUTION

Without a doubt, what launched the video game industry so strongly in its early years was competence satisfaction. Early arcade games were not graphically realistic or technically complex (especially compared to today's games). Nonetheless, they had a significant ability to capture and hold the interest of players through progressive challenges, sparking the cultural phenomenon of video arcades and beginning a widespread gaming trend among both children and adults.

Early Games and the Satisfaction of Our Need for Mastery and Competence

The first truly successful arcade game, *Pong*, was originally conceived as a training exercise in computer programming because it was considered far too simple to be an interesting game. It has virtually no story, no flashy graphics, no compelling "content"; a blip of light bounces back and forth between two rectangles on a black-and-white monitor, mimicking a game of ping-pong. In theory, it's not terribly exciting.

Although a seemingly sparse idea, the developers added some elaborations to the gameplay that made *Pong* highly effective in satisfying the need for competence. Instead of the ball moving at a constant speed, it moved faster as you got better. It required faster and faster decision making and reflexes. In an uncanny way, the game became harder just when it was in danger of becoming boring, sustaining a sense of challenge and engagement. With merely a few black-and-white blips, *Pong* created an elegant formula for competence need satisfaction that earned millions of quarters for its creators and paved the way for an entire new industry.

Other games followed in just a few short years, including such classics as *Donkey Kong, Asteroids*, and *Space Invaders*. Each of these used a similar challenge formula: Keep the premise of the game simple to engage players easily, and then keep them engaged by accelerating the level of challenge as players gained mastery. As a kid in the 1970s, I remember regularly visiting Station Break, a large arcade in New York City's Penn Station. Along one wall there were at least a half-dozen *Space Invaders* machines lined up shoulder to shoulder, and during rush hour, there were lines five people deep at each machine waiting to play. Although we stereotype games as the domain of the young, these lines were comprised mainly of business executives, holding their briefcase in one hand and a quarter in the other. Picture it: New York City's business elite, briefcases in tow, waiting in line to stare at a nine-inch black-and-white TV to zap brick-shaped aliens! Why were these relatively simple games such a phenomenon with the movers and shakers of New York City? Because they satisfied a fundamental need (competence) that is valued by all of us, regardless of age. Common beliefs notwithstanding, video games have never been simply an amusement for the young.

Let's dig a bit deeper into exactly how arcade games satisfy our mastery needs so well. We've defined competence as the experience of overcoming a challenge or extending our abilities in a meaningful way. If we return to our example of dunking a basketball at regulation height, several things are necessary. First, we need to have clarity about the goal at hand ("jump high enough to stuff this ball through that hoop"). If we are uncertain about what we are undertaking, it is harder to act meaningfully or to feel a sense of mastery, even if we succeed. In this regard, *Pong* and basketball dunking both present us with a pretty clear goal. But that's just the first step.

Next, we also have to feel that the challenge itself is not overwhelming. Frankly, I have never persisted in trying to dunk a basketball at regulation height, simply because I know I don't have the personal height or the vertical leap to succeed. I just look silly, so no thank you. In other words, when tasks seem overwhelming, there is little motivation to pursue them.[3] We have to believe that although they are challenging, we *can* and *will* eventually succeed.

Finally, there needs to be clear feedback on our actions that makes us feel we have learned something useful each time we engage in a challenge. Frankly, it is possible that with the right coaching and training, I might be able to dunk a basketball at heights greater than I currently can—if there was a feedback mechanism after each of my attempts (perhaps through a coach or a more talented friend) that allowed me to improve without making me feel ashamed of failure. For example, it's probably best if my friend doesn't laugh at me when I career into the hoop post, having completely missed the backboard (we could all probably use a few more friends with that kind of self-restraint).

Essentially then, competence satisfactions are most often achieved by (1) pursuing challenges that stretch our abilities but that we believe we can overcome (optimal challenges) and (2) receiving meaningful informational feedback on our actions (i.e., information that is useful and nonjudgmental) that allows us to learn and improve, whether or not we succeed the first time out.

If we think about that for a minute, it seems fairly straightforward, yet can be so difficult to achieve in our day-to-day lives. We all have a variety of tasks we must do that provide little challenge, whether it's standing over the copier at work or taking out the garbage at home. We also have things that seem overwhelming or leave us unclear on how to proceed, such as a major new assignment at work or school. Even when we turn in that assignment, feedback is often days or weeks in coming (if at all) and often does not feel terribly helpful in improving our performance. Certainly there are deep and rich competence satisfactions available to us in many areas of life, but it is often a challenge to find them (or feel like we have the time to pursue them). In other words, getting satisfaction of competence needs is often an uncertain and drawn-out process.

Not so with video games. Their simple but powerful psychological appeal lies in the efficient way they allow us to feel mastery. Arcade games created a formula for satisfaction that has several key ingredients.

First, these games are *simple* and *clear*. *Pong*'s original instructions read in full: "Avoid missing ball for high score." That's it. Even those inexperienced with video games (pretty much everyone in the 1970s) could immediately imagine getting the hang of that. Put differently, with most arcade games you don't have to invest a lot of time in learning how to play in order to start getting some satisfaction from the gameplay itself. Keeping *Pong* simple served an important motivational need: It eased us into the idea of video games without overwhelming us and created the opportunity for engagement with a new kind of interactive media. New arcade games created many different challenges (Jump over that barrel. Shoot those aliens. Eat that dot.), but keeping the in-game goals clear has remained a key ingredient in their success.

Next, arcade games provide us with nearly instantaneous feedback on our actions, allowing us to continuously learn something useful to fine-tune our performance. Those blips, beeps, and flashes may run the risk of annoying those around us, but as we play, they provide steady and instantaneous information on our successes and failures that allows us to learn and improve. Simply put, good video games take us by the hand and teach us how to get better at them, giving us continuous feedback and extending our mastery satisfaction. And as we'll see shortly, today's games envelop the player with mastery feedback at multiple levels, further deepening their value and appeal.

Finally, video games grow alongside us to keep us optimally challenged. As we get stronger in our skills and able to clear taller hurdles, we naturally want to face something new. Video games happily oblige us by raising the bar. They keep pace with our growing mastery, offering us new challenges just when we're ready to move on from old ones. Because good games can assess our skill level and adapt the challenges they present with the speed of a computer, they seem to be an almost perfect coach—pushing us at just the right pace to give us a sense of accomplishment without anxiety.

Clear goals, useful performance feedback, and optimal challenges that stimulate but do not overwhelm us—this probably describes what we'd wish not just from a game, but from our jobs and most activities in life as well, right? This demonstrates the fundamental nature of our need for growth through experiences of competence. Arcade games came along and offered this to us for 25 cents. Not a bad deal! No wonder they were a hit in the 1970s and have continued to be played ever since. Chances are you have some version of an arcade game in your pocket or purse right now (hint: check your cell phone). Maybe it's an interesting option for you the next time you're stuck in a long line at the bank or the Department of Motor Vehicles?

While this rich stream of competence feedback often creates in the gamer a flow of highly satisfying gameplay, an opposite impression can easily emerge to outside observers of the same game. The whirring graphics and frenetic activity can seem overwhelming and impossible to track, creating in many the feeling that they don't understand games or simply would be unable to play them successfully. Here again, competence motivations are at work: When we perceive an activity as being overwhelming, we intrinsically feel a decrease in our motivation to engage. As observers, we have not experienced the artful training the game has no doubt already given the player, nor the feedback, tools, and inputs that have allowed them to grow to a more advanced level of play. Just as ramping up the challenge too quickly can create feelings of frustration and anxiety that will turn off a player, so does observing a game we've never ourselves played. This no doubt leads many observers to not want to play.

There is an important age gap in this that is also worthy of note. We are still in a generational transition in which many of the observers of today's gamers are the "boomer" generation of parents, grandparents, teachers, and policy makers who did not grow up around games and who therefore did not develop the competencies and skills required for mastery. They are simply disengaged from the experience of games and mistakenly believe that games can be understood simply by watching (à la television or movies). But this is as silly as a child saying to their parent that they do not have to practice the piano this week because they watched a video of Van Cliburn playing at Carnegie Hall. In games, observing does not provide the challenge and satisfactions of competence, nor the experience of mastery that accompanies even the most far-fetched themes (e.g., stomping giant mushrooms). Having not entered that sphere, observers look on from the outside, sometimes with curiosity and sometimes with a sense of disgust and alienation, wondering what could possibly be so darn interesting.

Although these games are simple and sometimes silly, they hold our attention so well by satisfying our need for competence in the ways we've described, which in turn brings a variety of positive benefits. For example, our research shows that experiencing satisfaction of competence needs when playing even these relatively simple games results in a short-term increase in psychological well-being. But simply the *act* of playing these games isn't enough—your competence needs (among others) actually need to be satisfied. Our data show that when players do not feel need satisfactions, whatever the reason may be, they do not have these boosts to well-being.

In passing, let us describe a simple experiment initiated by a student we worked with named Paul Knowlton that shows how feeling competence at video games can be a boost to well-being. Paul had participants come into a laboratory setting where they were asked to perform a very stressful task. Without going into the details, the stress task worked—most participants became more anxious and unhappy as a result of the experimental manipulation. Some of them were then given an opportunity to play a very simple video game, and that game was preset to be either easy to master or very difficult. Those who played the easy version felt their anxiety drop away—they quickly shed their negative mood, returning to the "baseline" levels they had prior to stress. Deeper analyses also showed that this reduction in stress was directly a function of the feelings of efficacy and competence they had experienced in the game.

Paul's study shows why games, particularly those simple or "casual" puzzle games on our cell phones, can be so appealing in the middle of our otherwise stressful lives. They are often intuitively mastered and in just a brief play period can reduce stress by satisfying the deep-seated need for competence we all possess.

Competence Satisfactions in Games Today

Obviously, games have come a long way since their arcade days. Video games now offer the rich graphics, complex stories, and vastly more complicated mechanics that early arcade games don't offer. Because they have grown more sophisticated and detailed, it's tempting to think we now need an equally complex psychological model to explain their appeal and motivational pull—one that yokes a new psychological idea to each new dimension of gaming. Considering that games become more elaborate year in and year out, that could get pretty unwieldy.

However, if our need-satisfaction approach is truly a fundamental model of player psychology, then we should see the needs in the PENS model (such as competence) showing just as much relevance in complex games as in simple ones. Like the law of gravity, it should be universal. To test this assumption in our research, we look at games of all stripes, ranging from the most simple to the complex, across many different genres, exploring how competence and the other PENS needs explains their appeal and value to players.

What we've found is that certain genres of games focus on specific need satisfactions more than others. Just as horror movies are designed to scare us and comedies to make us laugh, certain types of games are designed specifically for competence satisfactions, whereas others focus on alternate needs. So while you might not think that *Guitar Hero* (a band game) and *Half Life* (a violent first-person shooter) have much in common, psychologically they share a focus on competence needs. Let's take a quick look at the genres that focus on competence, and then we'll explore each in more detail:

- **Musical Performance/Band Games**. A relative newcomer to the video game landscape, musical performance games require players to accurately recreate musical or dance performances using novel input devices such as guitar controllers and floor pads. These games are some of the purest modern examples of competence/mastery games, and include *Guitar Hero, Rock Band*, and *Dance Dance Revolution (DDR)*.
- **First-Person Shooter (FPS)**. Sometimes referred to simply as "shooters," these games are named for their visual perspective and fundamental gameplay mechanic: Players move through the game from a first-person perspective (i.e., as if looking through the "eyes" of the game character) and work through a chain of progressively more difficult challenges, usually involving a combination of combat and puzzle solving. Examples of famous FPS titles include *Doom, Halo, Half-Life*, and *Call of Duty*.
- **Sports/Driving**. As the name implies, these games recreate races and sporting events, literally putting players "into the driver's seat" or onto the playing field. While, like many genres, these games are becoming increasingly complex and offering opportunities for multiple need satisfactions, the core game offering of

this genre is primarily competence/mastery satisfactions achieved through gameplay challenge.

- **Platformers**. These games get their name from early arcade and home games that require players to maneuver their on-screen character around obstacles and challenges, often by jumping on and off of platforms as they navigate the game world. The best examples of this genre are the traditional Mario games (e.g., *Super Mario Brothers*) as well as the *Sonic the Hedgehog* series. Modern examples that place the player into more sophisticated 3-D worlds include *Super Mario Galaxy*, *Little Big Planet*, and *Prince of Persia*.

Again, it may seem odd to group such wildly different kinds of games together, but as we discuss each of them, the similarity in their motivational dynamics will emerge even though the context for the games (i.e., setting, story, and aesthetics) are often worlds apart. What they share is this: Each of these genres prioritizes competence experiences through challenge and rich performance feedback.

Musical Performance

We'll start with a relatively new genre of games—sometimes called "band games"—because they are a great contemporary example of competence satisfaction. Band games ask the player to pick up an instrument or a microphone (the game controllers) and recreate musical performances. Other games, such as *Dance Dance Revolution* (*DDR*), require you to dance to the music rather than recreate it. But the mechanisms for competence satisfaction are largely the same.

Guitar Hero is the game that popularized this genre. You play using a special game controller that is shaped like a guitar; gameplay involves covering rock classics and recreating performances by pressing keys at precisely the right time. While true rock-and-roll legends were born of creativity, the gameplay in *Guitar Hero* is ironically conforming: Players are not given the freedom to improvise performances and are penalized for not playing the right notes *exactly* where and when the game tells them. But what makes *Guitar Hero* so much fun for players is that the competence satisfactions it provides for correctly executing increasingly complex note sequences are rich and multilayered.

Guitar Hero expertly achieves this on three levels (see Figure 2.2). First, there is the immediate feedback that players get on each and every strumming of their virtual guitar; through colorful flashes and sounds, the player sees and hears immediately whether or not they hit each note correctly. Just like the bleeps and blinks of arcade games, these create mastery feedback loops in *Guitar Hero* that instantaneously and consistently provide competence satisfactions throughout the game. We call these kinds of competence feedback mechanisms *granular competence feedback* because they have a one-to-one relationship to each of the player's individual actions.

Building on this granular feedback, *Guitar Hero* then layers a second type of competence satisfaction into the gameplay. Just as pinball machines will give various score bonuses the longer you keep a single ball in play, *Guitar Hero* rewards players more when they have an unbroken streak of successful notes. Various score multipliers, visual cues, and the roars from the crowd powerfully communicate to the player that they are "in the zone." We call this *sustained competence feedback*. The game is recognizing not just your moment-to-moment success, but your skill and ability at being consistent. Just as sports statistics often keep track of records like "most consecutive" free throws or field goals, *Guitar Hero* rewards players in several ways for increasing their overall accuracy in hitting the right notes and extending a sequence of successful notes longer and longer. As with most video games, your "score" becomes a piece of information you can use to gauge your performance and another benchmark for you to clearly see the progression of your skill.

Finally, unlike arcade games where every time you play you begin at square one, *Guitar Hero* allows players to feel a more permanent progression and lasting recognition of their abilities. As you successfully complete songs, you progress in the success of your musical career, allowing you to play bigger and better venues on your way to becoming a stadium-rocking star. When you get back from a business trip having not played for a week, you can pick up the guitar and know your past accomplishments are not lost or forgotten as you walk back onto the stage and look out across the sea of virtual fans. This is what we call *cumulative competence feedback*—recognizing the more permanent growth in the player's abilities in ways that don't disappear when you press the "off" switch.

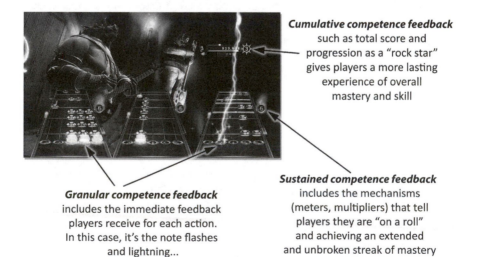

Cumulative competence feedback
such as total score and progression as a "rock star" gives players a more lasting experience of overall mastery and skill

Granular competence feedback
includes the immediate feedback players receive for each action. In this case, it's the note flashes and lightning...

Sustained competence feedback
includes the mechanisms (meters, multipliers) that tell players they are "on a roll" and achieving an extended and unbroken streak of mastery

Figure 2.2 Three flavors of competence feedback in *Guitar Hero*. (*Guitar Hero: Warriors of Rock.* © 2010 Activision Publishing, Inc.)

Table 2.1 Competence Satisfaction in Band Games

Band Games	
Context for Challenge	**Musical Performance**
Optimal Challenge: What Scales?	• Difficulty of songs • Complexity of required chords and player actions
Examples of Competence Feedback Mechanisms	• **Granular:** Visual/auditory cues for each note • **Sustained:** Score multipliers and "rock" indicators • **Cumulative:** Tour/career progress

Notice that one of the key ways that *Guitar Hero* provides this dense network of competence feedback is through its onscreen display (called the "user interface" or "UI" in geek speak). Game worlds can provide us with detailed feedback that we can only wish for in other activities in life.

Imagine, for example, that as you line up that golf shot, you can see in your field of view a real-time wind speed and distance indicator. As you're adding the ingredients to bake a cake, a counter tells you exactly how much sugar you've put in, second by second, so you don't overpour. While trying to impress someone on a first date, a "funny meter" tells you precisely how well that joke went over (rather than having to guess whether that was just a sympathy laugh). Wouldn't it be great to have this kind of "heads-up display" for life? This is precisely what *Guitar Hero* and every good video game provides—an experience of enhanced information that empowers us as we take action and make choices.

We can now see clearly how *Guitar Hero* provides a rich, multilayered environment for competence need satisfactions that engage us both second by second and over the long term. Players can fire up the game for a satisfying song or two and not only feel like they "nailed it," but can also see exactly how to improve their performance (granular and sustained competence) and also know that when they turn the game off, they are one step closer to virtual stardom (cumulative competence). All of that can be accomplished in about 15 minutes.

Table 2.1 summarizes the competence satisfaction formula of *Guitar Hero*. We'll use this same format to look at other genres, noting how they use different contexts but similar mechanisms to satisfy competence needs.

First-Person Shooters

There is little doubt that first-person shooters (a.k.a. "FPS" or simply "shooters") are among the most popular and controversial of the video game genres. FPS games comprise a solid proportion of the video game market, with sales of popular titles such as *Halo* reaching into the hundreds of millions within days of their release, eclipsing the sales figures of even the biggest Hollywood blockbusters. As the name implies, FPS games are primarily about psychologically intimate combat—intimate in the sense that (1) the game is played in the first person rather than observing from behind an avatar (i.e., third person) and (2) the player is asked to climb "into the trenches" of a conflict, facing it close-up. FPS games are about being in the thick of things, armed to the teeth.

If just one genre were chosen as the poster child for the anti-violence crowd, first-person shooters would be it. When parents watch worriedly as their kids tear through a video game world with guns blazing, chances are it's an FPS. They're called "shooters" for a reason: The primary challenge of these games involves themes of combat and killing, usually with big, nasty guns. The early shooters that defined the genre, such as *Wolfenstein* and *Doom*, made the bad guys you killed really bad guys (*Wolfenstein* = Nazis, *Doom* = literal demons). Today's FPS games have greatly improved in graphics and realism, and the core formula for these games has remained largely unchanged: Throw the player into a hostile environment and give them lots of guns to battle their way out. Let's take a look at this genre's underlying structure of motivation and satisfaction.

Doom: Combat as a Context for Challenge

Doom is widely accepted to be the first "killer app" (ahem) of the shooter genre. Although there are earlier examples of FPS games, *Doom* gathered up millions of new FPS fans through its well-balanced sequence of challenges and strong granular feedback to the player on their developing mastery. In understanding why *Doom* is such an engaging and motivating game, we can understand universally the motivational draw of the FPS genre, which, like *Guitar Hero*, lies largely in competence satisfaction.

First, *Doom* presents the player with a strong context for taking action. The player is a veteran marine with a noble spirit who has been banished to a Mars outpost for refusing to kill innocent people on a superior officer's orders. Once there, an experiment in teleportation goes horribly wrong (don't they always?) and a portal is opened between the Mars outpost and the Netherworld. The denizens of hell race through, and it's up to our hero to save the universe. The player must single-handedly defeat increasingly nasty demonic invaders, ultimately travelling back to Hell itself to seal the deal. While the story does give the player a context for their actions, it is the gradual progression of challenges as the player marches into Hell that provides the strongest motivational pull of *Doom* and virtually all successful FPS games.

That progression is the key. When *Doom* begins, you are armed only with your trusty pistol. But the enemies you confront early on aren't terribly overwhelming, and you learn you can dispatch them successfully. These early victories ease you into the rules of the game and increase your confidence that you will rise to the challenges ahead of you. With each hellish opponent you fell, there is a small victory won on your road to the larger goal. While game developers sometimes refer to drawing the player forward as a "breadcrumb" design structure, from a competence standpoint, these moment-to-moment victories are more like a trail of chocolates—each providing a small bite of satisfaction as the player succeeds and progresses toward the larger victory.

It's tempting at this point to get into a discussion about what motivational role the violence itself plays in these games, but as we are devoting a full chapter to this topic later, we'll save that discussion. Simply put, our research shows that motivational dynamics such as competence satisfaction are what make violent gameplay enjoyable, much more than the blood itself. When it comes to enjoyment, players actually don't care that much about the blood—mainly it just lets them know that they hit their target and got the job done. In other words, it gives them granular competence feedback that they are succeeding, moment to moment, just as we saw in *Guitar Hero*.

It may sound bizarre to compare *Doom* to *Guitar Hero*, but remember that we're focused on psychological dynamics and not content *per se*. Granular feedback and progressive challenge are key mechanisms of satisfaction in both kinds of games. FPS games like *Doom* use armed conflict as the context of challenge. But regardless of whether the story takes place on Mars, in Hell, or in 19th-century Montana, there's a pretty standard formula:

1. You find yourself in a situation that requires fighting against a formidable opposing force.
2. This opposing force threatens something very significant (the entire world, your one true love, etc.).
3. Overcoming the opponent (and thus saving the world, etc.) ultimately falls directly into your hands.
4. You become increasingly more powerful in your ability to meet the enemy and succeed (e.g., bigger, cooler guns and/or abilities).

It is easy to see in this formula how FPS games set the player up for competence satisfactions through a series of intense challenges through combat. Early FPS games were almost uniformly a matter of "run and gun," meaning the player needed to move through maze-like environments and blast through enemies without being blasted in return. The result was an exhilarating gaming experience, but also one that could be quite exhausting—many an FPS player ends a play session with shaking hands, a racing heart, and a smile on their face. Where does that satisfaction come from?

One place would be the game's focus on optimal challenge, which we saw so effectively put to use in arcade games. FPS games have several ways in which they sustain this feeling of challenge. Architecturally, they are structured in sequential levels, similar to the chapters in a book. These levels are virtual environments (i.e., "maps") that the player moves through as they progress. To keep the player challenged as they increase in their skill, the game's maps grow in complexity and difficulty as the player advances through the game.

Like *Guitar Hero* (and unlike other genres that we'll explore), shooters don't traditionally give players a lot of choices about how to move through these maps. In fact, they often push the player through a predetermined pathway on each map, requiring you to kill or be killed by bad guys along the way. It's as if the player is moving through a series of railroad cars, with the doors locking behind them as they progress from caboose to engine. This "forced march" structure is one way that FPS developers build challenges and emotional excitement; when the dust clears and you are standing, slightly breathless, at the end of the map, you feel a sense of satisfaction at having conquered those who stood in your way. Just like the exhausted athlete who has scored the winning point, reaching the end of the map alive soundly satisfies our feeling of mastery. After we've caught our breath, we ask, "What else you got?" The FPS game obliges our desires by dropping us into the next, more challenging map.

Puzzles and Pacing

Lest you think that FPS games are 100 percent flying lead, zero percent creative thinking, there are many types of challenges in the modern shooter that involve contemplation as a side dish to carnage. As you might imagine, getting shot at is an intense experience even when it's virtual. Because a good FPS game can take 10 to 15 hours to play through from beginning to end, game developers know that too much white-knuckle action wears players out, even if it's fun. To give them an engaging breather, FPS games offer more cerebral puzzle challenges alongside the heart-pounding combat.

As an example, perhaps in order to proceed from one level to the next you have to discover clues that will help you locate a hidden object or figure out how to scale a seemingly insurmountable wall. Or perhaps discovering the secret combination to a locked door requires you to remember and integrate various clues you have encountered along the way. Often developers will use these elements of puzzle solving to reveal a plot point in the game's story, setting up the rationale behind the next big battle. Psychologically, these puzzles slow down the emotional action while still engaging the player's intrinsic motivation to master a new situation. As a parent, you may be surprised that these kinds of challenges exist in FPS games, but they do. It's what your kids are up to when you don't hear a lot of screaming, gunfire, and death gurgles.

Boss Battles: Combining Puzzles with Combat

Some of the most intense FPS gameplay, and subsequently satisfying moments of success, emerge when players are confronted with particularly difficult battles against uber-bad guys, often referred to as "bosses." Just like the guy down the hall from your office who won't give you a raise, bosses in video games stand in your way and require extra effort to overcome. But unlike real life, in FPS games you are allowed to use explosives to conquer them.

It may seem logical to classify these special battles, which are often the most spectacular in the game, as combat challenges. But at their heart, a good boss battle is another form of a puzzle. Bosses are rarely defeated in the same way as garden-variety bad guys, and often the entire arsenal of weapons you've collected will not be effective if all you do is mindlessly open fire. Instead, you have to find the boss's Achilles heel—that special weakness or strategy that will knock him down. This can be a painful process of trial and error (and frequent deaths), but in turn it leads to significant "ah-ha!" experiences and grins of satisfaction when you discover the winning formula. Here again, FPS games are focused more on challenge over player choice (i.e., more competence than autonomy), requiring the combination of both brains and brawn to find a specific solution. The result is a significantly strong experience of mastery.

The game reinforces this by acknowledging the player's conquering of bosses in the game's story line, often by granting increased status and player admiration by the characters in the game ("Good work Smith! You defeated Captain Toughguy!"). Boss victories also often come with rewards that increase the player's power and capacity, preparing them for new adventures ahead. These are important ways in which FPS games provide cumulative competence feedback to players—the game recognizes the player's skill and accomplishments in ways that persist even when the battle itself is over. Put differently, good games only "raise the rim" when the player is ready and confident they can jump higher.

Before turning to other competence genres, let's summarize the dynamics of competence satisfaction and challenge in FPS games, see Table 2.2.

Table 2.2 Competence Satisfaction in FPS Games

FPS Games	
Context for Challenge	**Armed Conflict**
Optimal Challenge: What Scales?	• Strength of player (weapons, abilities) • Strength of opponents • Difficulty of maps/puzzles
Examples of Competence Feedback Mechanisms	• **Granular:** Blood and enemy reaction when hit • **Cumulative:** Increase in strength, reputation, and receipt of new weapons and skills as player advances

Driving/Sports

Next, let's consider driving/sports games. We'll focus on driving games as they provide clear examples of competence feedback that also predominate in sports simulations such as football and soccer.

In a similar fashion to the games described before, driving games are designed to stretch the player's abilities and offer them increasingly challenging activities synchronous with their skill. The new player is offered fairly simple tracks to drive, with gentle turns attached to wide straightaways, racing against peaceful computer opponents who seem to be more interested in pacing than racing. As you succeed in these early races and your competence grows, you unlock more difficult courses—those with hairpin turns and obstacles—and are pitted against opponents that drive with Richard Petty–like precision. As you win or place, these games integrate all three kinds of competence feedback (granular, sustained, and cumulative), satisfying your mastery needs and increasing your motivation to drive some more.

In the immediate gameplay experience, there is the granular competence feedback of the feel of the road and the sense of speed, often delivered in a tactile way through the rumbles and resistance of game controllers. This is what Robert White (one of the first motivational psychologists to describe the idea of mastery) would have called *real effectance feedback*[4]—the efficacy of your actions is experienced directly. Some game developers have enhanced this not only with steering wheel controllers, but also with full-form driving seats that rumble and simulate skid, drift, and momentum in response to your speed and control on the road.

When looking at these important kinds of cues, we distinguish between *visceral* and *representational* competence feedback. Visceral competence feedback is direct feedback that simulates or emulates "real-world" feedback, such as the rumbling of the road beneath you or the roar of the crowd. Representational feedback includes things like your score or a numeric "power meter" display; these elements also provide useful competence information, but do so indirectly through a representation of your ability and achievement. As we'll see in later chapters, while both types of feedback are useful in supporting competence, visceral feedback has the advantage of feeling authentic and contributing to deeper immersion and a feeling of "presence" in the game world.[5]

In addition, sustained competence feedback is achieved quite naturally by maintaining speeds and timing each race (a precise reflection of racing in the molecular world). Avoiding missteps (e.g., collisions or miss-shifting) results in higher and more sustained speed and better overall times. Just like sustaining a flawless performance in *Guitar Hero* where there are no missed notes, a perfect execution on the racing track deepens the competence satisfactions that come from knowing that you "nailed it."

Cumulative competence feedback is also integrated on multiple levels. After each race, you see how well you did compared to your opponents (e.g., win,

Table 2.3 Competence Satisfaction in Driving/Sports Games

Driving/Sports Games	
Context for Challenge	Competitive Sports
Optimal Challenge: What Scales?	• Difficulty of challenges (i.e., track complexity, obstacles, handicaps) • Skill and difficulty of opponents • Complexity of player actions required to succeed
Examples of Competence Feedback Mechanisms	• **Granular:** Smoke, sound, rumbles, and representational feedback from on-screen meters • **Sustained:** Increasing roar of the crowd and other environmental feedback • **Cumulative:** Increase in abilities, advancing in tournaments, and improving win-loss records

place, or show). When this feedback is presented in a way that provides you with information on how you can improve your performance, it draws you back to the starting line. In addition, most modern racing games let you develop your "career" as a virtual racer, increasing your abilities and giving you access to more effective and powerful cars to match the more tortuous tracks. Aggregate scores analogous to the driver ratings used in NASCAR represent your performance across the season and give you new goals to stretch toward. In short, the density of goals to reach, both near-term and long-term, are rich and plentiful.

Finally, despite the impressiveness of computer opponents, there are few rivals more challenging (or wily) than the guy sitting next to you. Both racing games and sports games are designed to allow direct competition between players, adding another level of challenge to the mix, as well as opportunities for other key need satisfactions (e.g., relatedness), which we'll discuss in detail shortly (see Table 2.3).

Platform Games

Platform games rose to prominence during the 1980s and early 1990s, and while they are no longer a dominant genre, they are still being created and enjoyed today. Even if you have never played a video game, chances are you are familiar with the rock star of platform games: a little red-capped plumber named Mario. In the mid-1990s, Mario was so popular that he was more recognizable than Mickey Mouse.[6] Just one of his games, *Super Mario 3*, made more than half a billion dollars worldwide, and that was more than 15 years ago.

Mario got his start as a supporting character in the arcade game *Donkey Kong*, but his breakout performance was *Super Mario Brothers* and its subsequent sequels. The latest installment, *Super Mario World*, was released in 2007 (16 years after the original) and was the highest-rated video game of that year.[7]

Table 2.4 Competence Satisfaction in Platform Games

	Platform Games
Context for Challenge	• Navigation of physical space (primary) • Combat (secondary)
Optimal Challenge: What Scales?	• Complexity of environments (e.g., levels, obstacles) • Strength of opponents
Examples of Competence Feedback Mechanisms	• **Granular:** Constant stream of micro-challenges (e.g., jumping, simple combat) • **Sustained:** Power-ups; Chaining actions successfully to overcome obstacles and reach new goals • **Cumulative:** Game "collectibles", score/points

Platform games get their name because of the core structure of gameplay, which involves using platforms at various heights to progress through obstacle-rich environments. A pivotal aspect of platform games such as *Super Mario World* is the increase in the game's complexity over early arcade games such as *Donkey Kong*; as Mario's world expanded, it filled up with more interesting obstacles and offered hidden content and rewards that could only be found through creative exploration.

Although there are enemies, combat, and even boss battles in platform games, the core mechanism of challenge and mastery satisfaction is *navigation*—getting from point A to point B despite the fact that fireballs, lava pits, and giant lizards stand in your way. Often there is a single solution to moving forward (making the game more like a puzzle), whereas other areas let you try out different strategies (e.g., zap the bad guys versus jump over them versus pick them up and carry them). In this sense, platform games such as the *Super Mario* series have evolved in their ability to satisfy not only competence needs, but also to satisfy autonomy needs through choice and discovery. We'll discuss autonomy fully in the next chapter, but it's interesting to note that over the 25-year development of Mario from *Donkey Kong* to *Super Mario Galaxy*, the graphics not only went from 2-D to 3-D, but the dimensions of gameplay have also increased. Mario has progressed from one-dimensional need satisfaction (competence) to two-dimensional (competence and autonomy), and is also improving relatedness need satisfaction through more in-depth cooperative play. We suspect, however, that the main motivational driver of platform genre will always remain its competence-related satisfaction (see Table 2.4).

The Player Hero: Competence Satisfaction in the Game's Narrative

In addition to the mechanics of gameplay that satisfy competence, a game's story also plays a role in fulfilling this need. While not all games have a strong story element, those that do invariably cast the player in the role of a hero of one stripe or another—the player is a special person who needs to face and overcome unique and significant challenges. The idea is simple: Killing demons is fun, but killing demons with the power of your mind in order to save the woman you love is *more* fun. The same game mechanics, nested successfully within a hero narrative, offer a significantly richer experience.

Much has been written about the "hero" as a psychological archetype, a construct that is deeply seated and resonates with our innermost wishes and consciousness. Carl Jung and Joseph Campbell have both described the common characteristics of hero narratives within literature, including elements of the hero as a special figure who yields unique power.[8] In games, as in literature and films, we see the depiction of a heroic protagonist time and again.

The need-satisfaction model we're describing provides a motivational framework for understanding the elegant way in which the hero narrative draws us in to stories and games, beginning with the competence/mastery heroes symbolize. Heroes are fundamentally masterful in their ability to overcome challenges and grow in strength and ability. Persevering through to an ultimate victory is a core thread of heroic narratives and provides a natural framework for the incremental progression of game challenges that optimally satisfy a player's need for competence.

In traditional stories we can, at best, vicariously enjoy the hero's exploits. But in video games, the heroic narrative does something else for players: From the very beginning, it supports in their minds the idea that they *are* a hero. The game *believes* in them and their ability (i.e., competence). Our research has shown that having support for competence by those around us and getting useful feedback on our growth and potential is an important contributor to both motivation and well-being. When video games put players into heroic circumstances, they are implicitly communicating a belief that the player can rise to the tasks ahead.

Batman represents a classic comic book hero who embraces the notion of challenge and becomes a masterful foil against evil. He begins as a small, helpless child (a vulnerability to which we all can relate), but works tirelessly at growing his skills and ability. In Chris Nolan's vision of the Batman narrative, as depicted in the films *Batman Begins* and *The Dark Knight*, Batman takes on his role as Gotham City's savior through much pain and struggle, because he knows that he is uniquely capable of doing so. Try as he might, he alone has the ability to push back the evil and chaos that would otherwise engulf the city.

In the video game *Batman: Arkham Asylum*, players can feel this power directly as the hero. The game enables players to experience the unique power of Batman to strike fear into the hearts of villains by silently attacking from above and disappearing into the shadows. While the mechanics of the game's combat system directly satisfy competence needs, it is also the ability to enter into the narrative world of Batman as the hero that further enhances immersion and satisfaction, deepening the game's value and the motivation to play. In the chapters ahead, we'll explore further how the other core needs in the PENS model are also integrated into the hero construct to successfully deepen player engagement.

GAME CONTROLS: THE PRICE OF ADMISSION

At amusement parks, your day starts standing in front of a small booth on the baking asphalt, buying a ticket that will get you past the turnstile and into the fun. As you stand there waiting your turn, you can hear the screams of delight and watch the roller coasters roar into the sky. You know that soon you will be riding them, too.

In addition to their purchase cost, video games have a second price of admission before a fun experience is possible: Mastering the game's controls. We saw how part of the success of early games such as *Pong* was their ability to keep the control scheme as simple as possible to minimize the cost of entering into the experience. This was a smart design choice given that games were completely foreign to most people 35 years ago, and we needed to be eased in gently.

But much has happened with games over 35 years. They've grown increasingly more sophisticated and complicated. Concurrently, there are greater demands on players to learn the more complex control systems often necessary to fully engage and succeed with video games. And for many players (and would-be players), this is a significant challenge in and of itself.

Many older adults today are amazed and even intimidated when they watch younger folks rapidly engage in games, quickly showing high levels of mastery. My three-year-old niece, who cannot yet read, was controlling her Nintendo DSi to take pictures, record sounds, and play games without any outside help (which she thoroughly enjoyed refusing) all within an hour of being handed the device. When the over-50 crowd sits down to try the same activity, frustration and confusion over how to control the action is often the result.

Like *Pong*, the control scheme in early home systems such as the Magnavox Odyssey and the Atari 2600 were very simple. The Atari, for example, had a control stick and a single button that could be used to play more than 400 different games. By contrast, today's PlayStation 3 controller has 15 buttons and two control sticks (controlled independently and simultaneously by each thumb), as well as multiple internal gyroscopes that add a further level of control by physically moving the device. There is even a keyboard that can be attached to allow for text communication within games. Simply put, this can be an intimidating device for uninitiated baby-boomers with an arthritic thumb for whom gaming is already a foreign concept. When people at any age are discouraged by a game's controls, they don't have the chance to feel competent at gameplay, because they can't even get to the real game. For them, the price of admission to the fun of games is so high, they often stay outside the turnstile.

We call this issue *control mastery*. This concerns developing the skill to translate your *intentions* into *action* within the game. When you want to run left, you can easily and reflexively run left. When you want to jump, you know how immediately and your character leaps into the air. For this to happen, you must master the controller and the "rules of action" for that particular game. This requires an investment of time and energy to master the control interface and learn the mechanics of a game, often before you get into the fun. It's an investment at the ticket booth that players hope will pay off once past the turnstile.

Video game developers refer to this acquisition of mastery of controls as the game's "learning curve." Games that have complex controls and mechanics are said to have a "steep" learning curve. Other curves, particularly for more simple or "casual" games (e.g., *Tetris and Bejeweled*) are quite short, allowing players to get right on the ride. Regardless, players do not typically enjoy this period of investment, but will put in the time in anticipation of the enjoyment the game promises to offer down the road.

Just as the amusement park ticket booth is a necessary first stop to fun, but not fun in and of itself, in our research we have studied how control mastery acts as a gateway to enjoyment and motivation in games. We have consistently found that having a stronger mastery of controls is related to increased enjoyment, but not by itself. Control mastery enables a greater potential for more intrinsic satisfactions such as competence and autonomy, which in turn result in greater enjoyment. If those deeper satisfactions are not present, mastering the controls really doesn't matter.[9] In other words, if there are no rides in the amusement park worth riding, it doesn't matter that you made it inside.

"CONTROLLING" INFLATION

Many game developers have recognized the significant issue of control mastery to game engagement and motivation. As a result, the last five years have seen an intriguing innovative trend in controller design—game controls are getting easier. A great current example is the Nintendo Wii, which decided to emphasize more simplicity in their games and controls rather than adding more and more "features." The Wii controller has half the buttons of its competitors and focuses on controlling games intuitively through movement. Want to swing your onscreen sword? Then swing your arm just as you would if you were a kid pretending to be Errol Flynn in *Robin Hood* (for our older readers) or General Grievous in *Revenge of the Sith* (for our younger readers). In fact, the Wii controllers are credited with bringing more and more older folks into gaming, with stories of virtual bowling matches breaking out in nursing homes around the world.[10]

This represents an interesting trend that bears watching. The Wii has been a tremendous success to date, outpacing more powerful and complex competitors in the marketplace. Lowering the "price of admission" and thus allowing more players to receive the satisfaction of games quickly has challenged the more-complexity-is-better evolution of game systems. While games will likely continue to increase in their sophistication, the innovation of easier and more intuitive control systems will better ensure that there is a ticket price that is available for all ages and levels of ability.

THE DATA ON COMPETENCE SATISFACTION IN GAMES

In our research, we closely examine how all PENS needs are being satisfied by particular games. The games we've talked about so far have one important element in common: the primary way in which they engage us and hold our attention is by providing experiences of challenge and mastery. Put differently, competence satisfaction is the primary contributor in making these games "fun" for players.[11]

However, just to prove our point that competence is a driver of people's motivation to play video games, we have done a few experiments. For example, working with our close colleague Andy Przybylski,[12] we brought naive players into a gaming lab at the University of Rochester. Over a few sessions, we had them each play four games of different varieties, randomizing the order of play. We did this because we wanted to be able to show that competence need satisfaction is a significant predictor of motivation for all players, regardless of the specific kinds of games they prefer. To show this, we used an advanced statistical technique[13] that allowed us to separately study (1) differences between players in their preference for different kinds of games and (2) the satisfactions within each game that makes people like them more or less. We wanted to empirically test whether competence satisfaction was important globally, irrespective of personal preference for content. And in fact, this is what we found—competence satisfaction was a consistent predictor of game preferences and desire for future play.[14]

In addition, across numerous studies, we've found that when competence needs are satisfied, players are more likely to value the game and continue to play it. In fact, having a strong experience of mastery from gameplay is a better indicator that you'll keep playing a game than simply feeling that the game is "fun." As we've discussed, fun is a very general term that can describe a variety of experiences, sometimes fleeting ones. Competence satisfaction gets at a deeper experience that reflects intrinsic and fundamental human needs and is also a key ingredient in why games are particularly good at keeping us glued to them.

But it's not the only ingredient. In fact, it may not even be the most important ingredient for the long-term engagement that often keeps players playing a game not just for a few days or weeks, but for months and years. Although arcade games were fairly one-dimensional in their need satisfaction (competence/mastery), as games evolved technically, they also evolved motivationally. New genres of games emerged that focus on different PENS needs, and as we'll see, even the game genres we discussed before are most successful when they combine other need satisfactions alongside competence. Next we'll look at another of the PENS needs that plays a large role in sustaining player engagement: the intrinsic need for autonomy.

NOTES

1. Ryan, R. M., and Deci, E. L. (2007). "Active Human Nature: Self-Determination Theory and the Promotion and Maintenance of Sport, Exercise and Health." In M. S. Hagger and N. Chatzisarantis (Eds.), *Intrinsic Motivation and Self-Determination in Exercise and Sport*. Champaign, IL: Human Kinetics.

2. Sansone, C., Weir, C., Harpster, L., and Morgan, C. (1992). "Once a Boring Task Always a Boring Task? Interest as a Self-Regulatory Mechanism." *Journal of Personality and Social Psychology, 63*, 379–390.

3. This is why for us backyard players who need a little help, someone brilliantly invented the adjustable rim.

4. White, R. W. (1959). "Motivation Reconsidered: The Concept of Competence." *Psychological Review, 66* (5), 297–333.

5. See http://www.gluedtogames.com for more examples of visceral versus representational feedback.

6. Iwabuchi, Koichi. (2002). *Recentering Globalization: Popular Culture and Japanese Transnationalism*. Durham, NC: Duke University Press.

7. As per overall game rankings at http://www.gamerankings.com.

8. Campbell, J. *The Hero with a Thousand Faces*. Princeton, NJ: Princeton University Press, 1968; Jung, C. G., *The Archetypes and the Collective Unconscious*, Collected Works, 9 (2nd ed.), Princeton, NJ.

9. Ryan, R. M., Rigby, C. S., and Przybylski, A. (2006). "The Motivational Pull of Video Games: A Self-Determination Theory Approach." *Motivation and Emotion, 30*, 347–364.

10. Georgia East, "Wii Bowling: In Boca Raton, Fierce Competition among Seniors," *Sun Sentinel,* July 31, 2010, http://www.chicagotribune.com/topic/fl-wii-seniors-20100731, 0,3276556.story.

11. Ryan, R. M., Rigby, C. S., and Przybylski, A. (2006). "The Motivational Pull of Video Games: A Self-Determination Theory Approach." *Motivation and Emotion, 30*, 347–364.

12. Pronounced "sha-bill-skee."

13. Hierarchical linear modeling (HLM).

14. Ryan, R. M., Rigby, C. S., and Przybylski, A. (2006). "The Motivational Pull of Video Games: A Self-Determination Theory Approach." *Motivation and Emotion, 30*, 347–364.

Chapter 3

GAMES AND THE NEED FOR AUTONOMY

uick quiz: Take a look at each of the pairings in Table 3.1, and for each one, pick the choice that most appeals to you.

Table 3.1 Pop Quiz

Which Would You Prefer?		
Lots of opportunities	*Or*	Limited choices
Freedom	*Or*	Constraint
Make your own decisions	*Or*	Have others tell you what to do
Do what interests you	*Or*	Do what you are told to do
Blaze new trails	*Or*	Conform to expectations

Did you choose anything from column B? Probably not. Column A may seem like common sense because that's how deeply we value things like choice, opportunity, and freedom from constraints. As psychologists, we have long been interested in *why* that's the case. Isn't it true that just imagining having more freedom and choice in your life brings with it a feeling of vitality and sometimes even longing? Don't we all find ourselves spontaneously daydreaming about this from time to time? This kind of natural energy is exactly the kind of thing we want to understand in our work.

In our research, we have conceptualized these experiences as evidence of an *intrinsic need for autonomy*. As with competence, we look at how autonomy needs energize and motivate people across numerous domains of life, including work, relationships, education, and health. We consistently find that when people experience autonomy, they are happier, healthier, and more motivated. And as with mastery experiences, people are naturally motivated to seek out and stay engaged with those activities that instill a sense of personal autonomy.

AUTONOMY: CHOICE AND VOLITION

Because it's easy to grasp that freedom and choice are intrinsically valued, there's a danger we'll stop there in understanding the concept of autonomy. But to understand the power of games in satisfying autonomy, it's important to be more precise in our definition to really capture what autonomy means and what contributes to its satisfaction.

First, it's true that autonomy is most likely to be satisfied when we feel we have interesting choices and opportunities, but this is different than "freedom." Yes, freedom implies that you are unconstrained in your choices and actions, but it describes your circumstances, not your state of mind. How many people retire each year and enter a state of "freedom," and then don't know what the heck to do with themselves? We all see people who technically have lots of freedom and choice, but somehow don't seem to be benefitting from it. Many people with loads of freedom lurch this direction and then that, but can't seem to make "freedom" work for them.

What's missing for many is the perception that there are interesting or personally valued opportunities to pursue and ready avenues and tools to go after them. Freedom itself isn't enough—you have to see *real* opportunities for yourself within your environment. We only truly feel a sense of choice when we perceive the situation as providing intriguing or valued alternatives or options, ones that we can actually explore and realize rather than just imagine. It's these real and meaningful choices—or opportunities for action—that contribute most to autonomy.

Going further, while these choices contribute to autonomy, autonomy itself is not dependent on always having "options." It is more fundamentally about acting volitionally, regardless of the level of choice that may be before you. At its heart, autonomy means that one's actions are aligned with one's inner self and values; that you feel *you* are making the decisions and are able to stand behind what you do. Even if you have only a single pathway open to you, you still feel autonomous if it is the one you want to travel down. Certainly, circumstances of freedom and choice facilitate being able to select and optimize one's preferences, but volition doesn't require that one have lots of opportunities. Indeed, it is often when an individual has a sense of mission and purpose that they feel most autonomous, even though they may not perceive a lot of options or specific choices.

For example, as the movie *The Dark Knight* comes to an end, we see Batman and Commissioner Gordon standing over the lifeless body of Harvey Dent (a.k.a. "Two Face"), who has just fallen to his death. As Gotham's crusading, charismatic, and effective district attorney, Dent was seen by Batman as the true savior of Gotham City—one who could inspire its citizenry without a mask. But after a devastating attack kills the woman Dent loves and leaves him terribly disfigured, he falters and turns to murdering those he feels are responsible.

Batman realizes that the only way to save Gotham is to protect it against the disillusionment citizens would feel if they learned of Dent's crimes. To preserve the righteous image of Dent, Batman decides to take the blame for Dent's wrongdoing and races into the night, hunted by the police. Gordon's young son asks why Batman is running. "Because we have to chase him," Gordon tells him, musing about the painful path that Batman must tread alone, "Because he's the savior we need, but not the one we can have right now."

Few would say that Batman felt "free" in this situation or that he had a lot of choices. In fact, he believed there was only one road for him to follow. Leaving Gordon, his steely gaze filled with a determined clarity, there is no doubt that Batman is acting deliberately—volitionally—as he drives away. Although constrained by circumstances, Batman is acting entirely from his own free will. Examples of this sense of purpose abound in other modern mythologies, from Frodo in *Lord of the Rings* to Sarah Conner in the *Terminator* series. Despite their constraints, these figures are being autonomous as they face formidable odds, and we appreciate their inner direction and bravery.

In our less glamorous lives, we see many examples of this kind of constrained, but volitional action. There are the new parents who have their "freedom" curtailed by the responsibilities of a young infant, but who wouldn't trade their new life for the world. The employee who is under pressure, but who believes in the value and importance of the project, acts volitionally despite the lack of choice at work. In our model, autonomy needs can certainly be enhanced when we have meaningful choices, but one can also feel autonomy when the only option open to you is one that makes sense to pursue, whether or not options are present.

The Value and Importance of Autonomy

As with competence, if autonomy is truly an intrinsic motivational need, we'd see it in many domains of life—deepening positive feelings and motivation where it is exists and seeing negative consequences when it is thwarted. Researchers around the world have published hundreds of studies looking at how autonomy operates to both motivate and sustain behaviors as well as to foster feelings of well-being and satisfaction. These studies offer strong support for autonomy as a fundamental motivational need. Let's take a look at some of the ways that autonomy impacts our energy and motivation generally before we dive into our exploration of autonomy in video games.

Autonomy in Education

School conjures images of things that we must do, which is why the spontaneous reaction to words like *homework* are not terribly positive. As such, parents and educators often discuss how to motivate education and learning. In collaboration with colleagues, we have conducted many studies looking at how the experience of autonomy impacts motivation for learning and educational success. The consistent finding is that when students feel that their autonomy is supported by teachers, rather than feeling that they are being controlled, there is greater sustained engagement,[1] better retention and learning,[2] and overall an improved sense of well-being in the student.[3] Learners, that is, are most engaged and perform best when they experience their teacher not as an authoritarian tyrant, but as a leader who understands, listens, provides choices, and supports initiative.

Autonomy at Work

Studies looking at the experience of autonomy at work have similarly found that employees' job satisfaction and productivity are significantly related to the degree to which they feel autonomous at their jobs and experience their managers as supportive of their autonomy in the workplace.[4] This doesn't mean that the "boss" is not in charge, but again it means that employees found in their work opportunities to make inputs, regulate their time or efforts, and that they feel they have a voice when things go wrong. No matter where they are in the hierarchy of the company, every worker feels better and produces more when they experience some sense of control and agency on a daily basis. As with education, it is when our intrinsic need for autonomy is facilitated by our circumstances that we see a natural energy and motivation emerge.[5]

Recently in a study of adult workers, we found that there are heavy costs to a lack of autonomy. This was reflected in a "weekend effect" in which working adults felt *so* much better on the days they were off work. They had more positive affect, fewer negative feelings, more energy, and even fewer physical symptoms like headaches or back pain. This may sound like a universal finding ("Thank God It's Friday"), but in fact where this weekend effect really happens most strongly is in those who feel lower autonomy at work. If you have a job where you experience a lot of volition, you are happier all week long![6]

Autonomy in Sports

In the last chapter, we explored the connection between video games and sports in relation to our need for mastery. Autonomy also plays a key role in sports motivation and engagement. Research has found that the enjoyment of sports, and the well-being that comes from playing, are significantly related to the autonomy one feels within the activity and how well autonomy is supported by coaches and parents.[7] In fact, studies even show that the more kids feel autonomy in gym class, the more they will be active outside of school, because the feeling of volition for being active sticks with them.

Autonomy in Close Relationships

We often think about relationships as being all about warmth and connectedness. But an ever-increasing body of research shows that the most satisfying relationships are those in which we feel autonomous and competent as well.[8] That is, we feel most intimate, most secure, and most happy around those people who do not try to control us, but instead support our sense of autonomy and choice. When we say that we want to "be understood" by those we love, we're expressing our innate desire for support in pursuing interests that are important to us.

In sum, it is hard to find any walk of life where greater autonomy is not associated with more satisfaction, energy, and sustained involvement. Autonomy has become an important consideration in motivating people everywhere—in medicine and health care, psychotherapy, vocational training, and religious institutions. Its power is ubiquitous. Gone are the days when B. F. Skinner's "beyond freedom and dignity" reigned—today we recognize that a sense of freedom or autonomy, and the dignity it affords, are a major factor in facilitating motivation. Taken as a whole, this research shows how autonomy satisfactions are a key element in the quality of our lives as well as in our motivation to sustain our engagement with activities in many domains. Let's get back to games now to see how they have emerged as such strong satisfiers of autonomy. As you might guess, it has a lot to do with how they excel at providing players with meaningful choices and facilitating volitional action.

Video Games and the Need for Autonomy

Describing autonomy at school and work sounds great, but let's face it, in the molecular world (a.k.a the "real" world), there are many things that get in the way of autonomy satisfactions with respect to both choice and volition. We know in theory that choices are always out there for us (and they really are). But contrary to the old saying, rarely does "opportunity knock." In reality, when we feel that longing to visit the pyramids or to go to culinary school, these notions seem pretty far away and unattainable. Indeed, rarely do we classify these thoughts as "opportunities" because this implies they are within our reach when in fact they seem like distant dreams.

There are also many challenges to feeling volitional in our day-to-day lives. Most of us don't feel a lot of autonomy on a daily basis, and in fact wearily deal with a long list of "have to's." Show of hands: Who out there doesn't feel like *everybody wants something from you*? Have that report on my desk by tomorrow, please see me after class, why haven't you finished balancing the checkbook—every day brings with it tasks and responsibilities that we need to accomplish, whether we endorse them or not (or even understand why we need to do them). We are all accountable to multiple authorities—spouses, teachers, parents, and bosses—for how we spend our time. Such obligations can easily constrain our experience of autonomy.

In contrast, within the digital worlds of video games, we see such constraints evaporate. The screen lights up and suddenly you become the center of the action. The characters in the game are waiting for you to speak to them, to decide what you'd like to pursue and how you'd like to spend your time. And the rules of reality that we all find so discouraging sometimes—the delayed gratifications, constraints, and unfair treatment—melt away. Rewards are freely and frequently given as we travel from one exotic locale to another nearly instantaneously. Think about the powerful satisfaction this gives to our basic need for choice and volition in our lives. While in the molecular world we hope for just a few moments to ourselves each day and dream of having more freedom to pursue our interests, in digital worlds there is a constant menu of opportunities from which we get to choose. Games have been designed specifically to provide us with a rich landscape of choice that is immediately available. Let's look at just a few ways games satisfy our autonomy needs through opportunity and choice.

DIMENSIONS OF CHOICE AND OPPORTUNITY IN VIDEO GAMES

Identity. Around the time the Internet was emerging, a classic *New Yorker* comic depicted two dogs, one of which was typing at a computer keyboard. He turns to the other who is watching and says, "On the Internet, nobody knows you're a dog." Over the last 20 years, virtual worlds have further expanded our freedom to shape an online personality of our choosing, building an on-screen character (or "avatar") from scratch. This includes selecting gender, race, physical appearance, clothing, biography, personal attributes (smart, strong, funny, etc.), and even supernatural or fantasy elements. Want to be seven feet tall or be able to fly? Now's your chance. With each generation of video games, developers empower players with broader freedom to build their identity.

Recently we were working with a developer whose comments told us just how much players' expectations had risen concerning character choice. They developed a game for the 9- to 14-year-old crowd in which players could choose their characters sex, shape, features, and clothes. But there were complaints that the wardrobe options were not extensive enough—kids highly valued the ability to create their own identity through clothes, hats, and other fun accessories. This youthful audience wanted more individuality within the game world, and they in fact *expect* it. They already know virtual worlds have greater freedom to provide options that are not available in the molecular world, where choice is restricted by access and cost. At the mall, you have to plead with your parents to get them to buy you that hat; in a virtual world, you have the freedom to make these decisions entirely on your own.

It appears that this effect is not just limited to the young. In virtual worlds that are inhabited primarily by adults, such as *Second Life*, inhabitants highly embrace the same commitment to digital fashion. Transactions for virtual goods are estimated at more than $1 billion "real" dollars a year and growing. And interestingly, during the recent "Great Recession" of 2008–2009, spending on virtual goods such as designer clothing and specialty items to customize your avatar rose significantly.[9] When the financial hardships of the molecular world restrain them, virtual inhabitants find another outlet for the need for self-expression and the feelings of autonomy this creates.

Activity. While games that focus on competence are constructed to present a carefully orchestrated series of challenges to the player, games that emphasize autonomy often let the player choose what activities and challenges they wish to pursue. Like a cruise director, these games present the player with an extensive set

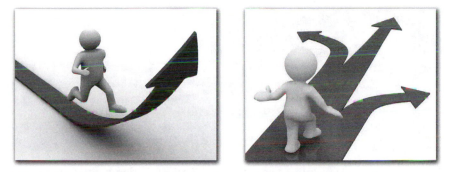

Figure 3.1 In most competence-focused games, there is only one path for players to take at any given time. By contract, autonomy-focused games satisfy players by giving them many interesting options from which to choose. (© 2007 John Kounadeas/iStockphoto (figure with multiple arrows) / © 2010 Sergey Ilin/iStockphoto.)

of choices and they make sure the player is always aware of options for interesting activities. After all, if you don't know about the shuffleboard tournament on the lido deck, it doesn't count as an opportunity.

Strategy. Yet another way that games satisfy our autonomy is by giving us choices over the strategies, solutions, and tactics we use to overcome challenges and succeed in the game world. Let's say you need to get past a locked door to find a hidden treasure. How will you tackle this? Perhaps you'll become an expert in lock picking and with silent and swift skill you swing the door open. Or maybe you prefer a less sophisticated approach as you jam a stick of dynamite into the lock and light the fuse, with a mischievous smile on your face. Games that focus on providing autonomy in the strategy of gameplay give you many paths to accomplish goals, allowing you the chance to experiment and explore different options (see Figure 3.1).

Open-World Designs. Looking for the best examples of games that excel at providing multiple avenues of autonomy satisfaction (e.g., identity, action, and strategy) brings us to games with an "open-world" design: After orienting players to the basic theme and mechanics of gameplay and giving them some suggestions as to what they might pursue, open-world games set them free to do what they please. For example, during the first hour of the game *Fallout 3*—a game set in a gritty, post-apocalyptic future world—players begin in a constrained underground "vault" and are introduced to the concept behind the game world, key characters, and initial story lines that they can pursue. After that, you are released into a vast open landscape filled with cities, people, missions, and dangers, and are free to go anywhere and do anything you wish. You can even earn good or

Figure 3.2 In the opening gameplay of *Fallout 3* (left), players are oriented to the game's narrative and their own abilities in a more constrained underground community. But they are soon set free to explore a vast open world (right) filled with the many opportunities for exploration, challenge, and action that can be highly satisfying to our basic need for autonomy. (*Fallout 3* © 2008 Bethesda Softworks LLC, a ZeniMax Media company. All rights reserved.)

bad "karma" for behaving maliciously or benevolently to those you meet along the way. But while the game gives you opportunities to pursue its story line, whether or not you do so is entirely up to you (see Figure 3.2).

The result of this structure is exactly what we'd expect from the perspective of our PENS framework. While the player is learning the game, autonomy need satisfactions are more muted. But once they are free, players give *Fallout 3* some of the highest ratings for autonomy satisfaction. This is an example of how games can be designed for autonomy, just as they can for competence. Shortly, we'll take a look at certain genres of games that emphasize autonomy satisfactions and explore how they sustain our engagement by giving us both interesting choices and meaningful reasons for taking action. The net result is a powerful satisfaction of our autonomy needs that, when achieved, can lead to a truly long-term relationship between player and game. In particular, the open-world designs that are pervasive in games today let players explore with a freedom few of us have in our day-to-day molecular lives.

VOLITIONAL ENGAGEMENT: THE HEART OF AUTONOMY

We've looked at how games provide players with significant autonomy satisfactions through opportunities and choice. But let's go a bit further in understanding our experience of autonomy, because choice is not the only path to satisfaction. Remember that feeling autonomous means that we are pursuing things that interest us and that we want to pursue. By contrast, we feel controlled when we are not interested in what we are doing and are simply taking action as a stepping stone to some other goal. We feel controlled by a boring job whose only value is a paycheck, or when we are worried we'll be punished if we don't finish a chore.

Even when others aren't controlling us, we often control ourselves—just doing something because we'd feel guilty if we didn't doesn't feel very satisfying or autonomous either. As common as these experiences are, they all represent situations of low autonomy satisfaction.

As we've explored, choice is one way in which our autonomy gets a boost because we feel more empowerment in what we're doing. But we also feel autonomous even when choice doesn't exist, as long as we personally endorse the path we're on. If we truly value the activity before us for its own sake—if it is personally interesting and important to us—we will feel autonomous even when choices and "freedom" are constrained.

If my wife is sick, for example, my choices in life would become quite constrained for a period of time. She needs to be taken care of, and this restricts my freedom. I need to stay nearby to get her medicine and other things so that she can rest and recover. But it is also true that there is no place I would rather be than by her side. I do not feel constrained or controlled—I feel quite autonomous in fact—because I value the path of caretaking that life requires of me.

Similarly, at the office there are many times when you must pursue a project that is assigned to you where you have no choice but to complete it. But if you understand and believe in its importance in helping the company succeed, if the reasons and rationale for needing to do the project are communicated to you, you are much more likely to feel autonomous while working on it. When we are consulting with companies on how to build motivation and satisfaction in the workplace, we often emphasize strategies of communication between managers and employees that maximize autonomous engagement in this way.

So too in video games, autonomy satisfaction can occur even when there are limited choices. Autonomy satisfaction in these circumstances depends on whether or not the game has succeeded in enlisting the player's interest, in getting them to "buy in" to the path ahead of them and the actions they must take. A bad video game will simply take the player's interest for granted, assuming they will happily move from one action to the next without needing to provide them with a strong rationale or reason. These games have characters that literally command the player to "Keep moving!" But a well-designed video game never drags or prods the player along in these ways. Instead, they use well-crafted stories and compelling rationales to awaken in the player an internal desire to walk the path ahead. We call this experience in games *volitional engagement* and it is strongly related to autonomy satisfaction even in games that are linear and do not technically provide a lot of choice or freedom.

This may come as a relief for game developers because building choices takes a lot of time and money and may not be possible given their available resources. While our data show that it's always a good practice to give players interesting choices where possible, when choices are constrained by a game's design, it is critical to focus on drawing the player into a deep interest in the actions they are required to take.

AUTONOMY GENRES

While volitional engagement is a strategy that even linear games can use, several genres of games make autonomy satisfactions their primary focus through a strong combination of choice and volition. Unlike the high-intensity, white-knuckle action of competence challenges and gameplay, games that focus on autonomy often involve significantly less screaming and jumping up and down on the sofa. Instead, their primary magic involves the ability to make you stare incredulously at the clock when you realize you have been playing for the last five hours straight. Even more so than competence, our data show that the satisfaction of autonomy needs is among the strongest predictors of long-term engagement with video games.

Three popular game genres that are autonomy-focused through a combination of choice and volitional engagement include:

- **Role-Playing Games (RPGs)**. Role-playing games inherited their name from their paper-and-pencil predecessors, in which groups of people would each play a character with specific skills that defined a "role." Players make choices about how to develop their characters (i.e., identity autonomy) as they progress, unlocking new abilities and opportunities as they go. Traditionally, these games have been fantasy-themed epics involving knights, wizards, and the occasional dragon (a.k.a. "men in tights" games).
- **Simulations (Sims)**. Remember erector kits? Malibu Barbie play sets? Legos? Simulation games give the player a set of tools and allow them to use the game world as a canvas for their own "vision" of an alternate universe. The most popular computer game of all time, *The Sims*, is the flagship of this genre, having sold more than any other computer game in history. In it you can build a family, pay your bills (or not), become a rock star, or simply hang out with your neighbors. A unique feature of these games is that they aren't about "winning" but instead focus on experimentation, discovery, and self-expression.
- **Turn-Based Strategy (TBS)**. TBS games are similar to simulations in that they give the player a broad set of choices and tools. However, TBS games do involve competition (usually against computer-controlled opponents) in the pursuit of goals. While this creates challenges within the game, the core value to players lies in the wide range of choices and strategies they can employ to achieve victory.

Let's take a look at each of these to see how they excel at autonomy satisfaction.

ROLE-PLAYING GAMES

Around the time Atari was plugging *Pong* machines into bars around the country, another kind of game was gaining popularity among millions of players around the world. *Dungeons and Dragons* (DnD) was first released in 1974 and involved a group of players embarking on a fantasy adventure in which each would "embody" a character with specific abilities. "Rockface the Fighter" might take the lead battling orcs in a murky dungeon while "Kevork the Healer" stood behind patching him up. As players succeeded in their roles, they had opportunities to increase their abilities. The game was played entirely old school—using paper and pencil and a complex series of tables, statistics, and multisided dice to determine the outcome of game challenges. In other words, the mechanics of the game were all about the math.

Conveniently for the video game world, it turns out that nobody loves math more than computers (except maybe the geeks like me who played DnD). The computational structure of RPG games made them well suited to the digital world of video games. Early multiplayer computer games—called Multi-User Dungeons or MUDs—emerged in the 1970s and thrived using the RPG structure. These games didn't have graphics but used text to describe the game world, events, and characters. Believe it or not, although rich graphics have been the hallmark of RPG games for years, these text-based RPG worlds from the 1970s and 1980s are still inhabited by tens of thousands of players worldwide.[10]

As discussed before, autonomy needs are most strongly satisfied when we experience both *meaningful choices* (in such areas as "who we are" and "what we do" in the game) and *volitional engagement* (i.e., do we endorse the actions we are taking, whether or not choice is present). Let's take a look at how RPG games so powerfully achieve these goals, starting with the facilitation of choice and opportunity.

THE EVOLUTION OF CHOICE: FROM WIZARDRY TO OBLIVION

Like their paper-and-pencil siblings, RPG games engaged players with the opportunity to customize the characters they would play in the game. Back in 1981, one of the earliest successful RPG titles, *Wizardry*, let players create a party of six adventurers by choosing from a variety of races, classes, and abilities, resulting in seemingly limitless combinations to explore. Will my fighter be more effective as a dwarf or a human? What if I combined three fighters with three wizards? Although the range of what you could do in the game was limited to crawling through a series of mazes, the ability to customize and combine characters was highly satisfying to player autonomy needs.

As RPGs evolved in the 1980s and 1990s, the expansion of computing power allowed developers to pack even more choice and opportunity into their games. This was most noticeable in the expanding menu of activities RPG games offered and how they were able to use graphics to more richly communicate opportunity to players. While early RPGs such as *Wizardry* relied almost entirely on text descriptions and simplistic graphics to convey their vision of the game world, modern RPG games, such as *Oblivion*, envelop the player in rich graphics that let them more immediately perceive multiple opportunities for action (see Figure 3.3).

Figure 3.3   Today's role-playing games (RPGs), such as *Oblivion*, envelop you in realistic landscapes that implicitly communicate open choice. (*The Elder Scrolls IV: Oblivion* © 2006 Bethesda Softworks LLC, a ZeniMax Media company. All rights reserved.)

Much of the increased sense of opportunity and choice comes from just being able to see and move within an open environment. In games today, a player can freely explore the landscape, choosing new directions that run far and deep. In the 1990s, the mountains you might see off in the distance were merely a backdrop—a set piece that could never be explored. In today's RPG games, you can actually ride to that far-off mountain and even climb it if you want! Interestingly, when we did a study of people's reactions to indoor versus outdoor visual environments, we found that just "being" in an outdoor setting "virtually" was enough to increase people's feeling of vitality and autonomy.[11] Outdoor environments—even when they are just on your computer screen—seem to increase your sense of possibility and your feelings of autonomy. Providing these kinds of worlds is yet another way that games, and today's RPG games in particular, speak to our intrinsic needs and motivate play.

QUESTS

Of course, while being able to explore lush virtual landscapes is nice, remember that autonomy-based games need to provide the player with interesting things to do in order to be satisfying. RPGs accomplish this by offering quests or missions that, when performed successfully, give the player various rewards and outcomes that shape his or her identity in the game.

For example, while you are galloping through the RPG countryside on your trusty steed, Mayor Wimpy of Victimville waves you over and tells you that the town desperately needs your help because Cranky the Disgruntled, a local warlord, is pillaging the town weekly and leaving barely enough food to survive. The villagers don't have money to offer you for defeating Cranky, but if you succeed, they will give you their most prized possession, the Ferrigno Amulet, which has the magical power to double your physical strength. Will you take on the task of defeating the warlord and saving the town?

Such quests have been a part of games for decades, but with each generation, RPGs get better at using quests to satisfy autonomy. The number of quests (and hence opportunities) in the typical RPG has grown remarkably as increased data storage enables more expansive games. Quests used to be offered to players in a more linear fashion, but leading RPG games now offer more free-form gameplay—the player goes in any direction they desire in an open world, finding different quests no matter where they choose to roam. This design, which is becoming more standard in modern RPG games, more deeply satisfies player autonomy and leads to greater engagement and immersion.

In addition, over the last 10 years, RPG quests have evolved meaningful ways to customize your play experience. If a player wants to develop a noble and charitable character, they have opportunities to do so by choosing certain quests or taking certain actions. If, however, they wish to travel a darker road and rule the land through merciless power, these choices are available to them as well. In this way, quests become a tool for shaping the very nature of who you are in the game, making them more meaningful and interesting. Offering a rich range of activities that empower you to directly craft your identity further increases autonomy satisfaction and motivation to play.

As an example, let's return now to the good Mayor Wimpy who is standing before us, his lip trembling in hopeful anticipation that we will agree to help him save the town. Will we take on the task, winning the love and admiration of the villagers and adding a powerful new amulet to our collection? Most early RPG games would have left us with this path alone. Today's RPGs, however, also give us the option to smile warmly at the good mayor, accept his task, and then negotiate a better deal with Warlord Cranky, perhaps even participating in the next round of pillaging. Savior or betrayer? The choice is up to you, and each has implications for how your character develops. This creates a dense tapestry of possibilities, deepening our experience of autonomy as we create a character who reflects our wishes and interests.

Games such as *Knights of the Old Republic* and the *Fable* series are great examples of RPG titles that expand choice to include the moral and ethical development of the player-character in these ways. In the *Fable* series, the choices you make have an impact on your character's appearance, reputation, and abilities. Evil behavior enhances sinister features, even horns; altruistic activities give one a halo's glow. Both shape the choices and challenges one is likely to face. The marketing slogan for this game emphasizes this volition in shaping your character: "For Every Choice, a Consequence."

Going further, RPGs succeed in providing strong autonomy satisfactions not only because of the choices they give players over actions and identity, but also by building volitional engagement through story development. For example, in *Fable 2*, you spend many hours exploring and fighting alongside your trusty dog. Our research on this game shows that players build a meaningful relationship with the dog that they find contributes to their overall satisfaction of the game (we'll discuss more about *relatedness satisfactions* in our next chapter). At a certain point, however, the player is presented with a hard choice in the narrative that means they would lose their dog in order to save others. Here it is the story that draws the player forward, providing a context for choices that brings them alive and gives the player more purpose and meaning in the actions they take. Similarly, *Fallout 3* uses early gameplay to not only orient players to the game features, but also to engage them in a story that will motivate them forward through a series of quests; in this case, the player's father has gone missing and it is his or her job to search the wide and dangerous world of the game in order to find out what has happened.

RPG developers vary on how much to emphasize an open-world design, or to instead volitionally engage the player through strong narratives. The most successful games manage to achieve both, hitting on all of the main avenues of autonomy satisfaction summarized in Table 3.2 below.

Table 3.2 Autonomy Satisfaction in RPG Games

Context for Autonomy in RPG Games: Freeform Character Development within an Heroic Narrative		
Opportunities for Action	**Level of Satisfaction**	**Description**
Your Identity	Strong	Many opportunities to customize your character along many dimensions (appearance, abilities, and moral/ethical qualities).
What You Pursue	Moderate to Strong	While some RPGs will still "funnel" players along a linear path, many have open-world designs with seemingly limitless content to freely explore.
Volitional Choices	Strong	RPGs combine meaningful choices with a heroic narrative that inspires personal agency in one's actions.

SIMULATIONS

The best-selling computer game of all time is *The Sims*, a game that is now in its third major release. By 2008, the franchise had sold more than 100 million copies, equaling billions of dollars in sales. And that's not counting the latest version, which is poised to add significantly to that total.

Obviously there must be something remarkably epic going on in *The Sims* to generate this kind of interest. One imagines jaw-dropping battles in which the player wields awesome cosmic powers, heady stuff compared with yawn-inducing everyday activities like going to work, cooking dinner, and paying the bills.

You might be surprised to learn that *The Sims* is actually about . . . going to work, cooking dinner, and paying the bills. It's not about controlling larger-than-life heroes, but about guiding common folk like you and me through the events of their lives, including mundane tasks like scrubbing the floor and taking a bath. That it sounds dull on paper may be why it took Will Wright, the game's creator, years to get the suits who fund new game projects to bite on the idea. Don't we play games to get away from all that? Isn't it bad enough that in real life I have to remember to take out the garbage, let alone remember to do it in a video game?

Yet this game has dwarfed the sales of every other computer game that came before it. Some of its truly die-hard fans (many of whom are middle-aged women with real-world homes of their own) schedule their vacations around the release of new *Sims* content so they can dedicate hours on end to playing it. Games like *The Sims* fly in the face of the idea that people play video games to escape the content of their lives, or the notion that games primarily engage us through spectacle. To the contrary, another highly successful game from Wright, *Sim City*, involves tasks like setting parking fines and connecting water pipes.

Wright himself often describes his products as less "game" and more "toys" that are designed to facilitate play. The concept of a toy is central to understanding how these games motivate. As play expert Stuart Brown suggests, a toy is more than color and stimulation, it is a device that allows for varied actions and challenges. Stimulation (such as watching some kind of spectacle) can be passive, but play with toys is active.[12] *Sim City* and other such games allow the player to engage in acts of creation and enhancement of their virtual worlds, representing an intrinsic expression of our need to author our lives and the outcomes around us.

How these digital toys compare with traditional forms of play is another interesting question that needs further study. Brown voices the reasonable concern that while play with computers can be stimulating and even facilitate some types of development, too much time in front of screens has us missing interaction with the "tug of gravity," and the physical and social nuances of material interactions. Nonetheless, play in video games shares the basis for fun in all play—enabling creative opportunities in which one experiences both freedom and mastery.

Games can also motivate players and elicit tremendous volition even when the content itself seems mundane. In *The Sims*, you can pursue many activities that are familiar even if they are not part of your actual molecular life. Always wanted to become a doctor? Wish you could trade up your one-bedroom starter home for a bigger spread, or at least get a new sofa and kitchen table? *The Sims* puts a wide range of possibilities before you and lays out a clear path to achieving your goals. In other words, *The Sims* lets you act with full autonomy, exploring a rich network of choices and opportunity and building a virtual "life" from possibilities that are completely within your control. It is this kind of rich volitional action that deeply satisfies players and keeps them scrubbing virtual floors and commuting to virtual jobs long into the night.

The quest structure that we see in RPGs is also operating in simulation games like *The Sims*. You may embark on the lifelong dream of becoming a rock star or take some cooking classes on the side. You can invest time into building relationships with the "neighbors" who live on your virtual street. You can fall in love, get married, and have a family. Simply put, simulation games like *The Sims* are about providing rich opportunities along multiple dimensions of both "who you are" and "what you do," but with even more headroom than in RPGs. In simulations *there is no story to follow*. There is only the story that you want to create, and you have the opportunity to bring as many different stories to life as you can imagine (see Table 3.3).

Table 3.3 Autonomy Satisfaction in Sandbox Games

Context for Autonomy in "Sandbox" Games: The Game Is a "Toy Chest" for Free-Form Imaginative Play		
Opportunities for Action	**Level of Satisfaction**	**Description**
Your Identity	Varies	Games like *The Sims* allow you to identify with a customized personality in the game (if you wish), where as other simulations are focused more on activities.
What You Pursue	Strong	The game world is a canvas with no predefined "scripting" of your activities.
Volitional Choices	Strong	Modern simulations excel at providing you the tools to build a self-directed story, along with enough structure (missions, goals) to not feel lost.

TURN-BASED STRATEGY

A close cousin of the simulation is the turn-based strategy game (TBS). These are a lot like an elaborate game of chess: You hover above the game world and choose the strategies and tactics you will use to reach victory. Similar to simulations, TBS games provide a wide-open menu of choices in both "who you are" and "what you do." A key difference is that unlike simulations, TBS games define specific goals and victory conditions for the player to reach. Simply put, simulations don't require you to compete and win, but TBS games do.

The game that best exemplifies the TBS genre is *Civilization*. First released in 1991, *Civilization* was an instant success and is frequently cited as being among the most engaging and replayable games ever made. Each game of *Civilization* begins by controlling a small band of loin-clothed settlers, looking to make a home in the vast wilderness of 4000 BCE. As you settle down to build your first city, somewhere in the mist other civilizations are also carving out their own place in the world. Each turn you have the freedom to manage your civilization and take it in whatever direction you wish. You may, for example, seek to build a dominating military force and wipe out your competition. Or you may choose to peacefully focus on building culture or developing advanced technology that can take you to distant planets. *Civilization* allows you to win the game through any of these paths by reaching various goals before competing civilizations beat you to it.

Unlike other game genres, in strategy games such as *Civilization*, you are not embodying an on-screen personality or avatar. Instead, you play as your society's leader—issuing orders and setting policies from high above. For this reason, these

Table 3.4 Autonomy Satisfaction in Strategy Games

Context for Autonomy in Strategy Games: Player Is an Empowered "Leader"		
Opportunities for Action	**Level of Satisfaction**	**Description**
Your Identity	Moderate	No specific on-screen personality; who you are is implied in your actions/strategies.
What You Pursue	Strong	There are many choices to be made at each turn with respect to directing the actions of your "citizens" and the various near-term goals you want to pursue.
Volitional Choices	Moderate/Strong	Long-range victory goals provide a sense of meaning, while strategy choices are fully in player control. Games that provide multiple paths to victory further deepen player volition.

games (as well as some simulation games such as *The Sims*) are often said to have a "God game" design: From your personal Olympus in the molecular world, you peer down at your digital subjects and control their lives. Table 3.4 summarizes the autonomy satisfaction matrix for TBS games along the same dimensions we've been discussing in other autonomy genres.

OPPORTUNITIES FOR ACTION: SPONSOR OF THE "WHAT IF" MOMENT AND THE REPLAYABILITY EFFECT

A key question in the psychology of games is how they inspire such dedication and long-term engagement with players. Indeed, gamers find themselves thinking about games even when they are not playing, talking about them with other enthusiasts and friends, and feeling a strong motivation to reengage games that they love time and again.

Our data indicate that one of the biggest contributors to the desire to reengage with a game over the long term is the experience of autonomy satisfactions. Like a great movie, an enjoyable competence game (like those discussed in the last chapter) might be highly engrossing and satisfying the first time through. But without strong elements of autonomy, such games are likely to be considered "finished" and put on the shelf once the player reaches the end. When we look at the relationship between players' need satisfactions and a longer player-game relationship, nothing predicts this more strongly than rich experiences of autonomy. No matter how satisfying games may be on other dimensions, players say goodbye to games without autonomy satisfactions much more quickly.

In our study of the genres discussed previously, we've seen this phenomenon recur many times. Regular players of these autonomy-focused games report longer gaming sessions and sustained motivation for play lasting months and even years. While the average play session for a FPS is usually not more than 30–40 minutes, a session playing an RPG or a game of *Civilization* or *The Sims* can last for several hours. In addition, players of autonomy-focused games are more likely to have been actively playing these games for years, and they often anticipate an ongoing relationship with the game long into the future.

Games like *The Sims* and *Civilization* enjoy a longer and more frequent relationship with their audience because the choices that they provide evoke an ongoing feeling of possibility and what we have been calling *opportunities for action*. In the molecular world, as I stand in the food court at the mall, my stomach growling in hunger, I probably perceive numerous opportunities for action: The dozen or so restaurants around me each offers me something meaningful (to slate my hunger), and just as importantly, each of these opportunities is readily apparent. In other words, if all those restaurants were on the floor below me and I wasn't aware of them, I would perceive zero opportunities for action and might easily head home for a sandwich. But when I can see a rich field of opportunities at the ready, I am not only more likely to enjoy myself, but also to consider coming back to try other choices in the future.

The exemplary autonomy games that we have reviewed here differ in many respects but share an emphasis on providing these "food court moments," rich in opportunities for action. In one study we did, tracking players over many months, we found that those games that emphasize autonomy through opportunities for action were more frequently thought about and more likely to draw players back to them. In particular, players reported that they would spontaneously think about:

- New ways to approach challenges and content that they had already seen (e.g., "What if I tried that with X instead of Y?")
- Interest in exploring the game world to find new areas and content that they may have missed ("What if I had gone left at that intersection instead of right?")
- Interest in playing through familiar game content with a new character and set of abilities ("What if I had snuck past that guard instead of beaning him?")

This "what if" effect is a key determinant in how interested gamers are in replaying a game again and again, and the degree to which games achieve this is directly related to how successfully they provide players with meaningful opportunities for action at any given point in the game. Opportunities for action are, in a sense, a key currency used by games to satisfy autonomy needs—they inspire the "what if" thinking that draws a player back.

AUTONOMY: THE SECOND PILLAR OF THE HEROIC NARRATIVE

In the previous chapter on competence, we introduced our PENS model of need satisfaction as a new framework for understanding why games are so often built around themes of heroism. We saw that heroes epitomize mastery and competence, showing extraordinary strength and effectiveness in their actions. Indeed, it is often these elements of effectiveness and strength that inspire us, not only when we play the hero in a game, but also when we watch heroes on the screen or even in real life.

At the same time, heroes also exemplify determination and some of the purest expressions of autonomy. In other words, they are simultaneously the embodiment not just of masterful ability (i.e., competence), but also of volitional action. Like Batman in *The Dark Knight*, heroes confidently follow their own compass and take the path that no one else believes can be taken. Sometimes this involves creating new opportunities and finding new solutions, and sometimes it means accepting the responsibility for what must be done when all other choices have vanished. Regardless, the hero's ultimate path is never one of conforming or indecision, but of willful and deliberate action. Thus, when players are cast in the role of the hero in video games, which they consistently are, they are invited to embody a truly need-satisfying experience that exerts a strong motivational draw.

We've seen how many games, such as *The Sims* and *Civilization*, provide a rich landscape of choice energized by a backstory designed to give the player a sense of purpose and fuel meaningful, volitional action. But even when games do not provide players with choice, it is often a well-crafted heroic narrative that sustains their autonomy satisfaction by inspiring determination and a willful engagement of the path to be followed (even if it is the only one available!). For example, in the FPS game *Bioshock*, players are enlisted to help stop an evil madman. They are constantly given specific instructions about where to go and what to do, but are also given a heroic rationale and a narrative that, while linear, is filled with interesting discoveries. Without a compelling backstory, the game would run the risk of feeling pretty pushy (as many unsuccessful games do). But the heroic narrative the game creates—the unveiling of worthwhile goals that rest entirely on *your* shoulders—supports the feeling of autonomous action even though in reality choices are quite constrained.

The point is that alongside their mastery and skill, heroes also embody the volition and choice at the heart of our intrinsic need for autonomy. They have good reasons for their missions and calling. When we hold a video game box in our hand and read the description of what it offers us, stories of heroism resonate with our need for autonomy alongside our desire for mastery. When the game we wish for truly satisfies these needs as we play, the net result is a highly valued and motivating experience.

WEAVING TOGETHER MULTIPLE NEEDS: GAMES THAT INTEGRATE AUTONOMY AND COMPETENCE

We've taken a look at the fundamental importance of both competence and autonomy needs and seen how certain genres of games emphasize each of them in their gameplay. However, our model is not about labeling games as one thing or another. Just as in life, in any moment of gameplay there is the possibility of satisfying not just one psychological need, but multiple basic needs simultaneously. Looking forward, we believe that there are no hard-and-fast rules about how needs are satisfied, even within the genres we've already discussed. Innovation and new design ideas are always shifting the formula for satisfaction, even while the needs themselves remain constant.

In fact, rarely do games today satisfy only one need to the exclusion of others. The most successful and valued games become favorites with players specifically because they have found a formula that satisfies multiple needs simultaneously. And as games as a whole evolve, they are becoming much more adept at engaging us through an integration of need satisfaction on multiple levels. Let's look at a few examples of games that have been exceptionally successful with players because their design satisfies both competence and autonomy needs simultaneously.

THE AUTONOMOUS FPS: *HALO* AND *HALF-LIFE*

We've presented FPS games as a genre traditionally focused on competence satisfactions rather than autonomy. The game defines who you are as a character and moves you through a predetermined course of events. However, many FPS games are now pushing past a singular focus on competence satisfaction to include other needs such as autonomy. Two of the most successful FPS franchises of the last decade, *Halo* and *Half-Life*, hit upon designs that were both immensely satisfying to competence and also gave players an experience of choice and opportunity. Interestingly, they each achieved this in different ways.

In *Halo*, a science fiction–themed FPS in which you play a super-soldier whose face we never see (Master Chief), there are plenty of great combat sequences and weapons to quench mastery needs and the thirst for challenge. But *Halo* also achieves autonomy satisfactions in its design of the world's geography. Unlike most FPS games, throughout much of *Halo* there is an open-space structure that gives players tactical choices about where they go and how that geography can be used in different ways to overcome game challenges. You may know that there's an army up ahead, but rather than being forced to march at them in a canyon, the landscape expands to allow you to decide how to engage them. Even if you succeed, autonomy's replayability effect kicks in: Could you defeat them even more effectively if you took a different path, using a new combination of terrain and weaponry? Because *Halo* gives you that option, players perceive opportunity and deeper enjoyment through autonomy satisfaction.

In *Half-Life 2*, the developers achieved autonomy satisfaction through a different mechanism. The geographical structure is constrained in a similar fashion to other FPS games, but players are given an innovative weapon/tool—dubbed the "gravity gun"—that opens up new opportunities and choices. While most FPS games provide a variety of weapons (and thus some element of choice), these weapons all have a similar mechanic: pull trigger → cause damage. The gravity gun breaks this rule. It allows players to pull objects toward them, pick them up and move them, put them down gently, or forcefully catapult them forward. This enables players to use objects in their environment in creative ways, instantly multiplying the opportunities for action. In most FPS games, your decision is simply to "shoot or not shoot"; in *Half-Life*, you can consider each situation more creatively. The net result is a jump in possibilities and opportunities for action when using the gravity gun, increasing "what if" thinking and a satisfying sense of choice.

In our research, the data show how games like *Halo* and *Half-Life* differentiated themselves psychologically from other FPS games in the satisfaction of both competence and autonomy, which subsequently leads these games into greater success with players (and the marketplace). To date, *Halo* and *Half-Life 2* are among the highest rated and most successful FPS games of all time.

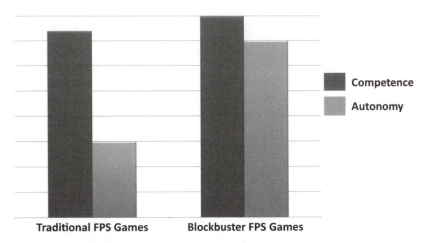

Figure 3.4 Traditionally, FPS games have emphasized competence satisfaction through intense challenges, but have sacrificed autonomy satisfaction in the process. By contrast, highly successful FPS games (*Halo, Half-Life,* and *Call of Duty*) have broken free of the tradtional formula, providing strong satisfactions of both competence and autonomy needs. (© 2010 Scott Rigby. Used by permission.)

Using PENS data from several studies, Figure 3.4 illustrates why this is so by showing the superior pattern of need satisfaction in *Halo* and *Half-Life 2* versus other FPS titles.

THE WHITE-KNUCKLE RPG: *DIABLO*

In the 1990s, the RPG genre also began to evolve a stronger mix of need satisfaction. *Diablo* was first released in 1996, and its success has led to numerous sequels up to the present day (as of this writing, *Diablo III* is in production). The story of *Diablo* involves the epic war between Heaven and the Devil (Diablo), with you as the story's hero called upon to make your way into the depths of Hell . . . hey wait, is this *Doom*? Nope, it's *Diablo*. I guess thrashing minions from the netherworld never gets old.

Diablo represents what has come to be known as the "action RPG," a game that combines traditional RPG choices in character development (autonomy satisfactions) with real-time movement and combat challenges (competence satisfactions). Like an RPG, you have the opportunity to customize who you are in the game to match your desired style of play. You can choose to be a hack-and-slash warrior, a wielder of dark magic, or some combination of skills that creates a personality that is truly unique. In addition, like most RPG games, *Diablo* is filled with magical items and armor that each grant special bonuses to your abilities, allowing you to even further customize and increase your power.

Unlike a traditional RPG game, however, *Diablo* brings real-time combat challenges into the game as a key element of its design and gameplay. Like an FPS or other competence-focused games, *Diablo* requires reflexes and the ability to think and act quickly in kill-or-be-killed scenarios. Amazingly, *Diablo* accomplishes this through a highly simplistic control scheme that allows players to stay deeply engaged in the action rather than learning and remembering complex controls. The net result is a game that brings players both the autonomy satisfactions of RPG customization and the more intense competence satisfactions that come from real-time combat. For players, it again represents a simultaneous satisfaction of multiple needs that increases value and enjoyment.

GRAND THEFT AUTO: THE OPEN-WORLD ACTION GAME

Another relatively new genre came into the mainstream with the release of *Grand Theft Auto* (*GTA*) in 1997. Although much derided by critics for its level of violence, what made *GTA* such a breakout success was the skillful way in which the design combined a focus on both competence and autonomy so successfully. In *GTA*, you take on the role of a criminal and have the opportunity to engage in many kinds of play, including armed combat, high-speed driving, and various quests to engage as you wish. In fact, although many decried the fact that the player was cast in the role of a criminal, consider what this provided the player in terms of choice: Criminals act with abandon, unconstrained by rules and often most content when flying in the face of them. And let's be honest, who among us doesn't sometimes fantasize about breaking out of the rules and acting without restraint? We may accept laws and conventions and see their value, but what we celebrate so often in fantasy is the character who *breaks* conventions, and whose actions are constrained only by his or her own will. In TV and the movies, it's become a cliché when the hero slams his fist down on the table and declares to his desk-bound bosses that "I haven't got time for your rules!" But it's a cliché for a reason—we love it.

In games like *GTA*, it's a worthy debate as to whether a criminal setting is the healthiest way to achieve this in a game, but you can't argue with the effectiveness of it. While *GTA* provided fewer choices than other games with regard to character development, it was simply unmatched in the breadth and variety of activities it made available to players. *GTA* allows players to unabashedly express themselves in creative and powerful ways.

It is no coincidence that each of these hybrid games was both a success in satisfying multiple PENS needs (i.e., autonomy *and* competence) as well as a blockbuster commercial success. Our model illustrates that as more intrinsic needs are satisfied in each moment of gameplay, overall enjoyment and motivation for a game (i.e., its value to the player) increases. With each development cycle, games continue to borrow design ideas from each other to create denser experiences of multiple need satisfactions, deepening their ability to draw us in and keep us engaged.

SUMMARY

In measuring the deep satisfactions that come from autonomy, we see time and again that the "fun" of games is not simply a function of competence and achievement, any more than a truly happy life comes from merely being a workaholic or a thrill seeker. It is in our very nature to need more than challenge to be satisfied over time. We intrinsically want to organize our own actions, to captain our own ship. We relate to the struggle for freedom and purpose in the stories we read and the movies we see because it resonates within us at a fundamental level. Video games give us the opportunity to spread our wings in a digital world and to soar with a freedom that the molecular world often does not provide. As we create and shape the character through which we act, we experience more meaningful satisfactions of autonomy that draw us into persistent play and loyalty to these digital worlds.

The strong draw into games, therefore, lies not in some mysterious "siren song" that we can't understand. The motivations to play reside in us at a basic level in the form of intrinsic needs that are always important to us and also often thwarted by events in life. The kid who feels chained to a desk at school and homework when home, the office worker stuck in her cubicle pushing papers, and the housewife with endless cycles of family chores all may feel a sense of liberty and empowerment in games that the molecular "real" world just doesn't offer. To be Magellan, Batman, or Lara Croft instead of a pawn in a mundane routine has a lot of psychological appeal to our need for competence and autonomy.

Some might see this as the same kind of escapism one finds in an hour of television or a good movie. But it's significant that in games we are not merely watching someone else's creation—we more directly *become* the hero. In game worlds, we take actions and make decisions that can often satisfy important and basic needs more powerfully because they follow from our agency. If I feel good because the actor in a movie helped someone, that's great. But how much more powerful it feels when it was *I* who took action and directly received the gratitude from someone who appreciated my actions.

From this perspective then, games are a virtual vehicle for the satisfaction of real needs, which has interesting implications for how we understand and relate to them. Whether these powerful satisfactions, readily supplied, are actual nourishment or just mental fast food is a question we will debate further. Yet before exploring that question, one important need is missing—our need for meaningful interpersonal connection to others. We have explored only two of the major components of what glues us to games in our discussion of competence and autonomy. We now turn to the final core need in our motivational model—our intrinsic need for *relatedness*.

NOTES

1. Connell, J. P., and Wellborn, J. G. (1991). "Competence, Autonomy, and Related-ness: A Motivational Analysis of Self-System Processes." *Self Processes and Development: The Minnesota Symposia on Child Development* (pp. 43–77). Hillsdale, NJ: Lawrence Erlbaum.

2. Grolnick, W. S., and Ryan, R. M. (1987). "Autonomy in Children's Learning: An Experimental and Individual Difference Investigation." *Journal of Personality and Social Psychology, 52*, 890–898.

3. For a recent example, see Jang, H., Reeve, J., Ryan, R. M., and Kim, A. (2009). "Can Self-determination Theory Explain what Underlies the Productive, Satisfying Learn-ing Experiences of Collectivistically Oriented Korean Students?" *Journal of Educational Psychology, 101*, 644–661.

4. Baard, P. P., Deci, E. L., and Ryan, R. M. (2004). "Intrinsic Need Satisfaction: A Motivational Basis of Performance and Well-being in Two Work Settings." *Journal of Applied Social Psychology, 34*, 2, 045–2, 068.

5. Gagné, M., and Deci, E. L. (2005). "Self-Determination Theory and Work Motiva-tion." *Journal of Organizational Behavior, 26*, 331–362.

6. Ryan, R. M., Bernstein, J. H., and Brown, K. W. (2010). "Weekends, Work, and Well-being: Psychological Need Satisfactions and Day of the Week Effects on Mood, Vitality, and Physical Symptoms." *Journal of Social and Clinical Psychology, 29*, 95–122.

7. Ryan, R. M., and Deci, E. L. (2007). "Active Human Nature: Self-Determination Theory and the Promotion and Maintenance of Sport, Exercise, and Health." In M. S. Hagger and N. L. D. Chatzisarantis (Eds.), *Intrinsic Motivation and Self-determination in Exercise and Sport* (pp. 1–19). Champaign, IL: Human Kinetics.

8. La Guardia, J. G., Ryan, R. M., Couchman, C. E., and Deci, E. L. (2000). "With-in-Person Variation in Security of Attachment: A Self-Determination Theory Perspective on Attachment, Need Fulfillment, and Well-Being." *Journal of Personality and Social Psy-chology, 79*, 367–384.

9. Ruth La Ferla. "No Budget, No Boundaries: It's the Real You," *New York Times*, October 21, 2009, http://www.nytimes.com/2009/10/22/fashion/22Avatar.html?_r=1&scp=1&sq=Second%20Life&st=cse.

10. Because they are also multiplayer games, we'll talk more about MUDs in the next chapter on the third of the intrinsic needs, relatedness.

11. Weinstein, N., Przybylski, A. K., and Ryan, R. M. (2009). "Can Nature Make Us More Caring? Effects of Immersion in Nature on Intrinsic Aspirations and Generosity." *Personality and Social Psychology Bulletin, 35*, 1, 315–1, 329.

12. Brown, S. (2009). *Play: How It Shapes the Brain, Opens the Imagination and Invigo-rates the Soul.* New York: Avery.

Chapter 4

GAMES AND THE NEED FOR RELATEDNESS

Everybody needs somebody sometime . . .

Dean Martin

At one time, playing video games was seen as a largely solitary, isolating activity—the lonely teen, staring into the screen, cut off from friends and social activities. But with each passing year, video games are becoming more and more a social world—a place to meet people, hang out with friends, and share experiences—often while storming a fortress or arming a spaceship. Today, a positive cultural buzz draws people together around gaming, catalyzed and propelled by the Internet's ever-increasing connectivity. Game developers recently christened a new category of games, *social games*, that taps into the blockbuster success of social technologies (such as Facebook) to create games entirely based on social networks of friends and family. But even within genres of games that have traditionally been single-player experiences, developers are focused on enhancing social opportunities—enabling players to more easily chat, collaborate, slay dragons, or build cities together, and collectively celebrate successes and commiserate over failures. And, because degrees of privacy are available, gamers can also share personal concerns and opinions from their lives outside the game itself.

Why all this effort to facilitate player interactions? Because players have made it clear that they enjoy games more when they can—at least at times—experience *relatedness*. In fact, it is impossible to understand the sustained motivation players have for games without focusing on this powerful human need for relatedness and the ways games satisfy it. Like our intrinsic needs for competence and autonomy, relatedness is the third need in our PENS model because it reflects a deeply intrinsic and fundamental motivational energy: Humans inherently seek to be connected with others and feel that they are interacting in meaningful ways. This need for relatedness naturally occurs in all of us, requiring no external incentive. We are simply evolved to connect and to feel like we belong.

Each of us expresses this need spontaneously as we seek out friendships or attention, feeling the happiness that results. We also feel this need's centrality in our lives when it is thwarted—by the pain of loneliness or isolation. In fact, interpersonal rejection is among the most painful of psychological experiences, giving testimony to just how deeply important relatedness is.[1]

Of course, there are "big" ways to satisfy relatedness needs. There is romantic love—the Romeo and Juliet "world of two" in which nothing else exists but amorous bliss. Although we have heard lots of stories of players actually falling in love in a virtual world and transferring that to the molecular world, games more commonly facilitate a different but very important form of relatedness, one that has been shown to contribute directly to well-being. It is simply called *companionship*.[2] In companionship, we are motivated to engage in mutually enjoyable activities from which we derive both pleasure and a sense of connectedness and shared experience. Companionship is obtained from pleasures as simple as trading stories or sharing hobbies, and research in the molecular world shows that it intensifies when people pursue common goals together, such as through sports or volunteer activities.

Video games offer a remarkably strong opportunity to instantly connect and experience companionship in these ways. Sitting here at my desk, I could enter a multiplayer game and be with friends in less than 60 seconds. As I log in, my network of in-game friends is notified that I am online. Many might shout greetings to me as I enter the virtual world—a tradition in most online social groups. And unlike meeting the "gang" at the food court at the mall, pelting each other with Taco Bell napkins would not be our only choice of activity. Our video game immediately offers us a menu of shared challenges to pursue together with opportunities to support, cooperate, and be rewarded in victory—all elements that increase feelings of meaningful connection and companionship. Even without an existing social group, multiplayer games facilitate the spontaneous creation of teams to tackle challenges. Simply click the "looking for group" button and the game itself will match you up with fellow adventurers, sending you off together to forge new friendships and shared experiences.

Because of this immediate ability to bring people together in shared worlds, video games supply a novel and efficient vehicle for people to experience relatedness. What's more, connecting with others in games has a lower "price of admission" and risk than relationships within our molecular world. To meet people in the real world can be difficult, often resulting in us mumbling weakly about the weather while we try to think of something more interesting to say. Video games remove pain and awkwardness by surrounding players with things to do together, such as group quests and adventures that serve as "next-generation" icebreakers. And because we interact with one another through avatars, games also decrease many factors that make us self-conscious—such as personal appearance—so we feel more freedom to just be ourselves. In short, games offer ready forms of relatedness that make companionship and feelings of belonging more accessible than ever.

Beyond companionship, relatedness needs are satisfied in even more subtle ways. On a good day, we experience relatedness satisfactions from many little moments, such as being recognized by the clerk at the grocery store or receiving a smile from a coworker when entering the office. Such flashes of appreciation and recognition light up people's emotional lives because they help us feel significant and connected to others, making an experience or a place enjoyable. The old adage "Service with a Smile" has motivational merit—it creates micro-moments of relatedness that draw us back. That smile tells us that we are valued.

In games, this recognition happens not only through other players, but also by the virtual characters who inhabit that world. Although it is most natural to think about relatedness as dependent on two or more people, our research shows us how computer characters ("non-player characters" or "NPCs") can enhance our relatedness satisfactions when they interact with us in meaningful and supportive ways. For example, when NPCs offer us a well-timed compliment or smile, players feel important and worthwhile. Just as a joke shared with your waiter can change your mood, a warm compliment from a computer character can also make your day, especially when it is specific to something we have actually done in the game.

This may seem a bit odd to say. Surely people know that computer characters are just lines of code. Even compared to a glancing exchange with your waiter—a *real* person—the relatedness from computer characters must, we imagine, be significantly shallower. In fact, for some people it may be troubling to think that we might experience deep feelings of relatedness from interactions with an artificial person. What a computer character says shouldn't matter that much! But we have very authentic emotional reactions to fictional characters all the time. We cry at movies. We become engrossed in a great book. In the next chapter, we'll explore this idea of immersion or presence in fictional worlds in greater detail. But it is possible, particularly through these small moments of "interpersonal" exchange, for computer characters to give us very real boosts to our relatedness.

To identify the key ingredients that satisfy relatedness needs—both in significant long-term relationships and glancing moments of interpersonal interactions—let's take a look at what must be present interpersonally in order to feel truly connected with others.

A Key Ingredient of Relatedness: You Matter

At the heart of all those happy interpersonal moments, both large and small, is the feeling that we *matter* to others. As the great American writer Elie Wiesel said, "The opposite of love is not hate. It is indifference."[3] Even during brief moments of interaction with those that we may never see again, we can feel relatedness operating powerfully.

Wandering lost through a confusing airport, we entreat an employee to help us find our gate. He sighs impatiently and, barely looking at us, mutters a curt "dunno" as he turns and walks away. We decide this person is clearly an insufferable jerk. More importantly, we feel even more disconnected and lost. In just a few seconds, this stranger powerfully crushed our belief—our *need*—that we matter enough for him to care.

"Excuse me," we try again with someone else, "Can you please help me?" This time we're met with a warm smile and a concerned listener who tries his best to help. By being attended to—by mattering in this small moment—our need for relatedness is met. Our whole emotional state changes in an instant, not only because we may get the information we need, but also because we are important enough to listen to. This encounter even makes us like this airport more because we experience it as a place wher those around us actually care.

We've all had experiences like this, and it highlights how powerfully experiences of relatedness affect us, not only in our more lasting relationships, but in the casual encounters of everyday life. In brief, when we look at the aspects of our relationships and interactions with others that support our relatedness need, we find three elements that are of particular importance in deepening satisfaction:

1. *Acknowledgment*—The first step to any feeling of relatedness is being acknowledged by another person. As with our friendly airport attendant, this can happen almost instantaneously when we make eye contact and receive a warm smile. It's further enhanced when we feel that we have one's full attention, that we are being listened to.
2. *Support*—Beyond acknowledgement, there is a desire to be supported. We want the other person to connect with who we are and what we're feeling, both cognitively and empathically. This requires that they not only understand us, but also that they facilitate satisfaction of our autonomy and competence, supporting these other important needs.
3. *Impact*—In addition to support, we matter to others when we see our impact on them. Healthy expressions of this might be as simple as the laughter of a shared joke or as complex as the deep emotional connection—what the social theorist Fairbairn called the *mature dependence*[4]—between two partners.

The common theme here is that we feel related when we matter—when we are acknowledged, when we are seen as significant, and when we get to express to others similar feelings and be understood. These are some of the basic threads that connect us.

VIDEO GAMES AND RELATEDNESS

Let's turn now to how video games satisfy our need for relatedness. As we previously noted, it may seem counterintuitive and even contradictory to talk about how most video games satisfy relatedness needs. After all, we've defined relatedness in terms of the meaningful connection *between people*—one in which we recognize the importance of others. But don't most games require that the player "unplug" from the molecular world of friends and family in order to immerse themselves into the artificial game world? If you've ever tried to get the attention of a gamer who is intensely engaged, you know what we're talking about. Short of setting their clothes on fire, it can be a difficult task to get even a moment of attention, let alone any true relatedness. Could there be anything more isolating?

In a later chapter, we'll talk about how video games can indeed contribute to social isolation. But for most players, our data show that meaningful positive moments of relatedness do exist in games. In fact, players find relatedness satisfaction not just through playing with other people (i.e., multiplayer games), but also in single-player games.

GIVING PLAYERS MOMENTS OF RELEVANCE

In traditional media—when reading a good book or seeing a great movie—we feel ourselves drawn into the story and connected to the characters. Although I've seen it many times, whenever I watch *Rocky* I am always on my feet by the end, cheering for him and swinging imaginary punches at Apollo Creed. But if Stallone looked out at me from the screen and said, "Yo . . . thanks a lot, I appreciate the moral support," I'm sure I'd fall over in a dead faint. In traditional storytelling, although we may get involved emotionally, we know that our reactions don't impact the characters. While they may matter to *us*, we simply don't matter to *them*.

This is limiting with respect to our relatedness needs,[5] because relatedness satisfactions entail that we matter to others. Unlike movies, here's where the interactive nature of games brings a deeper potential to satisfy relatedness, even when one is playing alone. Characters in traditional media *act for* us; characters in video games also *react to* us. In the video game world, Rocky *can* look out and thank us. He can even ask us to join him as his corner man. Or, we might instead root for Apollo Creed and help him actually win the fight. In other words, *we matter to the characters and events in video games*. And as we see them acknowledging us, feel them supporting us, and have the experience of impacting their "lives," our relatedness needs are satisfied—because after all, isn't that the kind of interactivity we most value from people, regardless of whether they are real or digital?

Going a bit deeper on this point, we often look at how well game characters (NPCs) offer the player the *experience of being relevant* to that character. In other words, how richly do NPCs express to players that they are needed and that their actions are appreciated (i.e., how much does the player matter?). There are several general ways in which this happens.

First, NPCs have the potential to speak to the player and act as a vehicle for motivating player actions. NPCs that express a positive belief in the player's ability and enlist the player's help in solving puzzles, overcoming obstacles, and completing quests and missions communicate a trust in the player's competence to succeed. For example, in our last chapter you might recall Mayor

Wimpy pleading with us to save his town from the evil warlord. In so doing, he communicates to us that we are both relevant and needed (relatedness) and also expresses a belief that we can meet this challenge of strength and courage (competence/mastery). That's already enough to make us feel a bit proud. In some games, if we take up the mayor's request, he may even accompany us on the journey and fight side by side with us in battle, thus allowing us to experience a significant moment together.

Unfortunately, in our work with developers, we often see games that miss these kinds of opportunities because they are trying to create a dark, gritty, and challenging world, and believe that in such a world everyone is rude and isolating. "Quit bothering me!" "Can't you see I'm busy!" "Get moving!" are just some of the quips thrown at players who are innocently trying to speak with these virtual curmudgeons. Sometimes these comments are programmed in simply as an after-thought, or to push the player in a desired direction. We suspect little thought is given to the emotional cost of using NPCs as cattle prods in this way. But this kind of heavy-handed dialogue, riddled with impatience and outright insult, rarely succeeds with players. Unless your game is entitled "Journey to the Depart-ment of Motor Vehicles," such treatment is probably hurting what the developer most wants—to create a satisfying and valued experience.

By contrast, a different kind of attitude exists in the NPCs of the most successful games. Sure, many great games have grumpy bad guys who provide the "dramatic tension" and set up the game's challenges. But when the dialogue from NPCs—whether a friend or a foe—shows respect for a player's abilities, there is stronger support of the player's competence and a greater opportu-nity for feelings of meaningful connection. There is also greater engagement with the game's content. When NPCs offer support to players, they are more likely to interact with them. Grumpy NPCs, by contrast, are more likely to be ignored.

A great example of NPCs being "programmed" to aid relatedness comes from an unlikely new source, a game called *Left 4 Dead* (*L4D*). In *L4D*, the developers made it possible for the zombie adversaries to disable a player, essen-tially leaving them helpless on the turf. But the NPCs have been designed to come to the player's rescue. Believe me, as someone who has been paralyzed by a mob of angry zombies, it leads to an authentic feeling of distress and subsequent relief and gratitude when your NPC teammate saves you from a gruesome fate. Sure you know that you are playing a game with purely fictional characters, but you also feel quite legitimately that you are part of a team that cares about your survival. Our data on the game confirm this personal experience: Players feel a closer connection to NPCs as a function of being directly supported by them. The experience of relatedness—that you matter—is often quite real and satisfying.

Game characters also satisfy relatedness needs by supporting players in feeling autonomy and facilitating choice. Conversations with NPCs present players with opportunities for action (missions/quests) and lay a strong foundation for the game's story, helping the player "buy in" to the path ahead of them (i.e., increasing volition). When the script between NPC and player supports autonomy (rather than controlling players or pushing them around), relatedness needs are enhanced. So for games that are deeply invested in engaging the player in their stories (i.e., building strong volition for the story line), it becomes even more important that they have an experience of relatedness to NPCs. In other words, autonomy support increases relatedness, subsequently enhancing the likelihood of really *caring* about what the NPC is saying and asking the player to do (i.e., the game's story).

NPCs also provide relatedness satisfaction simply by recognizing and acknowledging the actions and accomplishments of the player. Here's how this works: You have just defeated Warlord Cranky in hand-to-hand combat, and having thus saved the small village of Victimville, decide to return there for a burger and a nap (warlord slaying works up quite an appetite). As you ride through town, you realize that things have changed since the last time you were here. All of the townspeople are smiling and waving at you. As you enter the tavern, the innkeeper announces the arrival of the "hero of Victimville"! Even the things you buy at the shops in town are less expensive. What makes the gratitude of the virtual townsfolk gratifying to you is that the impact you see on "others" is accurate—it reflects your *actual* actions and decisions. It reminds you that you did indeed save these people and their (admittedly virtual) lives. Although they may be virtual, their gratitude is not arbitrary. Their reaction feels authentic because it is in response to something you actually did for them. In fact, it may feel more genuine than many real-world experiences, such as the plastic "welcome to MegaMart" smile we get from a greeter at a superstore (who we may suspect couldn't care less); see Figure 4.1.

Great single-player experiences with NPCs (such as in *Oblivion)* succeed with players partly because they provide thoughtful contingent reactions that successfully yield relatedness satisfactions. When the dialogue with an NPC meaningfully changes, when they react with happiness, anger, or sadness based on the player's individual choices, players feel they have a meaningful impact. In other words, they matter. As the artificial intelligence of NPCs continues to improve—potentially simulating more precisely the variety and emotional dynamics of our molecular world social interactions—games and their digital actors will have a growing opportunity to satisfy relatedness needs in ways not previously possible through other forms of linear storytelling.

In summary, each of these kinds of interactions between player and NPC is an opportunity for the player to have what we call a *moment of relevance*. Each one increases the chance that relatedness needs will be satisfied and that the game will be valued more highly. This relevance, of course, is often powerfully achieved through the game's story, which leads us back to our conversation of the "player as hero."

Figure 4.1 Greetings to the hero who saved us all! Games like *Oblivion* have NPCs that support relatedness through "contextual feedback" based on player actions. (*The Elder Scrolls IV: Oblivion* © 2006 Bethesda Softworks LLC, a ZeniMax Media company. All rights reserved.)

RELATEDNESS: ANOTHER MOTIVATIONAL PILLAR OF THE HEROIC NARRATIVE

In the last chapter on autonomy, we looked at Batman's decision to take the blame for crimes he did not commit as a strong example of volitional action, enabled by his strength and competence (in Gordon's words, "Because he can take it."). But there is yet a third thread in this story that also resonates deeply with us: Batman acts out of a commitment to others who depend upon him. The meaningful relationship that Batman has with Gotham City and those close to him (Alfred and Gordon) is an ongoing source of his energy to suit up each night. Indeed, it is the severing of his relationship with his parents that sows the seeds of Batman's very existence. A big part of what makes him a hero is his ability to stand in the face of personal loss and retain his relatedness—his meaningful connection to others.

Because there is rarely a story of a hero without villains, it is also interesting how relatedness distinguishes between the two. After all, whether blowing up innocent people or *stopping* the blowing up of innocent people, both the Joker and Batman are really good at what they do (competence). But while Batman takes actions that are energized by his connection and relatedness to others, the Joker acts out of isolation and without a thread of meaningful connection. In fact, in *The Dark Knight*, he uses relatedness to manipulate us—fabricating various heart-wrenching stories about how his disfigurement was the tragic result of betrayal by those he loved. When we first hear the Joker describe having been disfigured by his alcoholic father, we feel sympathy because it resonates with our intrinsic need for relatedness. But a bit later he changes the story and claims he self-inflicted his injuries to hold on to the love of his wife. In that moment, we feel chilled—this man not only has no emotional connection to others, he is using our intrinsic need for such connection to prey upon us. It instantly becomes easier for us to see him as an unsympathetic psychopath (albeit one who is fun to watch from the popcorn-munching safety of our theater seat).

We do not get off the hook as easily with the hero-turned-villain Harvey Dent. Dent is a courageous ally of Batman in the fight against crime, until the woman he loves is killed by the Joker. His despair breaks him emotionally, corrupting his commitment to Gotham and choking off his relatedness to all around him. He "lives to see himself become the villain" because of this failure of relatedness, and it is also for this reason that we have sympathy for him until the end. We can empathize with the idea that losing those you love dearly can shatter us, precisely because relatedness is a deeply felt intrinsic need.

It is also worth noting that the woman Dent lost was not only loved by him, but by Batman as well. Batman had known and loved her for his entire life. Further still, Batman's intention to save her was manipulated by the Joker to ensure that it was she who died. And yet, what distinguishes Batman from Dent, what serves as the currency of his courage and strength, is his ability to sustain his connection and commitment to those who depended upon him. Simply put, it is relatedness that ultimately distinguishes between hero and villain.

It is in the heady froth of heroic narratives such as this that we see all the core needs of the PENS model brought vividly to life. Because games so often cast us in the role of hero, they also afford us the feelings of gratifications only heroes usually get to feel—among them, the gratitude and respect of others. This in turn helps us understand the appeal of playing a hero and the strong motivational pull of the heroic story. Simply put, hero play is simultaneously fulfilling multiple intrinsic needs. And like Batman's relationship with Gotham City, building relatedness with the virtual inhabitants of the game world is a key element of their value and enjoyment.

Relatedness in Multiplayer Games

While everything we've discussed in this chapter so far can be experienced in a single-player game, many video game players will tell you that much (if not most) of the fun comes from playing with others. Multiplayer experiences—or interpersonal play—generally comes in two flavors: playing the game with those who are physically with you (what we sometimes call "couch play") and playing with others who are connected to the game from a remote location somewhere else in the molecular world. Games can also have both these kinds of play happening simultaneously, increasing the richness, and complexity, of interaction.

One thing we've emphasized is that relatedness is largely a function of how much we feel supported by others, in particular with respect to our own competence (mastery) and autonomy. This means that many games that you might not think of as "relatedness" games, such as violent first-person shooters, can be highly satisfying of relatedness needs when basic needs are supported in multiplayer play. Let's look at some flavors of interpersonal play and how they enhance multiple needs in the PENS model.

Cooperative Play

Relatedness is most clearly at work when two or more players team up to play cooperatively. Traditionally, this play takes place between friends or family members sitting side by side (couch play), although with the advent of high-speed networking, many games now offer players the opportunity to team up for cooperative play no matter how far apart they are. While we've seen that single-player game experiences can satisfy multiple needs very well, cooperative play weaves in even deeper opportunities for satisfaction, because by its very nature there is a remarkable motivational synergy in teamwork.

How Teamwork Synergizes Competence and Relatedness. In chapter 2, we saw how games create a fertile field for competence and mastery through challenge. When games integrate cooperative play into the experience of challenge, this catalyzes need satisfactions in two important ways. First, cooperative play allows each player to overcome challenges that would be impossible if playing alone. In other words, cooperative play extends the range of competence satisfaction that is possible for players, raising the bar and their potential for mastery. In a single-player game, you may be able to take down a single powerful enemy. But by teaming up, you can conquer an army of them.

The elegant part of this scenario is that the challenge itself, an element usually associated with competence, also directly enhances relatedness needs. In facing a shared challenge that can only be overcome by teamwork, the situation instantly communicates to each player that he or she matters to the others. Challenge heightens each player's experience of being important to his or her teammates and highlights every action as a potential "moment of relevance" in helping everyone achieve victory. Simply put, challenge itself deepens the potential for relatedness.

Genre Example: Massively Multiplayer Online Games (MMOs)

In 1999, Sony launched a fantasy-based, multiplayer RPG game called *EverQuest*. It was not the first multiplayer fantasy game, and as we'll see in a moment, certainly not the most successful. But at the time, its success was staggering. More than 100,000 people were playing the game at its peak. The game allowed thousands of gamers to play the game simultaneously, interacting with one another around the clock. Many players were *living* in the game, sometimes 12 to 14 hours a day (or even longer). No other game had ever achieved this kind of dedicated grip on such a wide mainstream audience. We were doing some work for Sony during *EverQuest's* heyday, and when I asked an executive there what the internal reaction was to the game's success, he said, simply, "It's transformed us as a company."

What would come next would make *EverQuest* seem quaint by comparison. *World of Warcraft (WoW)*, first launched in 2004, has more than 10 million players, or roughly 100 times the population *EverQuest* did just a decade ago. Like its predecessor, *WoW* is a persistent virtual world that many players inhabit simultaneously; in our research, active players regularly spend more than 20 hours per week—almost three hours a day—playing the game.

EverQuest and *WoW* are examples of a relatively new breed of game known as *massively multiplayer online games* (MMOs).[6] In its core design, *WoW* is similar to the RPG games we discussed in the last chapter on autonomy, and it enjoys all of the benefits of that genre—notably a rich open world of opportunity that satisfies our intrinsic need for choice and personal volition. In fact, putting aside the multiplayer aspect of *WoW* for a moment, its detailed and varied environments, quests, and character-development choices make this game one of the most successful games ever at satisfying autonomy needs, which our research shows has contributed greatly to the sustained interest of its players. But *WoW* also weaves in many kinds of interpersonal play that synergistically satisfy relatedness and competence too, particularly through cooperative play and teamwork. The end result is a game that "hits on all cylinders" motivationally, creating a deep and enduring loyalty in its audience.

Us against the World: Competence and Relatedness in "Endgame Raids"

Despite the vast amount of content in *WoW*, most of its dedicated players have long since seen it all. In particular, experienced *WoW* players spend a good deal of their time repeating things that they have already done before multiple times. These players are said to be in "endgame": They are no longer engaged in the usual RPG tasks of exploration and advancing their characters' core skills, and are instead repeatedly focused on highly specialized content. In many games, once you've done it all, it's time to call it quits and move on. So what keeps *WoW* players so engaged?

WoW accomplishes this through extremely challenging content and fights with very powerful enemies (i.e., "boss fights") that can only be conquered through highly coordinated team efforts called "raids." Relatedness needs are enhanced by ensuring that all players have a role to play that is important to the others.

Some players have the job of doing massive damage, while others' role is to heal the team to be sure no one dies. If one player doesn't do his or her part, all will fail—thus creating an instant crucible of mutual dependence and relatedness (i.e., everyone matters).

But our data show that competence needs are also highly active because of the difficulty in defeating bosses and overcoming obstacles. Interestingly, these experiences do not satisfy autonomy needs—at their peak, raids are an intricate combat ballet that leaves little room for improvisation. But remember that the core RPG design and open-world structure of *WoW* already provides plenty of autonomy support whenever players desire this. Raids fill in the need-satisfaction picture; complementing *WoW*'s core satisfaction of autonomy are these epic battles that instead emphasize relatedness and competence.

A personal story from another MMO highlights the synergistic relationship between competence and relatedness. About three years ago, I returned to a *Star Wars*-themed MMO to play some additional content that allowed players to pilot their own spaceship and tackle increasingly difficult challenges in open space (shooting down enemy fighters, protecting conveys, etc.). There was a series of challenges that had to be accomplished in order to reach the top rank, which once achieved, gave you access to a variety of new kinds of spaceships. As with most game mechanics focused on competence, the challenges were increasingly difficult.

The final challenge was virtually impossible to achieve as a solo player. It required attacking and destroying a large flagship that was protected by many support ships. It only appeared in space occasionally, and there was limited time to attack it before it disappeared. As I had not played the game in some time before returning, I really didn't know many players (and have never been terribly good at organizing teams anyway). Several times I tried to defeat this ship by myself, and each time was blown to smithereens.

On my penultimate attempt, I did manage to completely disable the ship's engines before I was once again turned into space dust. Suddenly, my communicator lit up with a message from another player:

"Nice."

It turns out that a small group of players had been watching from a distance, plotting their own strategy of attack. By disabling the ship, I had given us all time to figure out another strategy. They invited me to join them on the next attempt. There weren't many of us, but by coordinating our attack we took out the ship in less than a minute. Each of our computer screens lit up with a spectacular explosion and the message that we had achieved the highest pilot rank available. We cheered and slapped each other on the back (virtually of course) for 10 minutes. I even ran out to find my wife and tell her of our exploits. You would have thought we just tore down the Berlin Wall.

To this day, years later, I remember the feeling of exhilaration at having achieved this. But what is really interesting is that although I hadn't played with those teammates before, and did not play with them afterward, I remember them well from just this one experience together. We all needed one another to reach that goal. We all mattered in an emotionally powerful way—so powerful that the memory has endured. This is the remarkable marriage of mastery and relatedness satisfactions that good games can provide.

I have many similarly powerful memories from other multiplayer games that I have enjoyed over the last 10 years. This one involved victory; others have involved moments when I was rescued by strangers, or when I felt the gratitude of helping others. But each of these memories has a same common thread: They always involved (1) teaming up with others, (2) working together to overcome a significant challenge, and (3) feeling camaraderie and connection as we pursued the goal. Although more than 90 percent of my time playing video games over the years has been playing solo (i.e., as a single player), 90 percent of my lasting memories from games consist of these interpersonal moments. This illustrates how cooperative multiplayer challenges can provide powerful (and memorable) satisfactions of both our competence and relatedness needs.

How Teamwork Synergizes Autonomy and Relatedness

Cooperative play can also act to enhance autonomy alongside relatedness. Remember that one mechanism for enhancing autonomy is providing interesting opportunities for action—enabling the player to feel that they have a variety of meaningful choices in the actions they take. Coordinating actions with another player multiplies the possible strategies and paths that can be explored to reach goals and overcome challenge. The combination to a safe is one metaphor for how this works: If a safe had just one number (i.e., a single player), you wouldn't have to try many options before you'd exhaust them all. By increasing how many numbers are in the code, you greatly multiply the possible combinations. Similarly, adding players to a cooperative multiplayer team greatly increases your choices, opportunities, and "what if" moments—all of which increase the potential for autonomy satisfaction.

Of course, all of this is dependent on the game design and the goals of its creators. Each game makes creative choices that, whether intended or accidental, impact the player experience. For example, by requiring highly choreographed play, *World of Warcraft* focuses less on autonomy satisfactions in multiplayer raid play and instead emphasizes competence satisfactions. In our research, we often see other game designs succeed because they have hit upon a formula that satisfies multiple needs at the same time, using relatedness to catalyze both competence and autonomy needs simultaneously.

Team First-Person Shooters

A good example of the highly engaging gameplay that emerges when multiple needs are satisfied is the "team FPS" game. Although many FPS games pride themselves on creating violent and often isolating single-player experiences, they can be transformed into powerful satisfiers of relatedness needs when offering opportunities for interpersonal play. We see this most strongly in FPS games that offer team versus team "war games," such as capture the flag or "kill or be killed" goals. Within these designs:

- The core FPS need satisfaction of *competence* is enhanced by the increased challenge of playing against an opposing team of real people (who as of this writing remain much craftier than computer opponents);
- *Relatedness* needs are strongly satisfied by the mutual reliance on teammates to look out for one another and work together to achieve the objective (i.e., each player matters and is highly relevant to the others);
- *Autonomy* needs are satisfied by enabling teams to constantly formulate and test new strategies to achieve objectives (i.e., maximizing "what if" creativity).

As a result, FPS games that offer well-designed team play are among the most successful in retaining customers and sustaining the engagement of players over months and years. Our data on game longevity show that fans of successful team FPS titles report a longer relationship with these games than FPS fans who simply play the single-player experience. In fact, team FPS players have some of the longest relationships with their games among all video game players, specifically because this kind of play has such strong simultaneous satisfaction of competence, autonomy, and relatedness.

Competitive Play

All of this relatedness talk may seem well and good in the touchy-feely world of cooperative play. But much of the time, interpersonal play has nothing to do with cooperation—it has to do with blowing the other guy to bits, or in the case of the controversial "finishing moves" in the *Mortal Kombat* series, literally ripping out your opponent's spine. Can relatedness exist in *this* sort of gameplay?

Before we discuss how even such competitive play can support relatedness, let's talk about other forms of recreational competition, such as sports or a good game of chess. Here too we see a seeming paradox between trying to vanquish an opponent, and in many cases also feeling closer to them as a result. This isn't always the case, of course, but it often occurs. Each week during grad school, a classmate and I would play racquetball. We'd go at it pretty hard, and it was quite competitive. Yet even though we were opponents looking to defeat each other, it was also an activity that we greatly enjoyed and that strengthened our relationship.

This would seem paradoxical without understanding the interplay of need satisfaction. In our competition with each other on the court, we each acted as a sharpening stone that enabled the other to improve. In all forms of recreational competition, including video games, your opponent ideally gives you the opportunity to increase your skills, that is, to improve your competence. Through competition we contribute to the competence satisfaction of the other and them to us, which creates the kind of meaningful and supportive connections that are a hallmark of relatedness. The other player gives us the gift of helping us become more masterful. This explains how interpersonal connections sometimes grow from even the fiercest competition.

Of course, other factors also come to bear in competition to either enhance or thwart relatedness and other need satisfactions. Good-natured competition of the sort my friend and I had on the racquetball court represents the positive motivational satisfactions (i.e., competence, relatedness) that *can* occur, or what we might call *constructive competition*. But when we feel our opponents are trying to tear us down as people—through taunts, cheating, and mean-spirited play—our relatedness needs are thwarted. This is *destructive competition*, where a rift in relatedness exists between opponents who feel irrelevant and/or oppressed by each other.

As in other areas of life, both kinds of competition exist in the world of video games. All competitive play is referred to as "player versus player," or simply "PvP" play. Just as constructive and destructive competition are mostly a function of the people involved rather than the activity itself, examples of both are found in virtually all games that offer PvP play.[7] For example, a game may allow you to challenge a friendly player to a one-on-one "duel" for some constructive competition. Alternatively, in many games, it is possible to ambush another player or even for a group of players to gang up on one opponent. Usually the latter scenario—often called *ganking*—reflects destructive competition. Although for some, even an ambush is experienced as part of the game and an opportunity to interact playfully with others in a virtual rough-housing session.

In other words, just as some people will thoroughly enjoy a good tennis match even when they lose, while others will angrily curse the heavens at every lost point, finding relatedness satisfaction in PvP play is largely a function of one's experience of the competition. Did competition with the other player feel like a sharpening stone, honing your skills? Or did it feel as if you were being put down and diminished by the experience?

We do believe that games can "stack the deck" in favor of relatedness in the way they are designed. The more they have a structure encouraging support and cooperation and discouraging destructive competition, the more players will feel their relatedness needs satisfied and be likely to return to the game. In fact, by thinking about relatedness in the mechanics of the game (i.e., the ways in which players can interact) and by emphasizing rewards for constructive competition, game designs will maximize relatedness and improve the enjoyment and engagement of players.

BRINGING IT ALL TOGETHER: A NEED-SATISFACTION REPRISE

We've now finished an overview of the three core needs in the PENS model, and have given examples of specific games and types of play that focus on each individual need. Along the way, we've touched upon the fact that games are getting better and better at satisfying multiple needs rather than being "one-hit wonders." Because competence, autonomy, and relatedness are each unique, games that satisfy more of these needs have incremental appeal, with each component building upon the value of the other. Enthusiasm and motivation for gaming is consequently growing stronger year by year. The basic psychological mechanisms we've discussed are one way to understand more clearly what underlies the intense connection between games and their players.

Next, we explore what results from these strong connections, beginning with how they facilitate deep experiences of *immersion* in a game world. Most gamers and developers would agree that among the greatest compliments a player can pay to a game is the simple statement "This game is *totally* immersive." Let's take a look at this idea of immersion and its relationship to need satisfaction and other aspects of the player experience.

NOTES

1. Baumeister, R. F., and Leary, M. R. (1995). "The Need to Belong: Desire for Interpersonal Attachments as a Fundamental Human Motivation." *Psychological Bulletin, 117*, 497–529.

2. Sarason, B. R., Sarason, I. G., and Gurung, R. A. R (2001). "Close Personal Relationships and Health Outcomes: A Key to the Role of Social Support," 15–41. In B. R. Sarason and S. Duck (Eds.), *Personal Relationships: Implications for Clinical and Community Psychology*. Chichester, England: John Wiley & Sons.

3. Wiesel, Eli. *U.S. News & World Report*, October 27, 1986.

4. Fairbairn, W. R. D. (1952). *Psychological Studies of the Personality*. London: Routledge & Kegan Paul.

5. This is not to say that we don't believe that traditional storytelling cannot satisfy relatedness needs. Although we have not yet examined need satisfaction in relationship to linear media in depth, we believe that it is quite possible that needs are satisfied through identifying with characters and imagining or "projecting" oneself into highly engaging stories.

6. Alternatively, these games are called MMORPGs: "massively multiplayer online role-playing games," although in recent years the "RPG" has been dropped as developers play with new kinds of game structures and formats that break from the traditional RPG structure.

7. One of the original MMO theorists, Richard Bartle, described a particular kind of player who made it a point to aggravate as many other players as possible. He labeled this kind of player a "griefer," because their style of play was specifically to cause grief to others. In our research, we find that those who engage in "griefing" have forgone satisfying relatedness needs through gameplay, and focus instead on the feelings of power and competence that they derive through attack on others.

Chapter 5

IMMERSION AND PRESENCE

I n his book *The Art of Fiction*, the American novelist and literary scholar John Gardner poetically describes how good writing creates for us a convincing "dream":

We read a few words at the beginning of the book or the particular story, and suddenly we find ourselves seeing not words on a page but a train moving through Russia, an old Italian crying, or a farmhouse battered by rain. We read on—dream on—not passively but actively . . . In great fiction, the dream engages us heart and soul; we not only respond to imaginary things—sights, sounds, smells—as though they were real, we respond to fictional problems as though they were real: We sympathize, think, and judge. We act out, vicariously, the trials of the characters and learn from the failures and successes of particular modes of action, particular attitudes, opinions, assertions, and beliefs exactly as we learn from life. Thus the value of great fiction . . . is not just that it entertains us or distracts us from our troubles . . . but also that it helps us to know what we believe, reinforces those qualities that are noblest in us, leads us to feel uneasy about our faults and limitations.[1]

What Gardner describes here is often called *immersion* or *presence*: The experience of being "drawn in"—even transported to—a fictional world through storytelling. We've all had these experiences in response to a memorable book or movie, that incredibly vivid and rich emotional engagement with a story that psychologically carries us to another place. Dreams, of course, have this quality naturally—within them, they are experienced as real even if we are flying through outer space or serving as the 10-foot-tall supreme ruler of Australia. Nothing is out of bounds. In this way, dreams give daily testament to our ability to experience authentic emotion even amidst the most fanciful fiction.

More than this, Gardner suggests that something substantive can be derived in this process: We "learn from the failures and successes of particular modes of action . . . exactly as we learn from life." That despite the fictional nature of the content, a good story can be as meaningful as "real" experiences and used as a vehicle for genuine growth.

In today's world of video games, in which we not only read or watch the action, but actively participate in it, this has even broader implications. Such meaningful experiences might include an eighth-grader learning history while trimming the sails in a virtual Spanish Armada, or a housewife picking up some bona fide piloting skills from a realistic flight simulator.

Understanding the threshold of immersion in media begins by taking a look at media itself. *Media* is derived from the word for "middle," meaning something that sits in-between. Whether that media is an 18th-century book or a modern video game, it sits *in the middle* between us (its audience) and the subject matter it presents. But for us to be truly drawn into those stories, we need to *forget* about what lies in the middle between us and them: The media itself, along with the wires and pulleys it uses to communicate with us, need to fade out of view. In other words, if you are thinking about the book you are reading *as a book* or mentally analyzing the film you are watching *as a movie* ("Why did they put this music in the soundtrack?" "Is that the end of Act 1?"), you are aware that your experience of the story is a mediated one—something sits between you and the narrative, keeping you from full emotional entry. This awareness suggests you're not immersed or "present" in the story itself; you are sitting outside of it, watching it through a window whose curtains and smudges distract you.

Contrast this with your experience wherever you are right now as you are reading this. In a cozy chair at home perhaps? Or on the subway commuting to work? Wherever you may be, your awareness of your surroundings is direct and immediate—the rain that falls against your window and the siren wailing off in the distance are part of your direct experience and are not being "presented" to you through some form of media. Your sensory experience cuts out the middle man. It is *non-mediated*, meaning that there is nothing between you and those experiences.

Technically, stories are always told to us through some third party (e.g., our TVs or books or video games), and so are inherently mediated. But when they are good, they evoke in us an "illusion of non-mediation."[2] They draw us in to an enveloping emotional embrace where thinking about them as mere fiction feels inadequate. We become immersed and present in their worlds, emotionally experiencing them as if they were *really* happening to us. The psychological distance between us and the story vanishes as we move from detached observer to intimate participant. Simply put, we are *present* in their worlds.

This ability to become immersed in story in this way is one of the great joys of being human. That we can imagine and enter fully into the imagination of others allows us to transcend our limitations and constraints, opening up new possibilities and imagining new areas of growth and connection. As we've seen in previous chapters, having experiences of growth and possibility is intrinsically motivating. It turns out that being fully immersed in the virtual worlds providing these possibilities only enhances those intrinsic satisfactions.

Much of the attention on immersion in video games has focused on its considerable multimedia power—the ability to create visuals and sounds with increasing fidelity and complexity. But any book lover can tell you that these elements are not required for immersion. As the Gardner passage illustrates, writers are strongly focused on the combination of language and semantics to evoke deeper cognitive and emotional involvement in their audience. Words alone create a strong psychological sense of place even without any stunning visuals. In C. S. Lewis's *Narnia* series, we feel the gentle snow on our faces as it falls through the forest canopy. Likewise, we wince through the withering heat and emotional suffering that envelops us in the pages of Dante's *Inferno*. Great books cease to be a medium for storytelling and become a portal to another place.

Marie-Laure Ryan describes one way that books conjure such "spatial" immersion: when they evoke a personal memory that merges with the story. She calls this the "madeleine effect" in homage to Proust's description[3] of vivid childhood memories being unearthed simply by dipping a madeleine cookie in chocolate: "In the most complete forms of spatial immersion, the reader's private landscapes blend with the textual geography. In those moments of sheer delight, the reader develops an intimate relation to the setting as well as a sense of being present on the scene of the represented events."[4]

Ryan describes this "blending" somewhat passively, but in fact it is the reader who is *actively* blending, weaving together fiction and memory into a personalized tapestry of the story. We've seen how we are energized in life by an intrinsic desire to grow and to elaborate our experiences (i.e., through our competence/mastery). Here it is at work again: We intrinsically integrate a story's eddies and currents with our own streams of experience. In so doing, stories and fictional worlds come to life as an imaginative workshop for our further growth.

Amazingly, it doesn't even matter that the stories we create for ourselves are real or even plausible. When we are immersed, our emotions trump the boring world of "facts." We check all the closets after seeing a horror movie not because we believe brain-eating zombies exist, but because our emotions don't distinguish the real from the imagined, even if our rational (and, we fear, tasty) brain does. The film philosopher Noel Carroll explored this idea, distinguishing between *beliefs*, which are what we hold to be really true, and *thoughts*, through which we freely contemplate any idea or concept, no matter how fanciful.[5] He suggests that emotional responses really do not distinguish between the things we contemplate and imagine (i.e., our thoughts) and our more grounded beliefs about what constitutes "reality." Carroll points out that there is an adaptive/evolutionary advantage in our ability to emotionally respond to both thoughts and beliefs, as it enables us to innovate and strategize even in relation to things that have not been experienced (or, as of yet, remain unknown).

The consequence of this is that we freely contemplate the fictional worlds presented by authors and filmmakers—no matter how improbable or fantastic—with emotional reactions that are very much "real." The great gift of stories is that we can try them on for size, reacting genuinely to their contents, as a means of expanding our own experience. As our previous example with the movie *Rocky* illustrates, we read beloved books and watch favorite films again and again, reacting emotionally to the tension of the story although we already know the "blow-by-blow" outcome. We willingly tether ourselves emotionally to the story's present despite our full knowledge of what's to come.

IMMERSION IS IN THE DETAILS

Of course, most of the foregoing requires that the story be a "good" story. For every such experience we have, there are usually many terrible books we read, movies we watch, and games we play for which the first thought is that we'll never see those hours of our life again, and our second thought is to warn our friends not to make the same existential mistake. There is much literary and film theory as to what makes for good storytelling, and exploring this would be a lengthy journey for which we are hardly qualified. Much has been written on these subjects by others, in particular on how to engage an audience emotionally from the creative perspective. But where this body of literature touches on our own work around immersion and motivation, we have noticed a common theme: To connect with the audience, a story must provide details that feel *authentic*.

AUTHENTICITY

Authenticity is another one of those words (like *fun* and *immersion*) that carries with it many possible meanings. At its simplest, authenticity means that something is the "real deal"—that it isn't a copy or imitation of something else, nor does it feel flimsy or "made up." Authenticity also implies a sense of trustworthiness and honesty—authentic people, for example, are not trying to be something other than themselves. Authentic experiences and places are those that are true to how things really are. You can relax and get closer to what is authentic precisely because it can be trusted, whereas there is a natural tendency to keep a distance, both psychologically and physically, from what seems fake or contrived.

Feeling that any particular situation is authentic is largely dependent on our past personal experiences. We naturally organize what we learn about the world into various frameworks—sometimes called *schema*[6]—which we subsequently apply to new situations that seem similar. Schemas are what allow you to walk into a restaurant you have never visited before and still know exactly what to do; your experience in countless other restaurants has taught you the process (waiting to be seated, being escorted to your table, and being handed a menu). Restaurants that operate this way feel familiar and authentic, even if they are new to us. Our schemas give us a foundation of competence, even in new situations, on which we can build.

The fun part is that schemas are not just limited to our experiences with the molecular world. We also develop them for fictional worlds. We just described this amazing ability we have to emotionally engage with make-believe material, where our emotions do not necessarily care about reality. Similarly, alongside our schemas for things like restaurants, we develop schemas for fiction. Or put differently, we even want make-believe worlds to act in ways that feel consistent, and when they do that, fantasy feels *authentic*.

Vampires are a helpful illustration. If you were to jot down a list of the "rules" about vampires, we bet your list would look something like this:

- Drinks blood
- Very strong
- Avoids the daylight
- Immortal
- Undead
- Can make other vampires

Now, if we see a movie in which vampires run around on the beach all day in broad daylight while growing old and eating Pop Tarts, that wouldn't feel authentic. Instead of feeling drawn in to this world, we feel put off, furrowing our brow and wondering what the writer was thinking. We may be willing to see if the story can give us a convincing alternate set of rules—after all, that's what innovative fiction does. But until that happens, we exist outside the story rather than being present within it. In other words, the lack of authenticity pushes us out of immersion. Even in fictional worlds, authenticity is dependent on things being consistent with our experience and understanding.

The same is true in video games, where inauthenticity results in great disappointment for players. For example, in an effort to give players an emotional jolt, developers will sometimes use what is known as a "monster closet," a device whereby something jumps out at a player unexpectedly (Boo!) Of this particular technique, one developer offered the following opinion [emphasis ours]:

> One of my personal, least-favorite game-design elements is the "monster closet," those in-game tripwires that release enemies suddenly when you pass a certain point, **even though the enemies clearly hadn't existed a few moments before**. Even if the walls feature doors that, presumably, could be swinging open, it still creates a feeling of fakeness to the game-world . . . **Real life doesn't have trigger points**.[7]

In our research on games, we often track such moments and the impact they have on the player experience. Looking at both biometric data (things like heart rate and arousal) along with player mood and immersion, we find a consistent pattern: Monster closets will elicit a "startle" reaction from players, but even in those who like to play scary games, we immediately see a negative impact on their enjoyment and immersion. Players want to be imaginatively engaged, and not reflexively poked.

This is the natural desire for authenticity at work. When our fictions do not make sense—when they do not behave in ways that feel logical or familiar—they simply don't feel *real*. Their rough edges poke us awake from the immersive dream, and this disappoints us because we can't engage with them in ways that are satisfying. Authentic fictional worlds, by contrast, facilitate our emotional acceptance of them and draw us in more completely.

In fact, having an experience of authenticity that immerses us is so valued that we try to help where we can, through that reflex to "blend" our memory with fiction we discussed earlier. By weaving into the gossamer strands of fiction the more substantive threads of our own experience, that fiction becomes more tangible and personally relevant. And as the richness of our memory infuses the story with subtle sensory and emotional details, there is a further deepening of its authentic feel.

Great storytellers accelerate this blending process by providing touchstones to the familiar. Words, images, or other structures that reflect our real world are integrated into the fictional landscape and facilitate a deeper connection. In *The Hobbit* and *The Lord of the Rings*, J.R.R. Tolkien created a broad alternate universe, Middle Earth, with incredible depth and breadth. Completely outside the stories themselves, he compiled full histories of fictional races such as Dwarves and Elves, each with functional alphabets and languages. But what makes his work so compellingly immersive is that despite the fantasy content, the structure of the world is remarkably familiar. Like vampires, elves are not real; but to the extent that they have a history and a unique language, they feel authentic because these are the qualities we associate with *real* races and cultures. As a kid, I remember looking at the Elvish alphabet chart in the appendix of *The Return of the King* and was immediately reminded of similar charts that adorned the walls of my grade-school classrooms. How easy it was to imagine pointy-eared children in Tolkien's Middle Earth learning their letters just as I did, creating for me a vivid picture of this world made more authentic by my own life history. In other words, the madeleine effect kicked in. Great storytellers know how to create those conduits of connection between the fictional and the real, and in so doing facilitate our immersion.

FROM STORIES TO GAMES: THE MOVE FROM AUTHENTIC CONTENT TO AUTHENTIC INTERACTION

Up until now, we've explored the ideas of immersion and authenticity within storytelling generally, with a primary focus on traditional forms such as books and film. But as we'll see in a moment, interactive media complicates these issues. Because the words on a page or the frames of a movie are forever unchanging, conveying an authentic world to the audience is entirely the job of the *content* of the story and how skillfully it is created and assembled. The writer or filmmaker creates a story that unfolds the same way each and every time. This is the great artistic challenge of traditional storytelling: creating a work that can engage and immerse its audience even though the work exists independent of that audience.

Not surprisingly then, studies of immersion in traditional media tend to focus exclusively on content. Does a book convince us of the authenticity of a place or character through the detail of its writing, or do the images of an imaginary city on the silver screen look real enough to us to evoke a feeling of presence? More recently, this focus has extended itself to digital media technology and how it approximates the sensory input of "reality" (through features such as screen size, image resolution,[8] and multi-channel sound). As we write this, 3-D movies are making yet another comeback, and even 3-D televisions are now available to graphically simulate reality more accurately. Presumably, this commitment to fidelity assumes that it is the *authenticity of content presentation* that primarily drives immersion or presence.

However, traditional media lacks a significant dimension of experience compared to video games and virtual worlds. Regardless of how beautifully crafted and rich in detail its content may be, the audience can only imagine participation in traditional stories. There is no actual participation. We don't expect the story to change based on how deeply we cry as we turn pages or how forcefully we jeer and hurl popcorn at a cinematic villain. With respect to having any real impact on the story, *the audience is basically helpless and irrelevant.* That's not meant as a criticism—it's just the nature of most forms of media.

The concept of authenticity helps us understand why this isn't ideal with respect to immersion. Unlike traditional media, our life is fundamentally interactive. We are not irrelevant to what happens around us and have perpetual "give and take" with the world as active participants (rather than passive observers). In big and small ways, the world gives us choices and reacts to our actions. For all its focus on 3-D razzle-dazzle, traditional media simply cannot replicate this important and authentic dimension of our daily lives.

On the other hand, video games and virtual worlds open this dimension to us, creating a new and powerful channel for the experience of authenticity and immersion. We've seen how we are intrinsically motivated to pursue opportunities and build relationships precisely *because* we want to feel relevant and effective. Virtual worlds have an edge over traditional storytelling in their ability to meet these needs. While books and film may present authentic content, they cannot directly interact with us in ways that are important to our need satisfaction.

Video games are all about this interaction, and we've seen that they are most satisfying when highly responsive to (and even dependent upon) the participation of the audience. Specifically, when it comes to deep engagement and fun, players value experiences of effectiveness (competence), volition (autonomy), and connections with others to whom they matter (relatedness). In fact, when it comes to satisfaction in life, whether inside or outside of virtual worlds, these are the experiences that really count. Research on human motivation and emotion has shown time and again that we seek these experiences quite naturally.

It follows that authenticity in games largely flows from how they interact with us, rather than their content alone. Despite the investment to constantly improve sound and graphics, the main contributions to immersion seem to lie elsewhere. When we look at what predicts immersion, we find that it is more strongly related to the game's authentic ability to react and interact with us in ways that satisfy the intrinsic needs we've discussed. Although content is also important, our data show that game mechanics that satisfy intrinsic needs have a larger contribution to immersion than factors such as graphics or high-fidelity sound.

What appears to matter most to players is authenticity in these interactive dynamics. What does this mean? Simply put, players want game interactions to reflect their most satisfying moments in "real" life—moments when they felt effective, volitional, and meaningfully connected to others. When games succeed at providing this, players feel immersed and present because the world is providing them with authentic and desirable satisfaction.

THE RESEARCH ON PRESENCE AND PENS

Physical Presence

Conceptualizations of presence or immersion within the realm of digital media have been receiving more and more attention over the last 15 years. Previously we talked about one popular definition of presence as the experience of being "transported" to another place. This idea has been explored with respect to many new technologies, ranging from high-definition television[9] to more high-tech virtual reality rigs that fully immerse multiple senses in a virtual space. In our own work on video games, we describe this idea of transportation into virtual worlds as the experience of *physical presence*: The video game player feels that they have taken a journey to the world on the screen from their actual location on the couch or wherever they may be in the molecular world.

Of all the ways in which immersion might be defined, this one seems the most dependent upon perceptual fidelity. Much of the effort to develop more sophisticated enhancements to graphics and sound are to deepen this feeling of transportation. Many game-development jobs involve designing the "physics" of game worlds—simulating the movement of objects to authentically mimic gravity, acceleration, and other rules in the molecular world. Outside of the games themselves, the average size, resolution, and technical capability of televisions and computer monitors continues to advance.

Along with others, our research on immersion suggests that these fidelity factors do indeed have a positive impact on the player's experience of physical presence. In more than 10 different studies we've conducted so far, players consistently report a greater sense of being "transported" into the game world (i.e., a greater experience of physical presence) when they perceive the graphics and sound to be of higher quality. Some of our findings also suggest that the importance of fidelity to presence is greater for certain game genres compared with others. Fidelity seems to affect satisfaction, and therefore presence, especially for players of FPS or "shooter" games, as well as intense action/adventure and racing games. This makes sense because such action-oriented games, where combat and quick strategic movements are critical, demand more detailed visual cues to allow players to react effectively. In other genres, such as MMOs, players often feel absorbed in fantasy worlds that are far less photorealistic or detailed. In fact, their unreal qualities may provide more room for suspension of usual beliefs.

Interestingly though, across all games these qualities were not what mattered most to the experience of physical presence. As we hypothesized, the experience of autonomy, competence, and relatedness satisfactions were among the strongest predictors of a player feeling physically immersed in the game world, even when compared to things like the quality of graphics and sound. In a series of studies involving several thousand gamers, a number of qualities of favorite games were rated. They included game graphics, sound, and other content features, as well as players' psychological experience of PENS satisfactions. No matter what genre we look at (e.g., RPG, strategy, or FPS), graphic fidelity and quality were less related to "feelings" of immersion (as well as value and enjoyment) when compared to need satisfaction.

This supports our belief that it is the authenticity of a game's interactive dynamics that matters most to immersion, rather than the fidelity of its content. Our data support the idea that even with respect to the specific experience of physical immersion, it is more important to feel that the world supports your autonomy and effectiveness rather than simply enveloping you in high-fidelity graphics and sound.

It has also been hypothesized that when you do feel this sense of physical immersion, it will increase emotional and cognitive immersion. Specifically, there's a belief that the psychological impact of video games is heightened when one is fully immersed. Researchers studying the potential negative impact of games on aggression[10] and excessive gameplay[11] (both of which are discussed in greater detail in the next two chapters) have speculated that the level of immersion may enhance these negative outcomes, exacerbating negative effects for those more fully immersed. While this is a reasonable hypothesis, little research has actually been done on the subject, and more effort is needed to bring a fair understanding to the issue.

Along these lines, our colleagues Netta Weinstein and Andy Przybylski and their collaborators conducted some of the first studies to look at the influence of immersion on the emotional and cognitive impact of virtual environments.[12] Interested in the motivational impact of natural settings, the research focused on how exposure to different kinds of virtual environments—specifically those depicting either man-made structures or more natural, outdoor settings—might impact how people interact with others and set goals in the "real" world. In this way, the research was also designed to look into how immersion influences the "carry over" of virtual experiences into everyday life. This is a particularly exciting area of research given that virtual worlds are increasingly used for training and non-entertainment applications in areas such as health care and education.

In the study, Weinstein and her colleagues found that when subjects were exposed to virtual environments with natural imagery (e.g., blue sky, streams, and trees), they were more likely to endorse goals that were pro-social (i.e., focused on the well-being of others) and more likely to have greater feelings of vitality. When they were exposed to virtual environments depicting buildings and cities, they were more likely to focus on self-centered goals, such as wealth and attractiveness. But the most relevant finding for this discussion is the impact that physical presence had on these carry-over effects: The impact of these virtual environments was significantly stronger when one experienced greater physical immersion in the virtual worlds being depicted (as measured by an immersion subscale of the PENS).

In additional follow-up studies, Weinstein and her colleagues explored in more detail how immersion enhanced these kinds of carry-over effects. They found that immersion in the man-made environments, which by definition consist of more constrained physical spaces, evoked lower levels of need satisfaction in PENS factors such as autonomy. By contrast, feeling more immersed in an open, natural scene was associated with higher levels of need satisfaction and a feeling of connection to nature.

Taken as a whole, this series of studies offers an interesting first glimpse into the role of immersion and its relationship to deepened experience. It demonstrates that immersion has a significant impact on how well virtual experiences "carry over" back into the molecular world. And it shows that it is the experience of need satisfaction that catalyzes the immersive effect.

Emotional Presence

A second dimension of immersion or presence in video games is the degree to which you have authentic emotional responses to your experiences in the game world. Do you feel sadness at the death of your good friend Mayor Wimpy, or angry when you learn that the son of the villainous Warlord Cranky engineered his demise? Perhaps you even feel some guilt when you learn that Wimpy's assassination was retribution for you dispatching Cranky in the first place? You may reflect with regret at hastily choosing the path of violence now that you've seen the personal suffering it has caused. Today's games have this ability to evoke a wide range of emotion, and they get better at it every year.

If the feelings a player has while playing a video game are on par with parallel reactions to events in the molecular world, the player is experiencing *emotional presence* in the game—a state of genuine feelings in response to fictional events. Of course, this kind of presence can manifest in response to any good story, whether told on the pages of a book, on the stage, or on the silver screen. But the interactive nature of video games deepens emotional presence by offering players more than emotional response. Games give us the potential to take action when emotions move us.

My first personal experience with this kind of emotional presence was in the early 1990s, while playing *Civilization*. Shortly before I was heading out to play soccer in the molecular world, I was deeply engaged in the video game, battling for world domination with India (these things happen in the game *Civilization* on a regular basis). Then the unthinkable happened: Gandhi nuked me. *Gandhi!*[13] I watched in dismay as the mushroom cloud rose above my city. My ability to chuckle at the historical irony of this was completely overwhelmed by my sense of shock and anger, as well as sentimentality for "my country." My people didn't deserve this sudden and deliberate attack of the worst kind. When I left the video game to head out to the soccer field, I was preoccupied with these emotions, busily plotting my revenge. I was determined to get the best of my virtual enemies and emerge victorious. I remember the feeling to this day, and not coincidentally, I'm also pretty sure my emotional distraction contributed to our loss of that soccer game.

What makes this a good example of emotional presence (in my video game, if not on the soccer field) is that my emotional responses were *within the context of the game itself.* Often you see gamers get mad *at* a video game, either because they lost or got killed or a button on the controller didn't do what they intended. This can spark extreme emotional reactions akin to passing a kidney stone—but we would not call that emotional *presence*, because it is not an emotion evoked within the context of the game. In fact, extreme emotional reactions *at* a video game (usually frustration or anger) are quite the opposite of immersion or presence—they pull us out of engagement with the game and set us up in opposition to "that damn game!" We saw earlier how much of the aggression that occurs while gaming can be attributed to frustration at the game controls rather than as an actor in its story.[14] In my *Civilization* example, I was not generally angry at losing or frustrated with my performance or the game's functioning. I was angry at virtual Gandhi. I was also sad and vengeful on behalf of my fictional digital nation—of citizens that I had never even seen, but for whom I felt a sense of responsibility as their leader. My emotions were taking place within the context of the story I was weaving within the game.

It may sound a bit ridiculous to suggest that this game was evoking anything akin to "real" emotions, but is the idea any more far-fetched than shedding tears as you read *Romeo and Juliet* or watch *Old Yeller*? Games simply enhance our innate ability to emotionally engage in fictional worlds by enabling meaningful participation. When we are moved by a traditional story, there is nothing to be done. But in an interactive virtual world, that emotional response is put into action within the story itself. In other words, our evoked emotions are not the end result of the story, but often just the beginning of *our* story.

As we noted in the chapter on autonomy, our emotional connection to a story contributes to our volitional engagement in a course of action. In the best games, feeling both effective (i.e., competent) and autonomous empowers us to thoughtfully plan and execute that course of action. It follows that deeper experiences of emotional presence, just as with physical presence, will occur when games satisfy the intrinsic motivational needs we've been discussing, and our research bears this out.

In several studies, we have assessed the construct of emotional presence through items such as "I have emotional reactions to events in the game as if they were real," giving players the opportunity to report on how authentically their game experience is evoking emotions. Our general hypothesis is that when players feel the game environment is facilitating the satisfaction of their motivational needs—when they have the opportunity to act with volition, mastery, and in relationship to others—their entire experience will be perceived as more authentic, including their experience of emotional reactions. And indeed, when intrinsic needs are satisfied, emotional presence is enhanced.

This can spontaneously occur in reaction to even the simplest aspects of virtual worlds. A moment ago, for example, we discussed our research on how depictions of natural environments can deepen immersion. These depictions don't actually require much action; they happen spontaneously in virtual worlds when players stop for a moment simply to enjoy the vista of a beautiful landscape or the warm colors of the setting digital sun. Just as the natural beauty of the real world can inspire us to take a break to simply enjoy, so too can the digital beauty of virtual worlds. And when these worlds succeed in satisfying intrinsic needs, players are much more likely to respond to their physical surroundings with authentic emotions.

This is something an open-world game such as *World of Warcraft* does very well. Each of the "continents" in the game varies its landscape from snowy mountains to vast deserts to wooded lakes. The world is also authentic to the degree that if you dive into such a lake, you see the familiar shapes of coral and fish mixed in with the game's fantasy elements. Although not photorealistic, these environments are both engaging and sometimes aesthetically beautiful. Once your two heroic authors rode our digital horses through rolling lush savannah countryside, with a sparkling blue sky highlighting the vivid colors and varied fauna of the landscape. There was a genuine emotional pleasure when we found ourselves crossing the border into this bright and expansive area from the misty swampland nearby. Even today, as we remember that ride, we both recall the feelings of exhilaration at the bright possibilities exploring this land offered in that moment.

Games can also evoke emotional presence through shared experiences with other characters or players—not only the direct interpersonal connections we discussed as part of relatedness, but the shared experiences that enhance and deepen authentic emotional reactions to events in the game world. Defeating a dragon by myself may bring tremendous satisfaction of mastery, but knowing you are fighting alongside another player catalyzes a deeper emotional connection to the battle and its consequences. Emotionally, the battle matters more—reeling one deeper into the virtual world. As compelling as our individual experiences are in games, when challenges are overcome together, such victories create a positive lasting memory of the game event that is as real and compelling as any memory, one that persists in bringing warm feelings long afterward. In fact, in one study in which we asked gamers to recount their most memorable experiences, many players recounted positive events that had happened months and even *years* earlier!

To those who are trying to understand the strong motivational pull of games, this can be an important piece of the psychological puzzle. Earlier we reviewed the ability of games to offer experiences with immediacy, density, and consistency. Years ago, public-service announcements for libraries promoted books as a means to "travel" to fascinating new worlds of imagination merely by turning the page. Today's video games fulfill this same promise in a richer way through their interactivity. Our research on immersion and presence clarifies why players become so deeply immersed, and why they greatly value that immersion despite the fabricated nature of virtual worlds.

Narrative Presence

A third dimension of presence we regularly assess is *narrative presence*. Narrative presence is the extent to which players feel they are an integral part of the story— that their actions influence the path and the outcome of the game's narrative. To return to the tragic tale of Mayor Wimpy of Victimville, emotional presence occurs when we feel sadness at his untimely death. But narrative presence occurs when we feel that we personally *played a role* in that death. For example, perhaps we feel that we are the direct cause of Wimpy's misfortune, or believe we have the opportunity to avenge him. In other words, how much influence do we believe we have on the game's narrative as opposed to being merely a passive observer along for the ride?

While narrative presence is possible in traditional media—by strongly identifying with protagonists and their choices—the experience is only vicarious. There is no actual opportunity to act upon a story and influence its outcome. If the author of the story "loses us" somehow, perhaps through bad plotting or character actions that do not appeal, our immersion is broken and we are disappointed. But there is nothing that we can do about this really. It's not our story.

By contrast, in games we can impact the story line. Once again, we *matter*. Every generation of games increasingly allows us to tell our own story through the choices we make when interacting with characters and content. These opportunities, in turn, energize a deeper experience of narrative presence.

It makes sense then that we'd find a strong relationship between intrinsic need satisfaction and narrative presence. After all, no matter how hard a game may try to cast the player in a central role, it can't achieve this if the player doesn't care about the people in the narrative (relatedness), or if the player doesn't feel capable of taking effective action (competence.) And perhaps most importantly, players need an experience of personal agency—or autonomy—allowing them to feel volitionally engaged and make the story their own. In other words, each element of need satisfaction increases the ability to shape a story in which one will truly feel ownership.

This may help to untangle some interesting debates about the importance of "story" in games. When we ask players what are the most valued or important aspects of their game experiences, they will often cite "story" at the top of the list. Many developers point to this as proof that players want a precisely plotted narrative that unfolds as they move through the game. These developers will spend a great deal of their time creating rich, movie-quality "cut scenes" or long segments of dialogue to move their narrative forward, borrowing from the traditional media playbook as to how to tell their story. Other game developers take issue with this, some going as far as saying that "story doesn't matter" and pointing to all of the ways in which players derive satisfaction from the gameplay itself, rather than the story wrapped around it.

In working with players, we find that when they cite "story" as important, they mean first and foremost that they want to be deeply engaged in the game, and not necessarily that they want the game to *tell* them a story (as in a book or a film). In fact, players are often suspicious of games that are based on strong existing stories, because they are worried that the developers won't give them freedom. Story, to players, means *their* story, and this is best achieved by players building that story for themselves, rather than simply taking their hand and dragging them through it. In fact, we see many games fail with players specifically because they have spent too much time *telling* the player the story rather than letting the player experience it in their own way.

That said, even the player's own story needs to have a context. Dropping them into an open countryside with a bag full of goodies may technically provide them freedom to create a story, but as they stand blinking in the sun wondering what to do, their choices don't feel particularly meaningful or interesting. Providing them a backstory—a reason to want to go somewhere and do something—kindles their motivation. Building narrative presence in games is the art of describing clear and compelling destinations, ones that are thoughtfully crafted to be meaningful, while simultaneously letting players feel they are behind the wheel on the journey to reach them.

SUMMARY

In the preceding chapters, we discussed the core motivational needs in our model and how different types of games emphasize various combinations of satisfaction. Subsequently, in our research on immersion, we find that a deeper sense of presence of all types (physical, emotional, and narrative) is related to not only how authentic the appearance and physics of a game world are, but even more so by how well a game satisfies those core needs. In fact, we've seen some remarkable evidence that need satisfaction is consistently among the most important factors in immersion, even when compared to flashier elements such as graphics and sound.

We understand these findings as a reflection of the core idea of the very first chapter: That the fun and immersion in games so valued by players is not primarily a function of content (as in traditional media). Instead, it lies in the potential of games' interactivity to meaningfully satisfy intrinsic motivational needs, drawing us into a powerful and present connection. Immersion and the experience of "presence" we've discussed happen when players find opportunities to act within the game world in ways that reflect their basic needs in the *real* world—actions that satisfy the need to grow and feel masterful in what we undertake, to feel autonomous in what we pursue, and to have a meaningful and relevant connection to others. Game experiences that achieve this cannot help but draw players into deeper immersion and appreciation, sparking rich emotional responses that lead many into long-term and highly valued relationships with their favorite games.

This may sound utopic in many ways, but all of this talk of immersion in games leads to another important question: What are the implications of being highly immersed in games with respect to other opportunities and responsibilities in real life? We are aware that up until this point we have taken a rather buoyant view of games with respect to their potential to engage us in ways that are both broad and deep. We hope that those readers who are more skeptical of gaming's psychological value have been able to hang in there with us, understanding that the goal to this point has been to outline a specific and more precise way to understand gaming's formidable motivational pull. If we've succeeded to this point, the motivational dynamics and draws of gaming are a little clearer and less mysterious, and you've been able to slip some new concepts into your pocket for understanding games.

We can now turn this same lens to many of the more controversial issues surrounding gaming. Just ahead, we'll spend some significant time discussing concerns of game addiction and violence, as well as discussing how gaming can encourage healthier behaviors, learning, and psychological benefits. Since we've spent so much time looking at how games can create rich and immersive worlds filled with genuine emotion—places that motivate players to return again and again—a natural place to turn next is the issue of its overuse. When does the time we spend in these compelling virtual worlds become too much time away from the real one?

NOTES

1. Gardner, J. (1991). *The Art of Fiction: Notes on Craft for Young Writers*. New York: Alfred A. Knopf, p. 31.

2. Lombard, M., Grabe, M. E., Reich, R. D., Campanella, C. M., and Ditton, T. B. (1996). *Screen Size and Viewer Responses to Television: A Review of Research*. Paper presented

to the Theory and Methodology division at the annual conference of the Association for Education in Journalism and Mass Communication, Anaheim, CA; Lombard, M., Reich, R., Grabe, M., Bracken, C., and Ditton, T. (2000). "Presence and Television: The Role of Screen Size." *Human Communication Research, 26*, 75–98.

3. Proust, M. (1913–1927). *Remembrance of Things Past.* Volume 1: *Swann's Way: Within a Budding Grove. In Search of Lost Time,* translated by C. K. Scott-Moncrieff, Terence Kilmartin and Andreas Mayor (Vol. 7). Revised by D. J. Enright. London: Chatto and Windus; New York: The Modern Library, 1992. Based on the most recent definitive French edition (1987–1989).

4. Ryan, Marie-Laure (2003). *Narrative as Virtual Reality: Immersion and Interactivity in Literature and Electronic Media.* Baltimore, MD: Johns Hopkins University Press.

5. Carroll, N. (1996). *Theorizing the Moving Image.* Cambridge: Cambridge University Press.

6. Anderson, A. C. (1984b). "Some Reflections on the Acquisition of Knowledge." *Educational Researcher, 13,* 5–10.

7. Stephen Johnson, g4tv.com, August 17, 2009.

8. Lombard, M. (1995) "Direct Responses to People on the Screen: Television and Personal Space." *Communication Research, 22,* 288–324.

9. Reeves, B., Newhagen, J., Maiback, E., Basil, M., and Kurz, K. (1991). "Negative and Positive Television Messages: Effects of Message Type and Context on Attention and Memory." *American Behavioral Scientist, 34,* 679–694.

10. Carnagey, N. L., and Anderson, C. A. (2005). "The Effects of Reward and Punishment in Violent Video Games on Aggressive Affect, Cognition, and Behavior." *Psychological Science, 16,* 882–889; Anderson, C. A., and Carnagey, N. L. (2004). "Violent Evil and the General Aggression Model." In A. Miller (Ed.), *The Social Psychology of Good and Evil* (pp. 168–192). New York: Guilford Publications.

11. Grüsser, S. M., Thalemann, R., and Griffiths, M. D. (2007) "Excessive Computer Game Playing: Evidence for Addiction and Aggression?" *Cyberpsychology & Behavior, 10*(2), 290–292.

12. Weinstein, N., Przybylski, A. K., and Ryan, R. M. (2009). "Can Nature Make Us More Caring? Effects of Immersion in Nature on Intrinsic Aspirations and Generosity." *Personality and Social Psychology Bulletin, 35,* 1315–1329.

13. Part of the appeal of civilization is that these kinds of surprises can happen, creating opportunities to overcome novel challenges. Every virtual leader in the game has the potential to push the button on you under the right circumstances, even those you might not expect.

14. See the discussion of our research on "control mastery" in chapter 2.

Chapter 6

DANGEROUS WATERS: THE ADDICTIVE UNDERTOW OF GAMES

To this point we've described the powerful ways in which games satisfy basic psychological needs within us, creating immersive experiences that are often great fun. Virtual worlds stretch before us an ocean of satisfactions, sparkling with multiple attractions. We've discovered how deep enjoyment flows from the experience of agency and self-direction (what we've called autonomy) that virtual worlds provide. The appeal is also fed by the mastery and accomplishment felt in being able to perform heroic deeds and magical acts, growing stronger and more renowned every day (competence/mastery). This enjoyment is taken deeper still by connecting with others who depend on you—and on whom you depend—in a virtual world of shared purpose and camaraderie (relatedness). These experiences immerse us in worlds of discovery, opportunity, and narrative in which we play an important and active part.

These virtual worlds are especially attractive when games feel more satisfying of our basic needs than other areas of life. Those who engage in video game *overuse*—or to use the more alarming label, video game *addicts*—all find a pull into games that overrides their desires to engage with the real world around them. Simply put, while the issue of what to call game overuse is still being hotly debated, we must acknowledge a basic fact: Some people are spending a lot of their limited time on this Earth in virtual worlds, and often too much time.

For example, many reports suggest that most adolescents in the United States are spending double-digit hours each week on games. That's more time than they spend eating with their families, doing homework, reading, or being physically active. But it is not just adolescents. A national survey conducted by the *Entertainment Software Association* (ESA) in 2005 identified the prototypical gamer as a 30-year-old male who averages between 6.8 and 7.6 hours weekly playing video games, with 46 percent of MMO players reporting that they have sacrificed sleep, work, social opportunities, or study to play games.[1] When people start dismissing work, friends, and health for an entertainment experience, we understandably need to sit up and listen.

But these statistics do not tell the full story. After all, average Americans spend a lot more time watching TV, which is neither more real nor typically more edifying. Yet among the population of gamers is a group of truly extreme consumers who play almost constantly. Estimates vary on the size of this group, but current data suggest that 10–15 percent of gamers fall into a pattern of video game overuse or addiction. Using criteria developed by the World Health Organization, one study at Nottingham University in the United Kingdom polled more than 7,000 gamers and found an addiction rate of close to 12 percent.[2] In other words, a startling 800-plus gamers in that relatively small study alone were deeply hooked on gameplay. In the United States, researchers have estimated that a similar proportion of gamers may be so affected.[3] We know a number of these players, and some of their personal stories will help put a face to their struggles with game addiction.

"Peter"

We met 24-year-old Peter during interview research on games and overuse. Peter lived in a small apartment with another male friend. He was a college graduate who was both academically and athletically talented. He was also a pretty good musician. Yet he defined himself as "addicted to games." As long as he could remember, Peter had been interested in video games. After graduation, when he had a job and the means to buy consoles and games himself, Peter told us he began playing "every spare minute." He had a decent job as a technician at a medical laboratory, but didn't feel particularly challenged in his work. He looked forward each day to getting home to his gaming, and when not working, he could almost always be found in the attic space he had carved out for this activity.

Peter certainly had opportunities to pursue a lot of social and leisure activities, but in his experience games were "usually just more fun" than going to movies or out to bars. He admitted that because his spare time had drifted into gaming, he was socializing less and had stopped playing sports altogether. Almost any time there was an opportunity to do something with friends, Peter weighed the trade-off between socializing and games. Games almost always won. He found himself opting out, even leaving activities early to get back to his virtual worlds. In the MMO games Peter often played, he reported feeling many of the same satisfactions sports had supplied, such as teamwork, competition, and accomplishment. But unlike sports, his gaming team was right there and always available.

Asked why he thought of his pattern of play as overuse, he answered, "Because I play so many hours. And I am constantly wondering what I might be doing if I were not sitting there playing." At the same time, Peter felt like he was enjoying himself. He comes across as quite functional and well adjusted, albeit a bit existentially guilty.

The question Peter was asking himself is, in fact, quite healthy to ask about any activity to which we commit our time: *What would I be doing otherwise?* It is a question great philosophers such as Kierkegaard or Sartre would be proud to ask, not to mention countless gurus on time management, motivation, and self-help. Are we filling too much time working, playing video games, shopping, or watching TV? Writing this book? Reading this book? Taking a stark look at oneself is always a scary thought. But for Peter, he shared that humming cultural sensibility that somehow video games are "not real" and therefore a *waste of time*. It is striking how something that was giving Peter a lot of happiness moment to moment was at the same time creating a dull ache in his soul.

"Evan"

I interviewed Evan at his father's suggestion, after telling me his son was a victim of what he labeled video game "addiction." I was curious, and Evan agreed to talk with me although he was reluctant. Shy and reserved, he was resistant to speaking in detail about his game-focused lifestyle.

At 27, Evan was living with his divorced father in a spacious, high-end, city apartment. Nominally a student, Evan's enrollments in school were part time, and it was clear he was not enthusiastically pursuing his degree. Periodically he'd take jobs, but he had trouble holding them down. Often late, always tired and disinterested, Evan was usually relieved when he would be laid off or outright fired.

In contrast to his outer lack of achievement, Evan was a different person in his room at home. Here he had a large desk area (made from two wooden doors placed in an L-shape over sawhorses). Two 30-inch screens were angled strategically toward an adjustable gamer seat, complete with a headphone rack and cup holder. There were shelves of equipment, mods, gamer manuals, and magazines like *Wired* and *Game Informer* strewn about. It was like walking into a flight simulator. On the wall there were two large posters; one was a detailed map of the travel routes through the virtual *World of Warcraft (WoW)*, the other a poster that depicted Kratos, the hero of the *God of War* series, slaying a giant Cyclops. The room was dark, with lights focused only over the desk area and game controls.

Walking in, Evan said, "My dad probably told you that I play too much." But I was interested in hearing about his game experience firsthand, as he was clearly dedicated to it. I turned the conversation to what he was playing, and explored why it was central in his life. He was a regular *WoW* player with multiple characters at the top level in the game. He also had a variety of other characters spread across several game servers, each with a different circle of friends and guild memberships. His anxiety about my visit and his initial reluctance to talk about gaming melted away as we began talking about the game itself. Evan was highly animated as we exchanged stories of favorite moments and experiences in *WoW*, and on almost every topic related to the game itself, he was both extroverted and articulate.

We spoke a lot about guilds—the social groupings within *WoW* and many MMOs—and here Evan was having some struggles. His primary avatar's guild had become focused on highly technical aspects of team play and on perfecting their ability to succeed in the complex dungeons that represent the most challenging content in the game. They had been recruiting serious players—those who were committed to playing for many hours on a daily basis—and that had changed the tone of the guild. The pressure was on: If you weren't available for an important dungeon event (those "raids" we talked about in chapter 4), people noticed, disapprovingly.

This created a complex situation for Evan that mixed unpleasant pressures with his other game interests. "Now I just feel they demand a lot from me," said Evan. He felt he could not leave the game without making his teammates angry. "It sometimes feels like going to work," he said. But at the same time, he felt like there were always tasks to do that held some value for him—some new equipment to try to obtain, or other items or achievements he could amass. He also had good friends in the game who he looked forward to contacting every day and who he couldn't imagine "abandoning." To Evan these were his best friends, and he was sure he was theirs as well. "They play as much as I do," he said.

Evan also had reason to feel a sense of accomplishment. I asked him to show me his principal character or avatar. For those like me who play *WoW* less frequently, Evan's image seemed like a golden god decked out in epic yellow armor that granted him far more power and ability than I will likely ever see on my own character. And his capacity to move, attack, and defend was awesome. He glowed a bit as we reflected on this. He was no doubt an amazing mage—the kind of mage I would want behind *my* avatar in a fight!

Evan was behind somebody's character a lot. By his own account, he spent about 60 hours a week in *WoW* (though his dad estimates more). But he spends time there outside of his actual play as well. "It's in my dreams," he said. In fact, some of Evan's most cherished life memories were formed in places like the virtual mountains south of the Searing Gorge or the lush green meadows in Nagrand. As he reflected on this, he looked up sheepishly and said, "Kind of sad, huh?"

Evan is not alone among game overusers in the periodic feelings of guilt and self-disparagement they have. Like most gamers, Evan knows that the time he spends in virtual worlds doesn't readily benefit his "real-world" situation. He gains few directly transferrable skills, makes no income, and doesn't feel that he contributes to the rest of the world in any substantial way.

But these feelings don't move Evan to change, because unfortunately he is also resigned to his situation. "It is not like I have a lot going out there anyway," he declares. In certain respects, he was right. Though intelligent and personable once talking, Evan was uncaring about his looks, disheveled, obese, shy, and without confidence. On the street, Evan felt like an anonymous being, living in an unsatisfying universe with unchallenging jobs. His "real" life was not all that eventful, and he was not significant in anybody's world outside his home. It is no wonder that he was shy and reserved upon our first meeting.

By contrast, in *Warcraft*, Evan experiences high adventure and strong friendships. In that virtual world, he knew where he was going and exactly what to do to be effective. Moreover, he had risen to the top. Within his guild, Evan declared,

"I am an important guy," meaning that others respected and relied upon him. And for Evan, it was only in his virtual world where such a statement—that feeling of importance and ability that we all intrinsically value—was true. He simply did not see realistic possibilities for obtaining this anyplace else.

By all accounts, Evan is an overuser—or, some might say, an addict. His overuse is related to the fact that he both loves games and also loves little else. There is a gap there in which the need satisfactions he achieves in games far outstrip his experience in other aspects of life. Like a black hole, he feels an irresistible pull into games, even though, in his own words, he feels that time spent there disappears into the blackness and "doesn't amount to anything."

He is an addict, as well, in the following way: Were we to pull the plug on his games, Evan would become depressed. In fact, he is likely *already* depressed, but continually masking it through gaming. Just as when drug addicts or alcoholics withdraw from their drug of choice, their underlying depression often emerges, so too is the case with many dysfunctional gamers. For these individuals, like Evan, video games may supply a kind of self-medication and mood-management function. In gaming, those already prone to depression, anxiety, or social isolation can very effectively take their minds off such concerns. Though it is also likely that an entrenched pattern of excessive play—as exemplified by Evan—only aggravates his plight over the long run.

Clark and Scott, authors of the book *Game Addiction: The Experience and the Effects*, summed up the problem that Evan, Peter, and many, many other gamers have. "Human beings get tripped up because video games provide draws that most people don't know how to balance."[4] This is a common sentiment expressed by those who study game addiction, as well as gamers themselves who are struggling with too much time in games—the feeling that games are offering such compelling experiences that other life activities and relationships suffer as a result.

Until now, a critical piece missing in the conversation about excessive play has been identifying exactly what these "draws" and enticements are. This of course has led many to make dramatic statements about the inherent addictive power of games, casting them in a fundamentally sinister light, but unable to zero in on the exact motivational pulls games afford us. Our discussion of need satisfaction in games finally helps better pinpoint these "draws," allowing for more precise understanding that can lead to greater empathy and empowerment to address the issue. By understanding games through their ability to strongly satisfy needs for competence, autonomy, and relatedness, we not only have a means of understanding what makes them so enjoyable, but what makes them ideal candidates for excessive play.

In the process, we've discovered something very important: Games do not exert their strong pull through some arcane or extraordinary means; they are not, as many have implied, prying open a Pandora's box of primitive aggressive emotion, but instead are providing the same kinds of need satisfactions that motivate gamers and non-gamers alike in all spheres of life. In fact, our data support the idea that games' motivational strength lies in very normal intrinsic needs that are operating for us all throughout each day. Games simply have developed a means for meeting these needs very effectively, which creates vulnerability for the many who become over-involved in gameplay.

REVISITING IMMEDIACY, CONSISTENCY, AND DENSITY OF NEED SATISFACTION IN GAMES

In chapter 1, we touched upon three qualities of games that greatly add to a player's enthusiasm: their ability to deliver need satisfaction with immediacy, consistency, and density. Few activities available to us have the capacity to provide need satisfaction with high degrees of any of these three—let alone all of them—the way that video games do. It is these qualities of need satisfaction that are largely responsible for the tendency for some to spend too much of their lives and energy on games.

Immediacy: The Ready Accessibility of Satisfaction from Games

We (the authors) are the last generation to have lived at least a good part of our childhoods without the existence of computers and video games. For me, child-hood play involved convincing my siblings or parents to drag out a board game like Monopoly, or organizing the many kids in the neighborhood for a game of Wiffle ball or an adventure through the nearby woods, perhaps to build a tree house or blaze a new trail with our bikes. Being a young kid in the suburbs, I was limited to what I could conceive of doing within a quarter-mile radius of my house, on the few connected residential blocks I had permission to roam with relative freedom.

The effort it took to arrange many of these activities was substantial. A ballgame required at least an hour of door-knocking to see who was home and willing to play. Even then you might not get a quorum. And of course, if the weather didn't cooperate (which was a 50/50 chance at best), you were out of luck altogether. Nonetheless, we invested this effort because arranging games in the molecular world required it—and options in digital worlds didn't yet exist.

As we develop from child to teenager to adult, organizing interesting things to do together gets even more complicated. People have responsibilities to their work and others that make arranging communal activities a challenge, sometimes involving weeks or months of forward planning. Want to go bowling? Let me check my book and get back to you on that.

In short, organizing enjoyable activities in the molecular world takes signifi-cantly more time and effort when compared to the virtual world of video games. With no more effort than the click of a button, you are there: running through a virtual forest on an exciting quest, racing your Ferrari against a formidable opponent, or flying to the farthest reaches of space. Virtual worlds are immediately available to us, not just whenever we want, but with the advent of mobile computing, also *wherever* we want. Soon new forms of games, called "augmented reality," will go even further—overlaying virtual content into the molecular world in an effort to make "real" life more interesting and exciting.

Herein lies the problem for many who become over-involved in video games: If satisfaction from the molecular worlds of work, friends, and family feels too far away to achieve, why not turn to a digital world that is so much closer? It is just easier to connect to a digital world than to many activities in the molecular world, creating a legitimate temptation to always turn there first. And as our lives become busier and busier, the pressure to allow our easy-access digital worlds to crowd out time in other activities and relationships grows even greater. For those like Evan who spend an unhealthy amount of time gaming, the immediacy of games has tipped the scale too far.

Consistency: Whereas Life Is Uncertain, Games Are Not

Adding to the immediacy of game satisfaction is the consistency in how they satisfy us. Games operate on the basis of reliable, predictable rules that once learned will deliver satisfactions of our competence, autonomy, and even related-ness right on schedule. Finishing a quest in a role-playing game will always give you the reward you have worked for, and the game won't pass you over for promotion. Your virtual baseball game is never cancelled on account of rain. Put differently, you can rely on the need satisfactions offered by virtual worlds much more so than the less predictable molecular world of ambiguity, tough luck, politics, the store being out of your favorite brand of cookies, and the countless other mundane disappointments we face each day.

For most of us, this is just the fabric of life. Psychologists know well that a big part of healthy emotional functioning is being able to persevere through the nat-ural ambiguity and unexpected obstacles, both large and small, that we regularly encounter. Life can "get the better" of any of us from time to time. But for those who are struggling with these challenges more chronically, the allure of predict-able and consistent virtual worlds can be particularly strong. When turning away from the video screen brings with it an aching realization that molecular life may not be as predictable, there is a natural motivation to stay within a virtual space on which you can rely. Unfortunately, as with any activity that becomes over-indulged, other important areas of life are crowded out and suffer as a result.

Density: Getting a Lot of a Good Thing

A final quality of games and need satisfaction that may represent their greatest strength—and hence strongest motivational pull—is their ability to satisfy needs early and often. Life in the "real" world not only makes no promises that it will be fair in how it satisfies us, it also can be frustratingly slow in doing so. We toil through weeks, months, and years of school on the promise of getting into a good college, which in turn promises years of more hard work to get a good job. We jump on the treadmill in the hope of losing a few pounds, only to watch the scale needle stubbornly dig in even after many weeks and tiring miles. We "grind" away at our jobs year in and year out, hoping one day that management will recognize our effort and reward us. Instead, we are overlooked.

While we sit at our desks staring at yet another boring assignment, one that has no connection to any meaningful satisfaction, our thoughts drift to the more interesting game we began playing at home last night. In our mind's eye, we see opportunities and growth in the game world as readily within our reach, perhaps mere minutes into gameplay. There's that quest to complete. There's a new strategy to employ to defeat our "enemies." There's the good feelings we'll have teaming up with friends to reach a challenging goal, thus reaping a literal treasure chest of unknown but meaningful rewards. By comparison, even the *thought* of playing the game can bring more satisfaction than the work in front of us.

For most gamers, these thoughts are counterbalanced by an understanding that effort and perseverance in all areas of life has its rewards. We work to provide for our families, and find great meaning in their security and happiness. We hop on the treadmill because we understand the benefits to our health and energy (and perhaps to our waistline). But for some, these satisfactions do not occur with a frequency and richness that can compete with the moment-to-moment satisfaction offered by games. Perhaps it's because they simply aren't experiencing enough satisfaction in other areas of life, or because they fixate on the stimulation games provide through rapid-fire moments of need satisfaction.

A direct analogy to these strong appeals is our long dietary history with sugar. In the course of evolution, we evolved to enjoy sweet tastes. Our preference for sweets emerged over hundreds of thousands of years as fruit- and berry-gathering primates. Foods of sweet flavor tended to be energy laden and nonpoisonous. And since sweets usually came naturally in the form of fruits, they were healthy, too. There was selective advantage in a psychological preference and desire for these foods, and therefore we evolved to find sweet foods attractive. That initially was good for humankind's survival—until our modern age, that is. That's when we started packaging sugar in a thousand forms, and offering it cheaply on a mass scale, soon giving us much too much of a good thing. In the form of candy bars, sodas, and corn-syrup-laced snacks, sugar has literally become a deadly habit for those who can't regulate their intake. Sugar is a key ingredient not only in many processed foods, but in the marketing strategies companies adopt as they consider new ways to boost consumption. Because of its sweet and enjoyable taste, these sugary foods can be a danger area for those who are vulnerable to over indulgence in the pleasurable experience they provide.

We have similarly evolved deep psychological needs for autonomy, competence, and relatedness, acquired through the process of selective advantage. Those who could self-organize and effectively act and connect with others were simply better able to thrive. But today creative people are finding new ways to facilitate these experiences virtually. This opens up a whole new universe for rich enjoyment, but at the same time has the potential to become a less nourishing form of satisfaction for the over-involved who forgo pursuing these same satisfactions from actual living. Video games, that is, may provide meaningful and enjoyable satisfactions when in balance with life, but become the oversized candy bar of the psychological diet for those who have difficulty in regulating behavior.

CLARIFYING THE PSYCHOLOGY OF GAMES' "ADDICTIVE" POWER

We have focused on the strong ability of games to satisfy intrinsic motivational needs, but there are other ideas about what exactly the sugar is in video games that makes the experience so sweet for so many. One popular theory in the media is the "dopamine hypothesis." Dopamine is a neurotransmitter that has a number of functions in the brain and is involved in mood, sleep, voluntary movements, and situations of reward. It is this latter function that draws our attention. A lot of experiments suggest that dopamine is released when unexpected rewards are obtained, and is inhibited when expected rewards are not delivered. Dopamine is associated with the "pleasure system" of the brain, often described as the system that provides feelings of enjoyment and pleasure to "motivate" or reinforce behaviors.

Dopamine is released by naturally enjoyable experiences such as eating tasty foods, physical intimacy, as well as when drugs like cocaine or the nicotine in cigarettes are ingested. Accordingly, many theories of addiction implicate dopamine, and suggest that in addicted persons, the dopamine mechanisms of the brain create strong cravings for the source of the addiction.

Although the dopamine hypothesis is intriguing, and no doubt brain neurochemistry is involved in *sustaining* addictive behaviors, in terms of explaining the addiction it offers very little. While it's kind of reassuring to blame our brains when things go wrong, such explanations often obscure the problem. We point to the connection between dopamine and pleasure from games, and by applying the paradigms of substance abuse erroneously believe we now understand the mechanism of game addiction. But mapping game addiction is more difficult than substance abuse in this respect: Whereas we can see the clear, chemical causal link between substances like cocaine and brain mechanisms of pleasure, video games are *not* themselves a chemical. They are a form of entertainment, one among many, that must be subjectively experienced in a certain way (i.e., pleasurable) before dopamine is even relevant.

The dopamine hypothesis thus tells us little about *why* games are pleasurable, leaving us with little increased understanding of game motivation. In fact, whether you are measuring dopamine or any other purely biological outcome (e.g., arousal, brain activity, and smile responses), none of these alone can explain the subjective emotional connection between games and pleasure in the first place. They don't tell us why we find various games and game activities enjoyable and motivating.

To do this requires psychological models (such as PENS), which provide the explanatory power needed to understand, empathize, and develop mechanisms for change toward healthier behaviors. Understanding activity in terms of its ability to satisfy intrinsic needs such as competence, autonomy, and relatedness is far more useful in understanding *why* activities such as video games become addictive, while other activities such as grocery shopping or lawn mowing usually do not. To understand addiction requires thinking about the psychological impact of activities and the qualities that make them so pleasurable and attractive.

Put a bit differently, any behavior can become the focus of an addiction, but those that are most engaging and pleasurable are more common magnets. Our review of the strong motivational satisfactions video games provide demonstrates why they have this magnetic pull. In addition, we've explored how games become even more engaging when they satisfy multiple intrinsic needs simultaneously, identifying how some of the most popular games combine competence, autonomy, and relatedness satisfactions to great effect.

When we look at video game addiction, we similarly see the strongest patterns of overuse when players are getting consistent satisfaction of multiple needs. We thus want to look first at where the addictions most flourish, and understand the psychology of those genres.

MMOs as the Center of the Maelstrom

Not every game has equal potential to be addictive. Games have to have the right ingredients to pull someone into a pattern of overuse. As multiple sources have testified,[5] at the center of the cyclone of addiction are the massively multiplayer online games (MMOs), which we discussed in detail in chapter 4, and which are the problem areas for players such as Evan and millions of others worldwide. With more than 10 million players at the time of this writing, *World of Warcraft* alone has many parents and spouses "worried about warcraft," as they watch family members disappear into this virtual world—and many others like it—for large portions of each day.

We have already described some of the reasons why MMOs are so attractive, particularly their ability to gratify multiple intrinsic needs. Through their open-world structure, they offer strong autonomy satisfactions via myriad choices and opportunities for action. In most MMOs, you design your own character, choose among many professions, and explore a large and varied landscape of content in the form of quests or missions. This kind of structure—also present in many RPG games—creates a strong pull to stay engaged with MMOs and increases the degree to which players think about these games when they are not playing (e.g., "what if" thinking), which in turn increases the frequency with which they return to the virtual world. In the chapter on autonomy (chapter 3), we mentioned that when we have players keep diaries on all their daily activities, both in and out of games, it is autonomy satisfaction that most strongly energizes thinking about games when not playing. For those who are over-involved with games, these kinds of thoughts can be intrusive and obsessive, creating a common pattern of anxiety and irritation when they are not playing or are kept from playing.

MMOs also provide competence satisfactions on multiple levels. In immediate gameplay, they allow players to engage a variety of challenges, from very easy to very difficult, enabling them to both stretch their abilities and also to demonstrate mastery and even dominance (resulting in strong experiences of effectiveness). In the mood for a challenge? Then load up your guns to face that all-powerful titan lord. Interested instead in feeling powerful effectiveness over your world? Then find a spot with weaker enemies and wipe out a dozen with a single blow of your awesomeness. Here autonomy in choosing your challenge mingles with many kinds of competence satisfactions, further enhancing overall need satisfaction and creating a stronger draw into the MMO world. Here you can find a place to exercise skills with as little or as much pressure as your heart desires from one moment to the next.

But that's not all. In addition, accomplishments and growth in MMOs are cumulative. While in early MMOs you could actually lose your progress when you failed at a task, developers soon learned that this made players unhappy. In the motivational language we've been using, those mechanisms thwarted players' intrinsic need for competence and growth. But in today's MMOs, you *never* lose ground—even failures do not take away your forward progress (e.g., gaining stronger powers, and new abilities) or the greater opportunities that accompany this increased mastery. You end a game session with clear markers of growth that cannot be stripped from you. Taken together, these various forms of immediate and long-term competence satisfaction are good examples of the immediacy, consistency, and density of need satisfaction that MMOs provide.

Finally, there is the added layer of relatedness satisfaction within MMOs. By definition, these games are filled with people who provide opportunities for meaningful connections between players. And remember that unlike many social situations in which you may not feel confident about starting up a conversation, MMOs provide plenty of catalysts for fun and cooperation in the form of group activities, quests, and social events—and no one needs to know how geeky or beautiful you really are! Once again, we see immediacy and density at work. MMO players quickly meet others and form bonds through mutual adventures that encourage support. And as we've seen in talking to serious gamers such as Evan, these experiences can be as emotionally engaging and memorable as those in the molecular world. Relatedness satisfactions add yet another enticement to not only play MMOs, but to spend most of your time there.

When I was heavily into *WoW*, playing in much of my spare time, it was the pull of relatedness that I remember most strongly. Playing solo for many weeks, I had fought my way deep into a cavern where I was looking for a particular object—a chest in the possession of an evil shaman. But when I finally located it, numerous other enemies surrounded my prize. I tried fighting my way through that group multiple times, only to repeatedly die. But after a few attempts, another player showed up, also on the same mission. She invited me to form a group to tackle the task together. Now, fighting side by side, we made progress, defeating all the enemies in our path, achieving the prize, and making our way back to safety. As we exited into the light of day, she turned to me and said, "Thanks so much, I couldn't have done it without you. You were amazing." Feeling quite genuinely proud, I echoed similar sentiments, and a friendship developed.

Through this personal experience, it struck me how the immediacy of meaningful connections is facilitated by MMOs. The developers make it very easy to form groups to accomplish shared goals that lead to camaraderie and strong connection. In addition, once you have had these experiences and made friends, it is very easy to reconnect with them. In my case, the first thing I did every time I logged into the game was to check for my new friend. And whenever we were online together, which was a lot, we spent time together helping each other in the various challenges the game presented.

It's worth mentioning on a broader level that the phenomenon of "social networking" is currently all the rage. It generally refers to applications and technologies that accomplish what we're describing—drawing people into closer communication and facilitating a feeling of meaningful connection and relatedness without requiring physical proximity. MMOs offer many of these tools, but also something more: You actually have things to *do* together. These activities draw you into new experiences and big challenges, and consequently strong feelings that create memories and "Remember that time!" kind of moments. This shared history deepens the value of the MMO game experience and keeps people coming back again and again. Moreover, because one's history and accomplishments are *preserved* in MMOs, memorialized by the game itself in a list of your achievements and accomplishments, there is something always to return to and reminders of what has transpired—an identity always in the making, complete with a social ties, status, and an open future to be filled in.

Again, in principle, there is nothing wrong with any of these things. In fact, for most players of MMOs, these qualities add tremendously to the value of game experiences, and there is a healthy balance of online friends and meaningful "real world" relationships. However, because MMOs are so good at offering immediate access to engaging interpersonal experiences, the pull into these worlds becomes so compelling for some people that it throws life out of balance. Any pleasurable experience releases "positive" neurotransmitters such as dopamine. But just as cocaine directly and immediately gives addicts that rush, so too the immediacy and density of intrinsic need satisfaction in MMOs—richly provided for all of the needs in the PENS model—leads some to overindulge and show signs of addiction.

UNFINISHED BUSINESS: ZEIGARNIK EFFECTS IN MMOs/RPGs

Although the strong need-fulfilling experiences of autonomy, competence, and relatedness are no doubt the most active ingredients in the addictive potion of MMOs, this last issue of providing plenty of "things to do" brings up an additional point about how games keep people glued to their screens long after they should be sleeping, eating, doing homework, or talking with their spouse. Family and friends of every gamer have heard that familiar refrain, "OK, I just need to find a stopping point," or "OK, I just need to finish this mission," or "I can't right now, honey, I'm in the middle of a raid," or a thousand similar put-offs. It is uniformly hard to log off because in MMOs, you are *always* in the middle of something, indeed usually in the middle of several goals simultaneously. Most MMOs allow you to track dozens of very specific unfinished goals simultaneously, each with their own promise of meaningful reward. This creates a feeling of ever-present unfinished business.

The *Zeigarnik effect* is a concept psychologists often invoke when they think about unfinished business. The term is named after Russian psychologist Bluma Zeigarnik, who had an insight in a restaurant in Berlin, Germany, in 1927, an insight that has made its way into the permanent jargon of psychology. She noticed how waiters will remember orders as long as the order is still in the process of being prepared or served. But once complete, they mentally let go of that order. She reasoned that they were holding the orders in their short-term memory, but doing so required effort and rehearsal. If we don't actively keep the memories alive, they just might disappear. But once the order is delivered to the table, it is finished and can be let go.

There are many implications to this simple effect. One is that the Zeigarnik effect reveals a tendency to experience tension and even intrusive thoughts about goals that one has engaged in that are left incomplete.[6] It appears to bother us whenever we don't finish what we start. Some psychologists refer to this as a *lack of closure*. By contrast, the completion of a task brings a feeling of relief and pleasure. In short, unfinished business heightens internal tensions, and completion of tasks releases it, which feels good.

MMOs are designed so that your list of tasks is never done. No sooner do you complete one, then two more pop up to take its place. Like a digital game of whack-a-mole, accomplishment only brings more unfinished business. As soon as you finish or "turn in" a quest, you are immediately offered another one with an even bigger reward. Or perhaps completion of one "unlocks" the opportunity to receive many new quests at once. Quests are often linked together in a series that helps move a story along, but never provides much closure. If I need to find 12 jewels to complete my quest, I will not stop at 11. Even when I have all 12, if yet another quest is then offered to me in the chain—perhaps finding the golden setting into which all 12 gems fit—then I will not be likely to quit either. And so it goes, while my dinner gets cold and my wife contemplates how heavy an object to throw at me.[7]

Adding to this, quest completion in many MMOs (as well as RPGs) moves your character closer to the next level of ability, which brings with it new strengths and opportunities. This is yet another kind of ever-present unfinished business that tugs at players' time. Most gamers (present company included) would only sheepishly admit to how many nights they stayed up to the wee hours of the morning to cross the finish line of a new level, subsequently feeling the satisfaction of competence and completion this brings—great at that moment perhaps, but punishing the next day at work or at school! And as you might guess, suddenly you are at square one of the *next* level, beginning the process all over again.

Adding to these Zeigarnik effects of unfinished business lies the interpersonal pressure to stay engaged in long and consuming tasks. When you are playing with others, there is often overt pressure not to leave. You are needed to finish complex and intense gaming sessions lasting many hours in order to let everyone reach the desired goal. If you leave, you will fail not just yourself, but others as well. You are leaving others in a lurch, perhaps resulting in feelings of guilt, frustration, and even anger.

So when we think about the structure of MMOs, we can think about their addictive properties in two ways. On a fundamental level, these games keep you returning because they satisfy multiple psychological needs, and they are especially attractive because of that potential. But on a moment-to-moment level, they also keep you in a state of incompleteness, pulling on you to play longer than you might otherwise have planned. Finally, as you engage in more and more complex tasks that require group participation and cooperation, social pressure to play for extended periods of time also enters into the mix. As you connect more deeply with in-game friends, you feel a greater desire to support them and to not let them down. But since at any given moment any one of them might have more free time than you, their requests for you to commit to an extended quest for which they have time and you don't can result in too much sacrifice for those who struggle with saying "no" and disappointing others. This is one way games pull those who are vulnerable into unhealthy levels of play. In many MMOs, there it is almost never a quick exit for gamers, like Evan, who commit to deep levels of group play. This helps explain why in our research of time spent gaming, MMO players, on average, spend two to three times more weekly hours playing their game than players within most other genres.

Multiplayer FPS: Enabling Deeper Need Satisfaction That Can Lead to Unhealthy Play

While we have focused on MMO games so far, they are not the only problematic area for game addiction. We have highlighted how games that "hit on all cylinders" in terms of need satisfaction (i.e., competence, autonomy, and relatedness) are often those that become the focus of addictive patterns of play. Another example of this can be found within the first-person shooter (FPS) genre, specifically team or multiplayer FPS play.

As we highlighted in chapter 2, FPS games do not historically excel at multiple need satisfactions. They are typically competence-focused games that when executed well have also been able to increasingly provide some experiences of autonomy that consequently lead to greater market success and enthusiasm (e.g., *Half-Life 2*, *Halo*, and *Call of Duty*).

However, FPS games are increasingly adding an online multiplayer component that can greatly enhance their need-satisfaction profile to include significant satisfaction of competence, autonomy, and relatedness—increasing their "motivational magnetism" and inviting strong attachment and the potential for over-involvement. Multiplayer FPS play adds to the core competence satisfactions of single-player modes in several measurable ways.

With respect to autonomy, multiplayer sessions, often called "matches," widen the range of opportunity and choice for the FPS player. While FPS games usually lead players down a more constrained path through the game's narrative, multiplayer matches take place in open environments (much like smaller versions of the "open-world" landscapes of RPG and MMO games) that greatly multiply player choice in their strategy and plan of attack as they face opponents. In addition, multiplayer games are filled with a wide variety of weapons and devices, providing yet another dimension of choice. Overall, these design elements magnify the opportunities for action that players have in the multiplayer FPS game world, drawing players into a deeper experience through the greater autonomy satisfactions they provide.

Adding further to the draw of multiplayer games is the interpersonal element. Just as MMOs entice players through shared experiences of challenge and conquest, multiplayer FPS games satisfy a player's relatedness needs by encouraging meaningful connections through teamwork, collaboration, and support. Players are not simply trying out new strategies and striving for mastery on their own, they are doing so together. In this way, multiplayer FPS experiences fuse opportunities (autonomy) to creatively achieve greater and greater dominance (competence) that are maximized by working together through mutual dependence and teamwork (relatedness). The net result, when successful, is a burst of satisfaction across all of the core needs in the PENS model that is remarkably memorable and compelling, motivating the team FPS player to play game after game. And of course, the kinds of interpersonal pressures to stay and keep playing we discussed for MMOs are also present in team FPS play.

Here again lies both the promise and the peril: For those who balance their gameplay with other activities in life, team FPS play provides exhilarating experiences. But the strong satisfaction from these experiences also creates a temptation for those who are vulnerable to over-involvement, allowing their gaming to crowd out other relationships and activities. Furthermore, because FPS games are so intense (as compared to the more mellow pacing of most MMO play), those who are over-involved in team play also subject themselves to prolonged experiences of stress, which may be physically as well as emotionally unhealthy.

It makes sense, then, to spend some time looking at the issue of "vulnerability" in players, which we believe is also greatly informed by the need-satisfaction perspective of PENS and self-determination theory.

VULNERABLE PEOPLE

There are many types of overusers. We opened this chapter telling Evan's story, which like all personal stories is unique in its own way. Nonetheless, his general profile represents an important "subtype" of vulnerability to over-involvement with games. Abandoned by his mother, rejected by peers, and alienated within academic and sport settings, Evan did not have a lot of psychological need satisfactions in life. Moreover, because his life had been riddled with conflict, attachment insecurities, and neglect, Evan had not developed much by way of self-regulation. He overate, slept sporadically, and undertook little responsibility. In short, he struggled with the self-controls that can lead to greater balance and happiness.

Our work in applying self-determination theory to general well-being has shown that persons whose basic psychological needs are met in their daily lives— through avenues of work, relationships, and leisure activities—are better able to autonomously regulate those activities. In other words, these folks exert control over themselves that is integrated into who they are and what they personally find important. They are more likely to say they are pursuing their daily activities because of something they personally value than simply because they "have to" or "should be" doing it. It's not so much self-sacrificing discipline, but more a willingness to do what is important, and being able to delay gratification enough to get there.

In fact, a large body of research suggests that the more you are provided with supports for autonomy, competence, and relatedness within your development— from your caregivers, teachers, and important others—the stronger your capacity to self-regulate in a healthy way.[8] When people who have these supports in childhood become passionate about a hobby or recreational activity, they will experience that passion in a more controllable way that is balanced with other areas of their life. In contrast, when an individual's daily life is characterized by less satisfaction or more frustration of basic needs, they are both more likely to be vulnerable to an obsessive focus on activities that are somewhat need satisfying, and they will be less able to control that passion.[9] In other words, one marker of vulnerability for overuse of video games is the degree to which we feel our intrinsic needs are supported in other areas of life.

A couple of years back, our own research team set out to further study whether our intuitions about this reciprocal relationship between density of satisfaction in and out of games held any water. Our first hypothesis was that more obsessive passion for games, rather than balanced or "harmonious" passion, would be associated with lower need satisfaction in everyday life. We also predicted that the more obsessively engaged players would have fewer satisfactions and benefits to well-being from gameplay. Results of our first published study on this topic support the ideas we've been discussing.

With our colleague Andy Przybylski, we collected data from well over 1,000 avid video game players.[10] Most were males in their twenties, but generally this group was representative of truly committed players. It was our expectation that in this group, low levels of need satisfaction in daily life would be associated with an obsessive passion for games—the feeling that play is something one *has* to do (rather than something one does out of a more volitional interest). By contrast, a person who has lots of satisfaction in his or her non-game world might still play a lot, but will not experience the same feelings of compulsion.

Our results showed just that. Low levels of basic need satisfaction in life increased the risk of a disordered pattern of play, characterized by feelings of compulsion and extended amounts of game time. But we found some other interesting things as well.

First, those players who had this obsessive passion for playing video games also seemed to draw *less* joy out of their play. Even though they were playing more, they were enjoying the time they spent in games less. They reported more inner tension following game sessions, and less fun while playing. By contrast, avid gamers whose lives had reasonable levels of need satisfaction reported less tension after playing, and even more energy and vitality. They also enjoyed playing more.

One shorthand way that many people use to gauge disordered play is how much time people spend playing games. So in addition to looking at players' need satisfaction from games (via our PENS), we also looked at the relation of hours spent playing to a person's overall well-being. Interestingly, hours of play were not strongly related to poorer adjustment and wellness generally. But more hours of play were related to negative outcomes if gamers were playing games out of obsessive reasons. We're continuing to look at this issue, but these findings indicate that it is not so much the quantity of play, but the *quality* of one's reasons for playing games that is important to well-being.

And consider this final finding: The poorer adjustment of compulsive players was *not* due mostly to the fact of playing the game, or the number of hours played, but rather to the absence of satisfactions elsewhere in life. It suggests that the extensive and obsessive play was perhaps *itself* a symptom of a deeper problem—a life that was lacking in important intrinsic satisfactions. This particular study does not sort out the cause-and-effect issue, which clearly will require further research. But our analyses did show that the direct negative effects of gameplay are small once you take into account the general levels of need satisfaction in these gamers' lives.

While our work includes mostly Western gamers, researchers internationally have found similar patterns. For example, Wan and Chiou[11] studied Taiwanese teens addicted to online video games. Their results, like ours, suggested that gaming out of true interest and enjoyment was *negatively* correlated with addictive inclinations. Results of a second study in this paper also showed more dissatisfaction with psychological needs in addicted players. Wan and Chiou suggested that the video game addicts' compulsive use of games seems to aim at the relief of dissatisfaction rather than the pursuit of satisfaction. By contrast, for nonaddicts, online games are primarily a source of satisfaction rather than a defense against dissatisfaction.

Findings from research projects like these are just a start. But they highlight a key point we have been making throughout this book: The psychology of gaming needs to be better studied before conclusions are drawn about gaming. For example, we see a lot of people blaming video games for their destructive psychological impact and addictive qualities. Surely the concern is a legitimate one, particularly because game designers, like all producers of media or any product, are getting better and better at making their games more attractive and absorbing. Many people have become over-involved in games in no small part because games are engaging and satisfying. But it is also true that overuse occurs not just because games are engaging, but because people of all ages become vulnerable to seeking game satisfactions too often when they have unsatisfying lives at home, in school, or at work. It is for those who have a strong contrast between an unsatisfying life and a highly satisfying virtual world where we believe a strong risk for overuse is most present. It is when this combination of factors come together that gamers can really get sucked in and stuck in game worlds. And although the gamers who show this pattern may also, like Evan, appear less well-adjusted, it may be a mistake to blame gaming as the root cause. Our data and that of others suggest that this maladjustment is largely due to their lives, not their gaming.

This doesn't diminish the need for a serious look at gaming and its role in addiction. While it may be a symptom, games can still aggravate or intensify dysfunctional living. Our observations also suggest a vicious cycle: The more one compulsively plays games to escape an unsatisfying life, the less those games actually satisfy, and the more the individual is separated from the sources of change and support (e.g., family and friends) that could lead to wellness. While this is not always the case (sometimes too much gaming *creates* the problems in life all by itself, as in our case study of Peter), we think all those correlations we see in the journals between gameplay and poorer adjustment don't always teach us much about the "chicken and egg" relationship between excessive gaming and a dysfunctional or unsatisfying life.

In addition, it's equally true that not all people who become game addicts are the basement-dwelling "losers" we picture in our mind's eye. Some of the most talented, capable, and engaging people we know personally have had struggles with spending too much time in games. They fall in love with what the real world doesn't offer—a high density of psychological need satisfactions that come from being a hero, accomplishing goals, and teaming up with friends to accomplish epic feats. Like all great and cherished memories, it is natural for all gamers to want to go back and experience some more of that excitement and triumph, perhaps with a special draw for those with a high achievement motivation. But for most of us, there is also substantial need satisfaction in the other areas of life that lets us find our way back out of games. We avoid that extra hour of gaming the same way we refrain from taking a third cookie; while we may be tempted, the presence of other values, concerns, and satisfactions enables us to hold a healthy balance.

LEAVING THE WORLD BEHIND: THE RELATIONSHIP TRADE-OFFS OF GAMING

Behind almost all overusers are others who are deeply concerned about them, those whom the gamers themselves are often neglecting. However rich and engaging my virtual world may be, when I go off to spend time there, I am leaving behind the others in my "real" life. Over extended periods of time, this can feel hurtful and even abandoning. Our wife or child may be physically nearby, but feel a world apart from us as we are deeply glued to our virtual world and oblivious to the other world in which we sit—and in which most of our family and friends reside.

Because my wife doesn't game, mostly I have been on the "leaving them behind" end of this scenario. But recently I had the opposite opportunity to be the one left behind, and I experienced firsthand what an unpleasant experience this can be. I was traveling with a friend who also enjoys games. Though this was an outdoor trip, focused on hiking and canoeing, I was surprised that he came fully equipped with his laptop and gaming gear, ready to play. He explained, "Hey, we are on vacation!" with a look that said this was a time for indulging pleasures like gaming. How could I object?

But inwardly I did. Often I found myself impatiently waiting while he "finished something up." We could have been out enjoying the open air, but he was instead using that time to be elsewhere in some virtual space.

It was during the evenings when I really felt it. We had a hotel near the base of a mountain, and before I was even in the shower, he was off to his laptop screen. From there, our social interactions became brief and entirely without depth. Mostly I saw the back of his head, heard him chatter with his online mates, and felt I had been left on my own despite his physical presence. Finally, I'd wander down to the local pub where people actually would talk with me! I kept wishing he would put it away, but feared I would sound too much like his wife (for whom my sympathies were now increased).

This is a common tale among the loved ones of gamers. At this moment, all around the world, parents, spouses, and friends are waiting for their gamer to log off. Because the simple fact is that when gamers are at play, they are probably not relating to you. Video games are simply too absorbing and too demanding of our attention to allow us to relate to anyone who is not in the digital world with us. And outsiders can't help but experience this as a pulling away from shared experiences with them, opting for games over a fun conversation, cooking dinner together, or tackling chores and projects.

A great source for seeing firsthand the negative impact of overuse on others are online groups like gamerwidow.com or *EverQuest Widows* (a popular discussion group founded by my cousin's wife). Scanning through these sites one finds plenty of extreme tales told by those living with gamers who are unable to control their play habits. Most striking is the extraordinary number of heartbreaking tales of frustration and helplessness in the face of a partner or spouse involved in obsessive gaming. In our work in the game industry, we have heard many gamers object to the words *addiction* and *obsession*, wanting to dismiss these concerns as yet another unfair attack on gaming by those who have an axe to grind. But one cannot read the many stories of overuse without acknowledging that there is a destructive potential here, and how "too much of a good thing" hurts not only obsessive players, but those who long to be laughing, communicating, and living with them.

"ADDICTION" OR "OVERUSE?" THE SEMANTICS OF DYSFUNCTIONAL GAMING

Interesting debates are churning as to whether gaming can be clinically addictive, and thus diagnostically in the same group as habits such as smoking, drinking alcohol, and gambling.[12] These debates were highlighted recently when a task force of the American Medical Association (AMA) took up this issue, deciding how the behavioral disorder of excessive video gameplay would be labeled or classified in the official diagnostic nomenclature. There are, it was argued, enough parallels between excessive gaming and the existing diagnostic category for gambling addictions to warrant the classification. Although the AMA ultimately decided not to apply the word *addiction*, and instead to focus on *overuse*, they emphasized that this was a tentative stance still awaiting more evidence and consideration.

Typically, an addiction has to have several properties. Among the open issues around gaming is that of *withdrawal effects*, because an addiction is defined in part by the short-term adverse physiological and psychological impacts of stopping. It is not entirely clear to what extent withdrawal symptoms are strongly associated with video game overuse, as some excessive users do not exhibit "cravings" for games if they are unavailable, while other users do. So far, questions such as this have led experts to refrain from viewing gaming overuse as an addiction in the strict sense. As with all aspects of the psychology of gaming, we hope that decisions about a "gaming addiction" classification will ultimately be grounded in a solid foundation of research rather than hyperbole.

On another level, this debate distracts the lay public from the real issues. Whatever the white coats ultimately decide, millions are concerned about excessive gaming and struggle with it at some level, whether in their own lives or in the life of someone they care about. There are simply too many anecdotal reports of players losing themselves to virtual worlds, and unable to pull themselves out, to deny that an issue exists.

For example, we met a young gamer named Jamie (then 18) who told us, "I love games, but I can't go near them now." He works as a waiter in a local restaurant. Clearly a bright guy, he exclaimed that "I lost more than a year of my life to *EverQuest*." During that year, his sophomore year of high school, Jamie rarely studied, skipped a lot of school, stopped sports, and basically never went out with high school friends. All of his free moments were spent in the game. His grades dropped precipitously, and this cost him a lot of life opportunities even though at the time none of those were in any clear focus. After bottoming out, Jamie spent the ensuing months in conflicts over his school problems and his gaming habits. Finally, his parents "pulled the plug" just before his senior year. Angry, but determined to graduate, he scraped by to finish school, and was now working the tables in the restaurant. Despite his struggles with his parents, Jamie realized how lost in cyberspace he had been, and seemed vaguely thankful to his parents for providing some of the self-control that he could not.

We have emphasized, and in fact devoted, much of our professional lives to the idea that we all have intrinsic needs for autonomy that in most circumstances are best supported by respecting personal choices. But sometimes we can become "trapped" within destructive habits and need the intervention, and support, of friends or family. Regardless of the reasons, for those who fall too deeply into gaming, professional help to moderate their excessive gaming is an important option to consider. As games grow in their sophistication and ability to satisfy psychological needs, their motivational pull will also increase, perhaps drawing even more players into the territory of addiction. It is logical to assume that because each generation has a deeper and more longstanding relationship with games, virtual worlds will continue to become a readily available and familiar place to retreat for those who are experiencing the vulnerability of emotional stress or malnourished needs.

But as with the positive aspects of gaming we have discussed in previous chapters, inoculating against and helping improve dysfunctional gaming begins with better understanding of its causes and dynamics. Our focus on the player's experience of basic need satisfactions explains the reasons for dysfunctional gaming as well as gaming's happier moments. By seeing clearly the satisfaction from games in the broader context of how basic needs are being satisfied by *life*, we believe that those concerned about gaming addiction can get a clearer picture of how to address this issue empathically and effectively.

NOTES

1. Entertainment Software Association. "2005 Sales, Demographic and Usage Data: Essential Factors about the Computer and Video Game Industry." Available at http://www.theesa.com/files/2005EssentialFacts.pdf.

2. Grüsser, S. M., Thalemann, R, and Griffiths, M. D. (2007). *CyberPsychology & Behavior, 10*, 290–292.

3. Ng, B. D., and Weimer-Hastings, P. (2005). "Addiction to the Internet and Online Gaming." *CyberPsychology & Behavior, 8*, 110–113.

4. Clark, N., and Scott, P. S. (2009). *Game Addiction: The Experience and Effects*. Jefferson, North Carolina: McFarland and Company, p. 8.

5. Peters, C. S., and Malesky, L. A. (2008). "Problematic Usage among Highly-Engaged Players of Massively Multiplayer Online Role Playing Games." *CyberPsychology & Behavior, 11*, 481–484.

6. Baumeister, R. F., and Bushman, B. J. (2007). *Social Psychology and Human Nature* (1st ed.). Belmont, CA: Thomson Wadsworth.

7. In the game world, there is a term for this. A common feature of combat in MMO games is *aggro*, meaning how much anger you have built up in an enemy, thus making it more likely to attack you. Perhaps predictably, the term *spousal aggro* refers to the amount of anger you are building up in your partner by spending too much time in your virtual world!

8. See review by Ryan, R. M., Deci, E. L., Grolnick, W. S., and LaGuardia, J. G. (2006). "The Significance of Autonomy and Autonomy Support in Psychological Development and Psychopathology." In D. Cicchetti and D. Cohen (Eds.), *Developmental Psychopathology: Volume 1, Theory and Methods* (2nd ed., pp. 295–849). New York: John Wiley & Sons.

9. Vallerand, R. J. (2010). "On Passion for Life Activities: The Dualistic Model of Passion." In M. P. Zanna (Ed.), *Advances in Experimental Social Psychology* (pp. 97–193). New York: Academic Press.

10. Przybylski, A. K., Weinstein, N., Ryan, R. M., and Rigby, C. S. (2009). "Having to Versus Wanting to Play: Background and Consequences of Harmonious Versus Obsessive Engagement in Video Games." *CyberPsychology & Behavior, 12*, 485–492.

11. Wan, C. S., and Chiou, W. B. (2006). "Psychological Motives and Online Games Addiction: A Test of Flow Theory and Humanistic Needs Theory for Taiwanese Adolescents." *CyberPsychology & Behavior, 9*, 317–324.

12. Dejoie, J. F. (2001). "Internet Addiction: A Different Kind of Addiction?" *Medical Review of Liege, 56*, 523–530.

Chapter 7

THE APPEAL AND PERILS OF AGGRESSION IN VIDEO GAMES

E ach passing year, game developers provide players with an expanding variety of games that offer a broad array of interesting choices and opportunities. But the truth is that in most games, whether you're playing a grizzled soldier or a fluffy cartoon character, you're probably killing things. For the majority of developers, some flavor of violence is a main ingredient in their design, if not the central point. The star characters of most best-selling titles, such as *Halo*'s Master Chief or *God of War*'s Kratos, are fundamentally engines of armed conflict and destruction.

For some games, even killing alone isn't enough. Many developers have decided that true enjoyment requires gallons of blood and scenes of brutal dismemberment. And they may have a point: When talking to a room full of gamers—not criminals or sociopaths, but everyday folk with jobs and pictures of their families in their wallets—nothing brings a smile more consistently than images of truly spectacular kills. Heads exploding, in particular, are a real crowd-pleaser.

Brutal deaths elicit smiles? Really? No wonder so many people are disturbed by violent games and the impact they have on us. We suspect that most of these same gamers would *not* smile at an image of a real person's head exploding on the pages of their daily paper. So why does the violence in games appeal to players, and what about it really is so "fun?" Furthermore, since the game industry seems convinced there are vast audiences that demand violent games, to which players do violent games especially appeal?

We've argued that the enjoyment of games lies in the deeper psychological needs they satisfy, which leads us to ask: What is so need fulfilling about beating, stomping, maiming, and killing? What is energizing and motivating about this kind of play? Is violence in games conveying some deeper satisfaction, or is it truly satisfying in and of itself?

There are other important questions to be asked as well. Given the pervasiveness of violence in many games, what effects does this exposure to violence have on players? This controversy burns hot right now, just as it has for television and film in generations past. But for games the concern runs deeper because games are interactive—players are not merely watching violence, but are *acting* violently as they play. We've discussed how interactivity is a key element to deepening immersion. So in terms of violent action, is there a greater negative impact in games, one with potential to blossom into actual violence more readily?

Here we want to consider both the immediate and long-term effects on players. In the short term, how does the arousal of virtual combat and intense competition impact body and mind? Games create a sense of immersion where emotions and feelings are quite genuine, but what are the implications of this in a virtual firefight, stressfully struggling to kill or be killed?

Beyond this, we want to understand what influence violent games might have on behaviors outside the game. Many game detractors and researchers argue that exposure to violent games is already turning our kids into bloodthirsty killers. Indeed, Jack Thompson, a lawyer who appears frequently in the media, has argued that video games helped *cause* mass murders such as Columbine, Virginia Tech, Dawson College, and other bloody sprees by providing a "training ground" for killing.[1] And he is not alone. There are many researchers who are sounding similar alarms, and politicians seeking—often successfully—to limit or outright ban violent video games on the premise of these negative impacts. Some highly credible researchers have even claimed that video games are a public health threat as serious as smoking,[2] a behavior that kills thousands annually. To them the negative impact of violent games is "unequivocal."[3]

Other credible researchers have, however, dismissed these claims as simplistic, arguing that they often reflect cultural bias and ideology as much as solid science.[4] Across the research, some see little evidence that video games are contributing to an increase in societal violence, or to the propensity for violence, noting that even as sales of violent games accelerate, serious violent crimes in youth are decreasing. They see extreme pronouncements concerning aggression as overstated and counterproductive, contributing to a "cycle of moral panic."[5]

Within this emotionally charged, rhetoric-filled controversy, it's hard to stay levelheaded. The debates are heated on one side by legitimate concerns about the influence of violent games and on the other by concerns for freedom of expression and personal preferences. And these value differences certainly influence how commentators interpret the emerging research data.

As with the last chapter on addiction, we will begin our exploration of the issue by looking first at the underlying psychology of the violent game experience, and proceeding from there. First, we need to understand why there is so much violence in games, and connect that to the appeal of combat and fighting to players. Then it makes sense to explore *to whom* violent games most strongly appeal, and some of the psychological dynamics underlying that attraction. As we'll see, although game violence adds appeal for some players, for others it's a clear turnoff. Once we understand players' motivation, we can better talk about the potential effects of violent games on real-life behavior.

PLENTY OF BLOOD TO SPILL

With few exceptions, the most critically acclaimed and best-selling games of all time feature combat and violence. In 2009, 8 out of 10 of the top-rated games were focused on violent gameplay, with the majority having violent themes (war, warfare, or fighter) in the game title itself.[6] There are endless similar ways in which you can slice the data on game interest and sales, but all of them support the basic fact that violence predominates the video game industry. Only the Nintendo Wii system, which focuses on "family fun," had sales primarily of nonviolent titles. But even here, graphically violent games (*MadWorld*) and commercial successes (e.g., *Metroid, Call of Duty*) can readily be found. In *MadWorld*, players can impale their enemies on signposts and fences, rip out internal organs, and execute them with chainsaws—family fun indeed.

WHAT COUNTS AS VIOLENCE?

Because reasonable people can disagree about what *violence* even means, let's clarify how we define truly violent content. Some games have fantasy violence with low levels of offensive blood and gore, such as *Mario* crushing walking mushrooms or the bloodless (but still warlike) ways of *Pokémon*. On the other end of the spectrum are games that strive for graphic, blood-soaked realism such as most high-budget FPS titles (e.g., *Gears of War*) and many popular RPG games (e.g., *Fallout 3, Dragon Age*). Although some researchers suggest that any violence, no matter how unrealistic, is problematic, it is clear to most observers that the intensity and graphic realism of game violence ranges from cartoon playful to darkly vivid.

Advances in technology allow developers of violent games to create greater and greater realism through sound and image. When describing a design vision they believe will be more immersive and enjoyable for their target audience, there is often a desire to simulate more graphically realistic—and presumably more engaging—combat. And indeed, sound and images are able to heighten player arousal. A recent study, for example, showed that a tense soundtrack can heighten stress and cortisol production,[7] magnifying the intensity of play. This emphasis on graphics and special effects often becomes the dominant focus within a game developer's budget, stealing resources from other areas (e.g., character development, gameplay mechanics) on the belief that fidelity in the sights and sounds of the game are what players value most. Although we've challenged this idea in previous chapters, it remains an entrenched belief.[8]

Adding to this, design teams often "amp up" the intensity of violent actions in particular, designing in more and more blood, louder shrieks of pain and suffering, and even playing violent events in slow motion, just so you don't miss a drop. Simply put, games are often designed out of a core belief that violence and gore are *inherently* enjoyable, with their graphic depiction being raised to an art form.

Perhaps this kind of hyperbole in games is an extension of what has been seen for years in movies and on TV. It's a common cliché of action movies that when the hero shoots the bad guy's car in the rear bumper, it explodes in a gratifying nuclear fireball. In real life, we're pretty sure car bumpers aren't made of TNT. But it's sure fun to watch from the safety of our sofas. In games, we see the same kind of exaggeration and an inflationary trend in violent images and actions.

Because degrees of violence vary, rating systems have been instituted with the goal of helping consumers anticipate how violent a given game might be. The industry-standard ratings come from the Entertainment Software Review Board (ESRB). Much like the Motion Picture Association's rating of movies (i.e., G, PG, PG-13, and R), the ESRB generates ratings focused on the age appropriateness of games with regard to both violence and sexual content. Although widely criticized for the logic of their criteria,[9] they supply a rough continuum along which games can be classified and compared. Ultra-violence (and/or explicit sexual content) warrants a Mature (M) rating in this ESRB system, meaning recommended for adults only. Games such as *MadWorld* are placed here. These ratings range down to "E for Everyone," where we find nonviolent titles such as *Tetris* or the very mild cartoon violence in *Pokémon*. Games in Europe are currently rated under the Pan European Game Information (PEGI) scheme that is based on age ratings, which like the ESRB rating scale has both its detractors and defenders.

This issue of what constitutes violence in games is also very important. Among the most vociferous opponents of video games are those who think all violence, cartoonish or not, models and facilitates aggressive behavior in children and adults. Others are more concerned with realistic violence and/or violence directed against human victims in graphic and detailed ways. They argue that this is a more plausible pathway through which games influence social attitudes and behaviors. Still others seem to deny strong effects and treat all categories of virtual violence as relatively innocuous.

Our own research on this topic has focused on the realistic depiction of blood and gore in video games, but from a new perspective: We became interested in how much these very graphic elements actually contribute to value and satisfaction in players. It's our contention that there's a lot of need satisfaction woven into many violent game scenarios—notably strong satisfaction of both competence and autonomy needs—that carries the real value of violent play. As with game overuse, looking at the relations of in-game violence to need satisfaction opens up some very interesting ways to understand the pervasiveness of game violence, along with new ways to relate to it or even circumvent it.

WHY DO PLAYERS LIKE VIOLENT GAMES SO MUCH?

Let's explore what makes violent games so appealing and enduring. We've already noted that an entire genre of games—first-person shooters—is based almost exclusively on intimate and bloody combat. While RPG/adventure games are not all violent, most invariably involve marauding heroes, who must kill to survive and progress. And in their modern incarnations, even these games are turning more graphic than their predecessors, adding in options for players to increase blood and gore to extreme levels. While popular but nonviolent games exist (e.g., *The Sims, Rock Band*), they are still in the minority. Even racing games often layer in combat options, enabling players to drop bombs and oil slicks to defeat others. When I first purchased *Guitar Hero*, a seemingly violence-free music game, I was surprised to come upon not only a "boss battle" at the end of my first tour, but to also discover the ability to disable my opponent's ability to play! Thus, even this popular music game draws from the time-honored video game tradition to attack first and ask questions later.

According to early commentators, the reason combative, violent content is appealing is that it offers excitement, sensationalism, and feelings of empowerment.[10] This suggests that players may like violence in its own right and find it fun.

But in our research, we suspected a different and more complex story. It is our sense that many of the popular games that contain highly violent content are not fundamentally appealing because they are bloody or murderous, but because at a deeper level, they offer satisfactions of the basic needs outlined in our PENS model: namely, competence, autonomy, and when fighting alongside others, even relatedness. Violent situations offer myriad opportunities for players to feel challenged to the utmost, demanding an exercise of skills, and to receive the confirming positive feedback that satisfies a need to achieve. Thus, competence satisfactions reign in violent games. In addition, many of the popular violent games offer considerable opportunities for players to choose among goals, destinations, strategies, and tools—that is, to experience considerable *autonomy* in their gameplay. As McCarthy, Curren, and Byron argued, "In all the tabloid-inspired furor over *Grand Theft Auto*'s questionable content, it is easy to lose sight of why it's such a successful game in the first place. People don't play it for the violence; they play it because it affords the opportunity to do whatever they please."[11]

It is truly novel to have an open environment where you get to be the gunslinger, bust into any bar or even police station, and do what you will. And to have the choice over the many spectacular ways you can dispatch your "enemies" creates many opportunities for action that stimulate enjoyable "what if" moments. In *Red Dead Redemption*, a recent action/RPG game replete with opportunities for violence, your cowboy can ride the Western landscape doing either good (saving a barmaid from assault) or evil (shooting and looting innocent ranch hands). The bigger and more varied your options and weapon arsenal, the more such choices and the sense of freedom that goes with them are enabled. Couple those choices with fantastic explosions that give you immediate feedback on your skill, and you have autonomy and competence satisfactions rolled into one.

Violence also creates a context for the more powerful emotional moments in multiplayer games that we've discussed in previous chapters. Cooperation and camaraderie is catalyzed within the "do or die" violent challenges of combat and victory, similar to the exhilaration experienced in sports and other forms of teamwork. Indeed, military experts themselves have found that there is tremendous bonding from acting as a unit in combat.[12] We see the same happening in multiplayer games based on raids and combat scenarios.

In short, we suggest that combat-related themes offer compelling narratives and opportunities for action, heroism, achievement, and group camaraderie that readily satisfy all three of our core psychological needs, which is what in large part makes them so engaging and fun. So this led us to ask an additional question: How much of the enjoyment yielded by combat and violent games is due to the violence *per se* versus the opportunities for need satisfaction that these combat scenarios provide?

We set out to discover an empirical answer to this question. In collaboration with our colleague Andy Przybylski, we did a series of six studies, published together in *Personality and Social Psychology Bulletin* in 2009.[13] First, in a couple of survey studies, we sampled avid video game players from online gaming communities. We had these regular players tell us what their favorite games were, and had them rate these games on dimensions assessing autonomy and competence, presence, enjoyment, and other variables reflecting their interest in the games. We also identified the ESRB ratings for each of these games, and in addition we developed and applied our own rating system for the graphic quality, realism, and intensity of the violence in each game. We were able to show with these surveys (involving approximately 2,500 gamers) that enjoyment and interest in playing or purchasing these games was strongly related to autonomy and competence experiences, whereas the level of violence was not at all predictive of these outcomes.

You can see this exemplified in Table 7.1. When features of games are allowed to compete to see which have the strongest relations with outcomes, there are positive relationships between autonomy and competence opportunities in the games and negligible or even negative associations between the amount of violence and the experience of enjoyment.

Table 7.1 Violent Content, Competence, and Autonomy Satisfactions

Violent Content, Competence, and Autonomy – What Predicts Positive Experiences? ("***" indicate a statistically significant relationship)

	R^2	Violent Content	Competence	Autonomy
Enjoyment	.27	−.07	.19***	.41***
Presence/Immersion	.25	.00	.14***	.44***
Likelihood to Recommend Game to Others	.18	−.07	.23***	.30***
Interest in Sequel	.11	−.08	.13***	.26***

Note: Multiple Regression Analyses, n = 923, ***p < .001.

But such survey methods are not by themselves as definitive as more tightly controlled experiments, and in this same article we presented four additional experimental studies. Within these experiments, we developed comparisons between violent and nonviolent (or less violent) versions of the same game, so that the only differences in the gameplay were the levels of blood and gore involved and the violent versus nonviolent "story" (or context) we gave them for defeating opponents.

We constructed our studies in this way because we felt that much of the past research done by others was problematic. In many studies, researchers have examined the effects of violent games by comparing entirely different games, one violent and one nonviolent. But these games often differ on many dimensions that could affect players' experience (themes, controls, and gameplay mechanics) rather than isolating the impact of violence alone. For example, violent games— such as top FPS titles—are usually more complex, have more difficult controls, and represent bigger development budgets that result in richer gameplay. From a scientific standpoint, therefore, many things could be affecting different experiences of these "high" and "low" violence games.

So what we did was to take the same game experience—identical with respect to the game world, mechanics, and features—and vary only the level of violence. For example, in one of our studies, players in one group were introduced to a very violent "kill or be killed" scenario in which they ran around with a rifle and killed computer enemies in a highly bloody fashion. In a second group, players were told that they were playing a game of tag and that tagging enemies would "transport" them back to a central base (i.e., essentially they would be "tagged out"). In this second scenario, we modified the game so there was no blood at all—enemies floated up and evaporated into the air when they were "tagged." Because the games were essentially identical apart from these differences, it allowed us to have a more precise and "clean" test of the role of violence and gore in enjoyment. Remarkably, all players, even those who one might expect to value violence, enjoyed these games equally. The extra blood and gore added nothing to their "fun" as long as other aspects of gameplay (the competence feedback, the opportunities to choose actions, etc.) were equivalent. In fact, across multiple experiments, once we accounted for basic need satisfactions, *violent content itself did not enrich enjoyment*, and layering it into similar games did not cause the average player to think those games were more fun! Tagging people out was just as much fun as shooting them in the head.

A lot of gamers we interviewed have been incredulous about these findings— and direct about their opinions! The most common comment goes something like: "Don't take the %#$& blood out of my *#&$* game, or I'll kill you, lol!" Clearly, players feel deeply about the issue. They believe a game with realistic violence is more fun.

But even with these players, as they talk at greater depth about their love of violence, it often becomes clear that the reason is not the gore *per se*, but the immediate and visceral feedback it provides. For example, Eddie, a shop manager we know who is also an avid gamer, put it this way: "I like seeing the damage I'm doing. . . . Like in *Gears of War*, when the armor comes flying off, or you see the wound, you know you are hitting him. In contrast, I remember playing *Lost Planet*—you could keep shooting at the bosses and you couldn't tell how much damage they had sustained. . . . the blood makes it more real and immediate." This is the visceral sense of competence feedback we discussed back in chapter 3. Another gamer told us: "If you are in a fighting game, you don't want it to feel like you're shootin' cardboard cutouts." Still another gamer, age 20, from one of our experiments, put it this way: "It's not the same if you have to look up at a monster's health bar to know if you are winning." One gets the sense from these comments that it is the clear and visceral feedback, the ability to directly and immediately experience the effects of your actions without relying on abstract representations that makes the realistic wounds and flying blood relevant to feeling effective (competent) and therefore meaningful and valued.

In chapter 2, we talked about the immediate competence feedback of this sort (e.g., the sounds of your tires squealing as you take a turn too fast in a racing game, to the rising cheers of the crowds as you hit your notes playing a band game). But in a war game, what would this feedback look like? Well, turns out it looks like bullet wounds, screams of pain, and lots of dead enemies. It is a *war* game, after all. Valerie Walkerdine, in her detailed observations of kids joyously killing in games, interprets it this way: "The power to kill and therefore *to have control*, to manage a defeat that *signals progress in the game*. . . . is, of course pleasurable [emphasis ours]."[14]

What our research shows is that if you strip out the violence but retain the feedback on effectiveness in the gameplay, you really don't lose much of the enjoyment or value. Put differently, most of the fun of violence comes from vividly experiencing the positive effects of your own spontaneous actions and strategies. War and combat in games simply achieves these positive satisfactions to intrinsic needs with a violent content "wrapper" of killing, blood, and destruction. Taken as a whole, this explains the paradox of watching otherwise normal and even compassionate people relishing the fact that they are wreaking havoc with a virtual sniper rifle.

Still, if the value added by gratuitous violence is so little, why do developers keep adding more and more violence? Well, first let's acknowledge that it *is* a compelling and dramatic way of delivering competence feedback. But beyond that, there are several reasons we see that may not have much to do with the actual value of violence to the player experience, but may have more to do with other factors in the marketplace and the general creative evolution of gaming.

To begin, there is already a fixed population of consumers in this "combat and kill" market, and they represent a primary group that companies aim to please. If you ask this core audience of young adult and teenage males to whom violent games are marketed what they value, they won't parse the motivational value of violence (that's for eggheads like us), they'll simply remember that the last good game they played had a lot of blood and destruction, so keep it up! This is what will show up in focus groups and general marketing opinion polls, understandably reinforcing the "violence is valued" position.

Moreover, most studios operate more or less on the "Hollywood" model. Inspired game designer convinces publisher-with-bucks to develop a game based on intuition and armchair "feel" for the concept. And like Hollywood, proven ideas are considered safer bets (*Friday the 13th* Part 27, anyone?). Past games, like past movies, become templates and shorthand for selling concepts. The stereotypic Hollywood "pitch" meeting involves explaining your movie in a minute or less based on a combination of what has already been done. (It's *Terminator* meets *Terms of Endearment*!) If it worked in the past, the recipe says, simply repeat and add more. In the case of violence, past games including violence can always be mimicked and elaborated, with even more spectacular graphics and bigger guns. And of course, because game designers are deep gamers themselves, they've seen it all. For their own project, they naturally want to do it bigger and better than it was done before.

But perhaps a more important reason for violence as a staple diet in video games is the fact that when it comes to engaging worlds for people to play in, stories of combat and war just *work*. It is hard to think of more ready themes or concepts in which one can embed multiple types of challenge, offer opportunities to connect with others in cooperative adventures, or provide choices over strategies and approaches, than combat and war. The obstacles and goals are clearly defined, and the mechanism for achieving them (i.e., shoot head—see blood) provides immediate feedback on success. We see this in TV where, alongside sports and reality shows (which are perhaps television's version of *The Sims*), the prime time airways are dominated by violent crime shows, and the movie and history channels with stories of war. Put differently, combat and violent adventures are a compelling and familiar context for entertainment media—both traditional and interactive.

Going further with this idea, sports, combat, and war provide scenarios in which one can be a *hero*, which we've noted is a remarkably powerful vehicle for satisfaction of all three core needs in the PENS model (competence, autonomy, and relatedness[15]). In these inherently violent situations, the clarity and intensity of need satisfaction embodied by the player-as-hero is elegantly maximized: Our mastery satisfactions reach new heights as we defeat entire armies single-handedly; our autonomy satisfactions soar as we embrace our quest single-mindedly and blaze new trails to achieve it; and our relatedness satisfactions peak as we fulfill the hopes of those who rely on us as their single and ultimate hope for salvation. Our research shows that these satisfactions don't *require* violence to be achieved, but it's hard to imagine more powerful ways to get there. Certainly that's why violence has played a key role in heroic storytelling for thousands of years, and why so many modern games continue to embrace violence as a central pillar.

It took Will Wright years to get a game publisher to believe that *The Sims* would be fun to play, because buying a virtual sofa and paying your virtual electric bill just doesn't sound like it will be nearly as fun as "emerging victorious from a life-and-death struggle to save the world"—even if it is.

TO WHOM DOES THE VIOLENCE ESPECIALLY APPEAL, AND WHO IS "TURNED OFF"?

We've discussed how the value added by violent content *per se* may be more negligible than many have imagined. Instead, it is the narrative context of conflict, potential heroism, and achievement that are big draws—alongside opportunities to experience autonomy, competence, and relatedness. But since we can embed need satisfaction in both high or low violence scenarios (as our studies indicate), who is it that *prefers* that games have blood and gore when they are making decisions about the games they would like to play? Truthfully, this is another area of game psychology that has only been thinly researched. But in our own work, we have explored at least one variable that seems predictive of a preference for violence—the overall aggressiveness of one's personality, or what we'll call *trait aggressiveness*.

Aggressive Individuals

Trait aggressiveness is a variable that captures a person's general tendency to be argumentative, to respond to provocation with hostility, and to be easy to anger.[16] Studies in psychology have explored both the backgrounds of people high in this aggressiveness trait, as well as many of its consequences. Our interest was in how those high and low in trait aggressiveness respond to video games with high or low violent content. Thus, in the studies described earlier, we included measures of trait aggressiveness. Some of the results were predictable and others surprising.

First, let us say what will hardly be surprising: If you ask people about what games they prefer to play, people high in trait aggressiveness and hostility are more likely to rate a game as more valued or more preferred if it has higher violent content. They prefer more blood. Oppositely, people low in trait aggressiveness show the opposite pattern; they are less likely to value games that are more graphically violent. This pattern is graphically displayed in Figure 7.1, which represents the results of just one of our studies, but is a good illustration of this effect.

Remember our study of a high-violence game of "kill" versus a low-violence game of "tag?" Just as in our other studies, when actually *playing* the game, people did not enjoy violent versus nonviolent versions of this game differently, regardless of their level of aggressiveness. But the high-aggressive group still stated a *preference* for the more violent version, indicated by their higher estimates

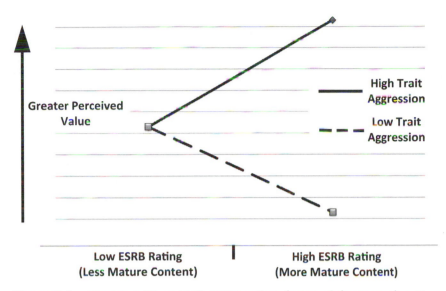

Figure 7.1 Games with a high ESRB rating (more violence and mature content) were of greater interest to those high in trait aggression and of less interest to those low in trait aggression. (© 2010 Scott Rigby and Richard Ryan.)

of the game's value. In contrast, people low in aggression tended to value the violent game less.

This suggests that developers have been driving themselves deeper down a road that appeals to an aggressive subgroup while simultaneously "turning off" another, perhaps even larger, demographic of those low in trait aggression. Little work has been done to identify the size of these populations relative to one another among gamers (i.e., we don't yet know the actual proportion of high versus low trait aggressiveness in the gamer population), but unless evidence emerges that gamers are higher in trait aggression generally (which seems unlikely), blood-based marketing designed to appeal to the game's "core" audience may be ultimately hurting sales with a broader audience of potential players.

What was most surprising to us was the issue of enjoyment: The more violent content did not add to game enjoyment for players, *even for the high aggressive group*. Although they stated that they valued violent content more highly in the abstract, it did not reliably add to their pleasure in actual moments of play. Thus, their preference for violence is not really the result of their *actual* gameplay experience. Instead, it may simply reflect that they identify more easily with the role of a violent action hero because they have higher trait aggression.

Our key point is that experiencing the violence itself within the game is not where the value lies. This is worthy of more consideration and careful study because it provides a different take on the idea that "violence is fun." What our research has demonstrated more fundamentally is that showing mastery is fun, and having interesting choices in how to overcome obstacles is fun. Violent gameplay, as we've seen, is a great vehicle for achieving this, but the violence may be beside the point. Or to put it another way: Violence, in itself, is not intrinsically motivating.

THE GENDER GAP

Another characteristic of people associated with preferences for violent games is gender. There are clear differences in the patterns of gaming between males and females. Sales records show that when it comes to games of combat, war, and fighting (e.g., *Mortal Combat, F.E.A.R.*), males are the primary consumers. When we move to RPG and MMO games that are less combat oriented and less graphic in their violence, males still predominate, but more females are in the mix. When we move to games like the *The Sims*, however—a game focused on less violent, and even nurturing themes—females are the main consumers. Females also make up approximately 39 percent of all game consumption (and that number has been rising), and we've already noted that the *The Sims* is among the most popular games in history.

Interestingly, however, when we have both males and females play games in our laboratory settings, we do not find big gender differences in the enjoyment of play, and this is so even for violent games. Anecdotally, when we watch males and females play, they both express satisfaction with success, whether or not it involves killing and blood. Again, the key is the satisfaction of intrinsic needs such as competence and mastery that all good games, both violent and nonviolent, are able to provide.

But there is a deeper story here. Society provides us with various scripts, ideals, and norms that differ for males and females. In a stereotyped view, men must grow up toward a model of competence, achievement, heroism, independence, and dominance. Women also must have some of these attributes, but there is also a greater social expectation that women have a caring and compassionate nature and be adept in relating with others. As Walkerdine[17] argues in her qualitative studies of girls and boys interacting with video games, girls are "supposed" to display an "abhorrence to violence to maintain a soft femininity." That is, it is less safe for them to express an interest in violence. Oppositely, Walkerdine observes that competitive and violent video games fit with what we expect of boys—to appear tough, independent, and focused on achieving. How much this is nurture and how much is nature remains a deeper question. But without a doubt, there is an invisible hand of culture at work, guiding boys and girls differently to value (at least explicitly) various kinds of games, and also influencing how they talk about them openly (highlighting yet another problem with focus groups).

This helps explain our own research findings, which also runs against the grain of "traditional" market beliefs about enjoyment with respect to gender expectations. In our lab where both men and woman play identical games and then report on their experiences privately (i.e., without social pressures present), we don't see a big gender difference in *actual* enjoyment of violent play, despite the gap that is assumed. To the extent these gender differences exist in game consumption in the real world, it may reflect the socialization Walkerdine (and many others) have observed.

Taken as a whole, the research reviewed here supports our general argument that we need more research and fewer assumptions about how personality and gender differences predict game experiences. Specifically for this discussion, how do such factors actually influence the preference for, and impact of, violent games? Traits such as aggression and hostility are apt candidates for further research, and we believe there are many others (e.g., sensation seeking), along with demographic variables (e.g., gender, economic circumstances, and culture) or individual background factors (e.g., history of family violence) that may ultimately have predictive value.

DOES VIRTUAL VIOLENCE BEGET ACTUAL VIOLENCE?: CONTROVERSY AND RESEARCH

In both the media and the social sciences, the most contentious discussions about video games concern their potentially harmful effects on players, especially young ones. We covered one of the major issues about video games in the previous chapter on game addiction. But an equally pressing social issue may be the concern that many video games *increase aggression*. Do violent video games actually foster violence in the real world?

Many detractors of video games believe that these games "teach aggression," and that exposure to them is a direct cause of real-world violence. Some researchers have agreed, implicating video games in specific acts of murder and violence as well as to the general moral deterioration and desensitization of society.[18] Perhaps *most* researchers believe that the evidence is at least clear enough to conclude that exposure to violent contents represents a risk factor for aggressive behavior, raising the probability of aggressive acts. Consider this statement by the *American Psychological Association*'s Jeff McIntyre: "The evidence (for media violence as a cause of societal aggression) is overwhelming. To argue against it is like arguing against gravity."[19]

Other researchers are defying this gravity. Some critics of the position that games teach aggression question the definitions of aggression, as well as the methodologies used.[20] Still others argue that the connection between video game violence and real-world aggression and antisocial behavior is anywhere from weak to nonexistent.[21] And of course, industry advocates are quick to point to the global downward trend in violent crime during the same period in which video games have been in their ascendancy.[22]

In other words, opinions range from alarmist to dismissive. In the heated atmosphere of debate, research is often interpreted stridently and perhaps with bias in an attempt to gain victory. Yet those who suffer in this skirmish are the many parents and policy makers who depend upon accurate and clear guidance.

VIOLENT CONTENT IN MEDIA, AND ESPECIALLY GAMES, AS A DIRECT CAUSE OF REAL-WORLD AGGRESSION

The most substantial evidence for the direct harmful effects of violent content in games comes from researchers who use *social learning theory* as the foundational framework to conceptualize their work. Essentially, social learning theory is founded in the idea that we directly learn behaviors vicariously, by observing those behaviors in others in our social (and, by extension, media) world. Some of the classic early experiments in this area were conducted by Albert Bandura and colleagues using a "bobo doll"—an inflatable upright toy (often in the image of a clown) that kids could punch and hit like a sturdy balloon. Using these dolls, Bandura's experiments showed that if children observed physical violence (either live or on television), they were more likely to punch the bobo doll afterward during a play session.[23] Bandura concluded that real-world learning was happening vicariously, simply by observing the behaviors of others.

A group of researchers applying this basic idea to explain the connection between real-world violence and video games includes L. Rowell Huesmann and Brad Bushman (University of Michigan), Craig Andersen (University of Iowa), and Douglas Gentile (Iowa State), among others. They not only claim that violent contents foster aggressive behavior, but as a group they have suggested that this conclusion is beyond any reasonable doubt. For example, some years back, Anderson stated that "debate concerning whether such exposure is a significant risk factor for aggressive and violent behavior should have been over years ago."[24] More recently, Huesmann stated that there is "unequivocal evidence that media violence increases the likelihood of aggressive and violent behavior in both immediate and long-term contexts."[25]

In support of their position, this social learning group has done some of the most methodologically varied and sophisticated studies on the violence question, ranging from experiments that examine short-term aggressive thoughts and behavior to longitudinal survey studies looking at the frequency of aggressive acts. For example, in a typical laboratory experiment, players may play either a violent or a nonviolent game. Afterward, they have the opportunity to punish another person (e.g., deliver a noise blast[26]). In similar studies with children, experimenters let kids play after being exposed to violent video games and watched for signs of aggression.[27] Consistent with Bandura's early experiments, findings from these studies suggest that short-term exposure to video game violence is significantly associated with increases in aggression.[28] Others have additionally reported that exposure to media violence may foster desensitization to violence[29] and decreased pro-social behaviors in social interactions.[30]

A central tenet of social learning theory is that people are fairly open to cultural programming, adopting and mimicking the scripts from the people and media models that they see in the world around them. Just like the kids with the bobo dolls, *people see, people do*. In Anderson and Bushman's language,[31] this is called *script theory*. Scripts are mental frameworks that link emotions and actions (or goals). Script theory says that when individuals watch violence in the mass media—or worse, perform it in video games—they develop aggressive scripts. And the more people rehearse these scripts, the more likely they'll put them into action out in the world. So beating up computer bad guys to reach your goals over and over again, script theory would say, would keep this model of violence active in your mind, increasing the likelihood that you'll swing your fists in other situations outside the game. Psychologically, in this view, "you are what you eat" with respect to the media you consume.

Script theory, therefore, grants the media a lot of power over us, which naturally raises concern and suspicion. After all, we widely acknowledge that media shape and influence our sense of politics, fashion, and countless other aspects of our lives. Is it such a stretch to believe that if we keep immersing ourselves in the vicious and aggressive worlds presented in many video games, pretty soon we will start living it?

It's a worthwhile question to ask. But as adamant as these theorists are about the violent effects of video games on everyone, and as logical as it may seem that mere exposure to violence fosters violence, there are other researchers who dispute this "direct effects" view and offer evidence to the contrary. For example, Christopher Ferguson and his colleagues[32] found no reliable link between exposure to violent games and real-world aggression. Why didn't it exist here, as it had for Anderson and others? The results from Ferguson's group suggested that trait aggression, family violence, and even simply being *male* were predictive of violent crime, but when these variables were accounted for, exposure to violent games did not add any predictive value on its own.[33] This led them to question the accepted conclusion that violent game exposure itself causes violent acts. Others have echoed the fact that despite laboratory research on video game exposure and aggressive behavior, there are no clear data that show that exposure to violent video games leads to more serious violence or crime.[34]

Anderson and colleagues have since released another analysis, one that attempts to answer the issues raised by those questioning their conclusion that violent games catalyze real-world violence. They again found that exposure to violent games was related to extra-game violence.[35] Commenting on these results, Huesmann suggested this new analysis "nails the coffin shut on doubts"[36] about these adverse effects of games. But what really seems to be without a doubt, given the active debate by researchers in this area, is that the debate has yet to be answered affirmatively.

We think this is such an important topic that it is premature to close the book on it. Researchers need to do more in order to bring parents, politicians, and gamers themselves a clearer and more reliable picture of violence in games. If we step back from the emotionally charged nature of the debate, we can direct more energy to really understanding the issue of violence, finding its possible impact, and understanding the circumstances that increase its risks.

We do believe it is important to consider the possibility, backed by growing evidence, that there are certain people who are at greater risk for violent video games amplifying or catalyzing their violent behavior. Although most people have a relatively intact capacity for self-regulation and controlling impulses, not all do.[37] Just as research shows there are differences between us in our risk for conditions such as alcoholism, it seems clear that the violence in video games may pose a greater risk for some individuals, facilitating their crossing the line into unthinkable action. Many scoff at Jack Thompson's rants linking violent games to mass murders such as those of Columbine and Virginia Tech, and indeed the strident tone of his words deflate his credibility. But the fact is that violent gameplay is a common thread in many of the stories of the troubled young men who have caused so much death and destruction. Do they belong to an "at-risk" group, perhaps identified by abusive backgrounds, antisocial personality disorders, or other factors that make violent games are a dangerous influence? If we don't consider that possibility, we run the risk of missing how a video game, while harmless to most, might be tragically toxic to a vulnerable few.

Researchers Patrick and Charlotte Markey recently reviewed evidence that violent contents do more adversely affect a subgroup of players.[38] Using what is called the "five-factor model" of basic personality traits, they found that individuals who were highly neurotic and low in both agreeableness and conscientiousness were those most impacted by violent content. In other words, the negative effects of game violence may be mainly relevant to individuals with a *specific* disposition. Such findings are clearly at odds with the social learning theory view that it is exposure *alone* that does the damage to "any child from any family,"[39] providing further evidence that the debate and our understanding of this topic are far from complete.

Like Markey and Markey, we also lean toward an interactive view of media effects. In part, this is merely because the vast majority of players are neither violent nor antisocial, even those who regularly play highly aggressive games. At the same time, children and adolescents who have not been socialized appropriately with respect to aggression, or for whom aggression has been modeled by caregivers, may be at greater risk of transferring the aggression they see in games into real-world actions. In addition, children who come from homes that are overly controlling, rejecting, or abusive—that is, those who suffer a *thwarting* of the basic psychological needs we have been discussing—may also be vulnerable to transfer effects. Evidence suggests that when these basic needs are thwarted in childhood, individuals are more prone to a variety of antisocial acts, including aggression and overall poorer self-regulation.[40] Although this has not yet been well studied, we think it is important for researchers to look at a variety of such moderating effects so that we can better understand what might be putting certain individuals at risk. And in the process, we can also learn what factors can help protect people from being vulnerable to violent games, along with other forms of violent media.

In the end, it comes back to a central theme we have emphasized throughout: Video games are still a relatively new and very complex media that we are just beginning to study and understand. With all due respect to McIntyre, nothing about them is as certain as gravity!

Need Satisfaction and the Violence Question: What's Next?

This chapter has touched on a number of questions concerning violence in games. Our main contribution to the conversation, when seen through the lens of players' intrinsic need satisfactions, is that violence itself may not be where the action is in terms of what gamers value and what contributes to a deeply satisfying virtual experience. On the practical level, this possibly opens up a little breathing room for game developers, perhaps giving them more freedom to step back and consider how the same satisfactions achieved by violent games can be realized by less-violent designs. Innovation, after all, is among the most cherished goals of game development, and the fact that enjoyment is not chained to gore will hopefully encourage some "out of the ammo box" thinking.

At the same time, we've also reviewed how violent themes are a very, very effective way to achieve need satisfaction, especially in providing an immediate sense of mastery and competence. Added to this is the emotional power of relatedness satisfaction that emerges when players rely upon each other during the stressful heat of battle. So it's no wonder that violent themes have endured and will likely continue in popularity long into the future, just as they have throughout the history of entertainment.

This may be disappointing to those who are concerned about in-game violence. But here we offer some words of encouragement: Our work suggests that the typical player does not like violent games because they are violent; they play them because they are fun. And they are fun *not* because of the blood and gore, but because games of war and combat offer so many opportunities to feel autonomy, competence, and the relatedness of camaraderie rolled into an epic heroic experience. We know it's hard to watch your teenager grinning from ear to ear as he or she blows people's heads off. But chances are the smiles grow from the mastery satisfaction this represents, and not the gore itself.

Nonetheless, there is some worthy and concerning evidence for negative effects of violent games, whatever motivates us to play them. Experimental research clearly indicates some short-term carry-over effects of violent games. While some meaningful criticisms of the research and its interpretation exist and have merit, the data generally support the conclusion that exposure to violent video games can increase aggressive thinking, emotions, and behavior immediately after play. Just as watching the *Three Stooges* has prompted many a brother (including mine) to poke his sibling in the eye, playing highly violent, emotionally charged video games amps up aggressive emotion in the moments following gameplay. But just how substantial and lasting these effects are, is, in our view, yet to be understood.

This and the previous chapter focused on some of the controversial and potentially negative dimensions of being glued to games—topics that fill much of the public discussion about video gaming and its relationship with healthy living. But there is another side to gaming that is growing by leaps and bounds each year: the development and use of games for purposes other than entertainment alone, such as enhancing learning and health. In the next chapter, we turn our discussion to some of these efforts and discuss the crucial role that motivation plays in the application of games to other areas of life.

NOTES

1. Thompson, J. (2007). "Massacre at Virginia Tech: Interview with MSNBC." Retrieved from http://www.msnbc.com/id/18220228/.

2. See Huesmann, L. R. (2007). "The Impact of Electronic Media Violence: Scientific Theory and Research." *Journal of Adolescent Health, 41*, 6–13.

3. Anderson, C. A., Gentile, D. A., and Buckley, K. E. (2007). *Violent Video Game Effects on Children and Adolescents*. Oxford, UK: Oxford University Press.

4. Grimes, T., Anderson, J. A., and Bergen, L. (2008). *Media Violence and Aggression: Science and Ideology*. New York: Sage.

5. Ferguson, C. J. (2010). "Blazing Angels of Resident Evil: Can Violent Video Games be a Force for Good?" *Review of General Psychology, 14*, 68–81.

6. *Metacritic*, 2009 game rankings, http://www.metacritic.com.

7. Hebert, S., Beland, R., Dionne-Fournelle, O., Crete, M., and Lupien, S. J. (2005). "Physiological Stress Response to Video-Game Playing: The Contribution of Built-In Music." *Life Sciences, 76*, 2371–2380.

8. And certainly with some justification. In our research, graphics quality does have an independent contribution to enjoyment and immersion, although as we've reviewed, the impact is smaller than many other areas, notably intrinsic need satisfaction. The stronger market justification for investment in graphics may be that developers must first sell a game before anyone can actually experience it, and graphics are a key element of that important process of marketing. Players often assume that the game with great graphics has a better budget and development team, and hence will overall be a better game. Unfortunately, they are often disappointed, even if the graphics helped initially convince them to open their wallets.

9. Gentile, D. A., Linder, J. R., and Walsh, D. A. (2005). "Media Ratings for Movies, Music, Video Games and Television: A Review of the Research and Recommendations for Improvements." *Adolescent Medicine Clinics, 16*, 427–446.

10. Johnston, D. D. (1995). "Adolescents' Motivation for Viewing Graphic Horror." *Human Communication Research, 21*, 522–552; Zillman, D. (1998). "The Psychology of

the Appeal of Portrayals of Violence." In J. Goldstein (Ed.), *Why We Watch: The Attractions of Violent Entertainment* (pp. 179–211). New York: Oxford University Press.

11. McCarthy, D., Curran, S., and Byron, S. (2005). *The Art of Producing Games.* Boston: Thomson.

12. Grossman, D. (1995). *On Killing: The Psychological Cost of Learning to kill in war and society.* New York: Little, Brown and Company.

13. Przybylski, A. K., Ryan, R. M., and Rigby, C. S. (2009). "The Motivating Role of Violence in Video Games." *Personality and Social Psychology Bulletin, 35*, 243–259.

14. Walkerdine, V. (2007). *Children, Gender, Video Games.* New York: Palgrave Macmillan, p. 88.

15. Rigby, C. S., and Przybylski, A. K. (2009). "Virtual Worlds and the Learner Hero: How Today's Video Games can Inform Tomorrow's Digital Learning Environments." *Theory and Research in Education, 7*, 214–223.

16. Buss, A. H., and Perry, M. (1992). "The Aggression Questionnaire." *Journal of Personality and Social Psychology, 63*, 452–459.

17. Walkerdine, V. (2007). *Children, Gender, Video Games.* New York: Palgrave Macmillan, p. 87.

18. Anderson, C. A., Gentile, D. A., and Buckley, K. E. (2007). *Violent Video Game Effects on Children and Adolescents: Theory, Research, and Public Policy.* New York: Oxford.

19. Cf. Mifflin, L. (1999). "Many Researchers Say Link Is Already Clear on Media Violence." *New York Times.* Retrieved from http://www.nytimes.com/1999/05/09/us/many-researchers-say-link-is-already-clear-on-media-and-youth-violence.html?pagewanted=1.

20. For example, see Grimes, T., Anderson, J. A., and Bergen, L. (2008). *Media Violence and Aggression: Science and Ideology.* New York: Sage.

21. Ferguson, C. J., and Kilburn, J. (2010). "Much Ado About Nothing: The Misestimation and Overinterpretation of Violent Video Game Effects in Eastern and Western Nations: Comment on Anderson et al." (2010). *Psychological Bulletin, 136*, 174–178. See also, Freedman, J. (2002). *Media Violence and Its Effect on Aggression: Assessing the Scientific Evidence.* Toronto: University of Toronto Press.

22. Entertainment Software Association. (2007). "Sales and Genre Data." Retrieved from http://www.thesa.com/facts/sales_genre_data.php.

23. Bandura, A., Ross, D., and Ross, S. A. (1961). "Transmission of Aggression through Imitation of Aggressive Models." *Journal of Abnormal and Social Psychology, 63*, 575–582.

24. Anderson, C. A. (2003). "Video Games and Aggressive Behavior." In D. Ravitch and J. P. Viteritti (Eds.), *Kid Stuff: Marketing Sex and Violence to American Children* (pp. 143–167). Baltimore, MD: Johns Hopkins University Press.

25. Cf. Anderson, C. A., Gentile, D. A., and Buckley, K. E. (2007). *Violent Video Game Effects on Children and Adolescents.* Oxford, UK: Oxford University Press, p. 4.

26. Anderson, C. A., and Dill, K. E. (2000). "Video Games and Aggressive Thoughts, Feelings and Behavior in the Laboratory and in Life." *Journal of Personality and Social Psychology, 78*, 772–791.

27. Cooper, J., and Mackie, D. (1986). "Video Games and Aggression in Children." *Journal of Applied Social Psychology, 16*, 726–744. Interestingly, they found an increase in aggression only in girls.

28. Anderson, C. A., and Bushman, B. J. (2001). "External Validity of "Trivial" Experiments: The Case of Laboratory Aggression." *Review of General Psychology, 1*, 19–41;

also, Anderson, C. A. (2004). "An Update of the Effects of Violent Video Games." *Journal of Adolescence, 27*, 113–122.

29. Bartholow, B. D., Bushman, B. J., and Sestir, M. A. (2006). "Chronic Violent Video Game Exposure and Desensitization to Violence: Behavioral and Event-Related Brain Potential Data." *Journal of Experimental Social Psychology, 42*, 532–539.

30. Sheese, B. E., and Graziano, W. G. (2005). "Deciding to Defect: The Effects of Video Game Violence on Cooperative Behavior." *Psychological Science, 16*, 354–357.

31. Anderson, C. A. and Bushman, B. J. (2002). "Human Aggression." *Annual Review of Psychology, 53,* 27–51.

32. Ferguson, C. J., Rueda, S. M., Cruz, A. M., Ferguson, D. E., Fritz, S., and Smith, S. M. (2008). "Violent Video Games and Aggression: Causal Relationship or Biproduct of Family Violence and Intrinsic Violent Motivation?" *Criminal Justice and Behavior, 35*, 311–332.

33. Olson C. K. (2004). "Media Violence Research and Youth Violence Data: Why Do They Conflict?" *Academic Psychiatry, 28,* 144–150; Ferguson, C. J. (2010). "Blazing Angels of Resident Evil: Can Violent Video Games be a Force for Good?" *Review of General Psychology, 14*, 68–81.

34. Grimes, T., Anderson, J. A., and Bergen, L. (2008). *Media Violence and Aggression: Science and Ideology*. New York: Sage.

35. Andersen, C. A., Shibuya, A., Ihori, N., Swing, E. L., Bushman, B. J., Sakamoto, A., Rothstein, H. R., and Saleem, M. (2010). "Violent Video Game Effects on Aggression, Empathy and Prosocial Behavior in Eastern and Western Countries: A Meta-Analytic Review. *Psychological Bulletin, 136*, 151–173.

36. Huesmann, R. L. (2010). "Nailing the Coffin Shut on Doubts that Violent Video Games Stimulate Aggression: Comment on Anderson et al." (2010). *Psychological Bulletin, 136*, 179–181,179.

37. Ryan, R. M., and Deci, E. L. (2000). "The Darker and Brighter Sides of Human Existence: Basic Psychological Needs as a Unifying Concept." *Psychological Inquiry, 11,* 319–338.

38. Markey, P. M., and Markey, C. N. (2010). "Vulnerability to Violent Video Games: A Review and Integration of Personality Research." *Review of General Psychology, 14*, 82–91.

39. Huesmann, L. R., Moise-Titus, J., Podolski, C. L., and Eron, L. D. (2003). "Longitudinal Relations between Children's Exposure to TV Violence and Their Aggressive and Violent Behavior in Young Adulthood: 1972–1992." *Developmental Psychology, 39*, 201–221, 218.

40. Ryan, R. M., Deci, E. L., Grolnick, W. S., and LaGuardia, J. G. (2006). "The Significance of Autonomy and Autonomy Support in Psychological Development and Psychopathology." In D. Cicchetti and D. Cohen (Eds.), *Developmental Psychopathology: Volume 1, Theory and Methods* (2nd ed., pp. 295–849). New York: John Wiley & Sons.

Chapter 8

GAMING BEYOND ENTERTAINMENT

It's a hallmark of life, both in the big and the small things we think about each day, that we distinguish between what's enjoyable and what's good for us. As I reach for the few remaining crumbs in a potato chip bag that 12 minutes earlier was unopened, I'm both happy to have enjoyed them and guilty because they aren't "good for me." Trying to balance the tension of potato chips versus broccoli, in some form or another, is just a regular part of life.

This book has been about video games as entertainment, and how their ability to satisfy intrinsic motivational needs lies at the heart of what makes them so fun and sustains such deep engagement in players. An undercurrent to this discussion is whether games are simply a guilty pleasure, or can be something more. We've suggested that game experiences can have some meaningful impact on happiness and well-being, while also discussing how they can be consumed in overindulgent and unhealthy ways. In both cases, we've identified the need satisfactions (i.e., competence, autonomy, and relatedness) that are behind games' remarkable power to engage us. Generally, though, we've stayed in the realm of virtual worlds designed purely for entertainment, or what most would consider the "games-as-potato-chips" category.

But there's a larger story to be told about virtual worlds, one focused on how they can achieve goals beyond entertainment alone. Games and virtual spaces are being engineered to emphasize learning (in traditional education and job training), to build greater awareness and social action, and to support people struggling with (or at risk for) disease. Collectively, these efforts are often called "serious games" to indicate that they are *not* of the potato chip variety, but instead seek to harness the potential of games to engage and motivate us to achieve something more.

We've noted at various places that the motivational theory underlying PENS (known in scientific circles as *self-determination theory*) has been applied in many domains outside of interactive entertainment—including the more "serious" domains of education, work, and health care. Just reflecting on the concepts of *competence, autonomy,* and *relatedness*, we suspect they resonate with most people as meaningful beyond games. And that turns out to be right. Social scientists have long studied how the same intrinsic needs that contribute to entertaining and engaging game experiences also contribute to greater satisfaction, engagement, happiness, and well-being outside of games. Throughout hundreds of research programs worldwide, data consistently show intrinsic need satisfaction to be extremely important to positive outcomes (e.g., better learning, improved health) along with sustained engagement.

This "sustained engagement" is one of the critical keys to the success of any effort designed to benefit people or reach important goals. Any teacher, employer, or doctor will tell you how important "engagement" and "motivation" are for their students, employees, and patients. In most cases, it's the whole ballgame: No matter how elaborate your efforts to reach people, if they do not engage and *stay* engaged with you, the probability of long-term impact is minimal.

And it's getting harder to achieve because our modern, wired, on-demand era has created a tectonic shift in the dynamics of engagement and motivation. In the last 20 years, the world of information, media, and services has fragmented into a billion pieces, each of which can be picked up instantaneously in one second and discarded for something else a moment later. In the era of the *Cosby Show*, we watched what was on three channels, went to class without cell phones, and dutifully filled our prescriptions knowing only what the doctor told us. Trying to hold our attention in those days was a cakewalk compared to today, where technology now empowers each of us to build a personalized experience anywhere and at any moment, from millions of available options.

By and large, society speaks positively of this shift and the vast opportunities it now affords us. And technically that's true. But just ask a teacher what he thinks of students having cell phones. Or a doctor what she thinks when a patient says, "I read on the Internet that. . . ." The advancements of the last generation have accelerated our need to really understand motivation and engagement and how to connect with those around us at a deeper level so we can hold onto them and accomplish something. If we want to successfully keep the attention of learners, employees, and patients in order to reach goals, it must be through meaningful satisfaction of *their* needs. Otherwise, they will move on—because it is so easy for them to do so. This is one of the profound motivational consequences of the new self-directed life: Anyone with a message will need to address intrinsic needs if they want to meaningfully engage us.

In this crowded world of choices, we've seen how games are particularly good at winning our attention. And throughout the book, we've seen why. They are great at satisfying the intrinsic needs that are so critical for sustained engagement. But looking beyond this fact alone, we see something else that is pretty exciting—the same needs we have been discussing as important factors in fun are also what lead to more success in "serious" pursuits too, such as better learning, more effective training, and more lasting change to healthy behaviors. These game structures surely provide a promising template for building applications that might engage us more effectively in non-entertainment areas such as learning and support. As we're about to see, the intrinsic needs for competence, autonomy, and relatedness we've described in PENS provide an alignment between what's "tasty" and fun in games and the more nutritional goals that serious games are trying to achieve. Intrinsic need satisfaction may just be the elusive "healthy potato chip," one that keeps people engaged while ensuring that real benefits occur.

GAMES AND LEARNING

A while back, my friends and I were discussing pirates. Not the creepy modern-day variant, but the fun "peg leg and parrots" kind found in *Treasure Island* or the *Pirates of the Caribbean* films. We were talking about what it would be like to be in a battle at sea, and I began holding forth about various types of cannon ammunition. Grape shot, of course, would be useful once you got in close, but a reasonable alternative might be canister shot for its shrapnel value. Of course, you couldn't beat round shot for getting some structural damage on a ship's broadside, but if you really wanted to take out the masts, chain or bar shot would be better.

Ever vigilant for symptoms of geekdom, my friends grew concerned. How was it that I knew so much about pirate ammunition (most of which turns out to be reasonably historically accurate)? Had I long ago written a paper about this for a class that somehow got stuck in my head? Did I secretly look up the information on my cell phone when nobody was watching?

Interestingly, nobody guessed the real answer: I learned it in a video game. In fact, it was only when my friends asked that I myself stopped to remember where I learned it. For a while I had been playing an online multiplayer game that was heavily focused on 18th-century ship-to-ship combat. It required learning and strategically deploying a variety of tactics, including detailed ship navigation (e.g., running speed, turning speed, and wind direction) as well as gunnery skills (cannon range and ammunition). In the course of enjoying the game's challenges, I had learned something real without being focused on the learning. And unlike the tests I took in school—where I crammed lists of geometry formulas and plant phenotypes into my head on Monday, dumped them onto Tuesday's exams, and forgot half of it by Wednesday—I had spontaneously retained a lot of my knowledge of ancient ammunition months after I stopped playing.

Steven Johnson writes about this ability of games to motivate learning of complex, even seemingly dry, ideas. He describes playing *SimCity* with his seven-year-old nephew. *SimCity* is a simulation game (a genre discussed in chapter 3) that requires you to plan and manage the growth of a virtual metropolis. Johnson writes,

> I was controlling the game, pointing out landmarks as I scrolled around my little town . . . After about an hour of tinkering, I was concentrating on trying to revive one particularly run-down manufacturing district. As I contemplated my options, my nephew piped up: "I think we need to lower our industrial tax rates." He said it as naturally, and as confidently, as he might have said, "I think we need to shoot the bad guy."

The question is why kids are so eager to soak up that much information when it is delivered to them in game form. My nephew would be asleep in five seconds if you plopped him down in an urban studies classroom, but somehow an hour of playing *SimCity* taught him that high tax rates in industrial areas can stifle development.

There are lots of such stories where game experiences are doing more than just entertaining us—they are also teaching us, sometimes without our even noticing. And Johnson raises a great question: Why *are* kids so eager and self-motivated to learn in games, when conventional teaching techniques seem so hard? And can this power to engage us be harnessed to teach things more useful than sinking 18th-century pirate ships?

It's a question many are trying to answer. In addition to our own research programs, we have received requests and made PENS available to dozens of research projects at universities and other not-for-profit institutes in the United States, Europe, and Asia. While some of this work focuses on traditional gaming, many researchers are hoping to find winning formulas for applying games outside of entertainment in the area of learning as a way to motivate deeper engagement and performance.

But they also recognize something else, sometimes through lessons that are hard-learned: Achieving engagement and spontaneous learning in a game isn't easy. It can't be achieved by simply wrapping game ideas around existing curriculum. The motivation to learn that comes so easily from *SimCity*—a game that isn't even focused on teaching—eludes most educational games that are trying very hard to teach. In fact, "educational games" have a pretty bad reputation as being uninteresting to play.

Solving this problem is a key focus of the "serious games" movement, which from now on we're going to call *non-leisure games*. To be honest, the label "serious" may be part of the problem because it creates a false "potato chips versus broccoli" distinction that unfairly stereotypes entertainment games as frivolous and non-leisure games as cod liver oil. Neither need be true. In fact, we've seen how entertainment games are often taken quite seriously by gamers, providing meaningful experiences that evoke "seriously" deep engagement (like the kind I found in my pirate game). This is exactly the motivational quality of entertainment games that non-leisure games are trying so hard to capture. And as we'll see, the same intrinsic needs are important to both.

LEARNING AS THE GOAL, BUT NOT THE FOCUS

Contemporary non-leisure gaming has its deepest roots in education, where interactive games labeled "edutainment" (education plus entertainment) began emerging in the 1980s. A frequent formula is to take an educational outcome (e.g., to learn math) and attempt to teach it by inserting it into a game. Unfortunately, these strategies are a far cry from the integrated learning of *SimCity* or my pirate game. Instead, they are more like my early, misguided attempts to give my dog medicine. I'd hide the distasteful pill in a bowl of yummy dog food, smugly assuming that because he has the ability to inhale a bowl of kibble in less than 15 seconds my method was foolproof. But 16 seconds later, I was always staring at a soggy pill at the bottom of the bowl. We all have a way of consuming what we enjoy and discarding what we dislike, even when those two things are in close proximity. And because we humans are pretty smart, too, we can easily sniff out when someone is trying to manipulate us by mixing unappealing learning pills into our games. That's why most educational software has the bad reputation it does, often ending up at a yard sale or being stored underneath the dusty exercise equipment we bought during a late-night infomercial. It turns out that wrapping fun around a nugget of learning is pretty hard to do successfully. We end up just nibbling around the outside and leaving the rest in the bowl.

Maybe though, it's a better strategy to reverse things and keep fun as the focus—seasoning fun with sprinkles of learning that enhance the fun's flavor. Let's go back to the pirate example. In that circumstance, I didn't set out to "learn about maritime history." And frankly, the developers weren't focusing on teaching as their primary goal. Instead, I found a good battle game that caught my imagination. To play it well involved lots of learning, and some of that learning was educational because the developers used a combination of accurate facts from history and sailing. In fact, the *incidental learning*[1]—the learning that just happened along the way without me intending it—was deep and abiding because it had meaningful value to me in satisfying intrinsic needs. Specifically, I *autonomously* chose to learn the material to achieve the satisfaction of greater *mastery*. And as a result, although I haven't played the game for over a year, I still remember most of what I learned. It stuck with me because it was a meaningful way to deepen my enjoyment of the game (i.e., to enhance its flavor).

Contrast that with the typical "quest" in a math game in which the problem has nothing to do with the quest. While bounding through the countryside, I run into a giant troll who says, "Tell me what the square root of 16 is, and I'll let you open the magic chest." There it is—the arbitrary pill in my food bowl. Even if I swallow it, this kind of conditional reward only underscores that they created the game just to make me do the math. And motivationally, that undermines long-term interest because it makes me feel manipulated.

Better would have been a treasure map, where the math was necessary to complete the quest. The learning in this case (i.e., figuring out the treasure map) is self-initiated and has purpose and meaning for the player. In the language of need satisfaction we have used throughout this book, whereas in the troll example our behavior feels controlled (and de-motivating), in the treasure map example, it feels autonomous and more motivating. In chapter 1, we gave a real-world example of this very difference: The *World of Warcraft* player who blogs about the math underlying his spell power is motivated to learn the math first and foremost because it *enhances* his ability to gain more mastery and enjoyment of the game.

It is not an arbitrary "gate" players must cross or a hurdle they need to clear. If it were, rest assured they would find a way around it—or, at best, forget it as soon as it was behind them.

That's where many learning games miss the mark. They assume that because learning is the goal, it needs to be the *focus*. But this simply communicates to players that you are trying to get them to swallow something distasteful, because why else would you need the sugary treat of the game? We are all well-attuned to these kinds of subtle manipulations, and we don't like them. Players (and learners) will always spot this technique regardless of how well the learning "pill" is camouflaged.

In contrast, if the focus is on the game and enhancing that experience in meaningful ways through learning, there are many opportunities for highly motivating experiences. As it turns out, what keeps people engaged with great entertainment games is also what deepens their learning as well. This is the synergy we noted before—that the ingredients that make games the most engaging are remarkably aligned with what makes for successful learning.

NEED SATISFACTION AND LEARNING: WHEN LEARNING STICKS

In previous chapters, we've talked a lot about how the "stickiness" of games—the experiences that sustain engagement with players and keep them coming back— is due to the intrinsic need satisfactions they provide. But for non-leisure games, the goals are more complex. Those who make learning games do not primarily want people to remember how fun the game was, they want the *learning* to stick around. Happily, it turns out that need satisfaction is critical not just to keep players engaged with the game, but to also ensure that the learning *itself* is deep and abiding.

In this regard, traditional education doesn't have the best track record. It has that "broccoli" vibe to most students. We can relate to Paul Simon singing about "all the crap I learned in high school." Truly, most of us studied, learned, and then forgot most of the facts and skills we were taught as soon as the test was over. Educators are aware of this, too, with educational researchers focused for years on better ways to make learning stick. It turns out that motivation, and specifically the satisfaction of intrinsic needs, is again an important part of the solution.

As an example, let's take a look at one of the needs we've discussed in detail: the intrinsic need for autonomy. When people engage in a learning task autonomously—rather than feeling manipulated or controlled—the facts they learn tend to stick around and retention is greatly improved. Some time ago, our colleague Wendy Grolnick, an expert in child development, did an experiment that showed this simply and elegantly. In this study, fifth-grade students came to a learning lab where they were exposed to classic social studies textbook material. To some kids she said, "Read this material and later we will give you a test on this, and the grade will go to your teacher." The kids were not surprised by this, as this is a pretty standard experience in school; why else would you read this stuff except to be tested! A second group of students was given the same text materials. But in contrast to the standard school formula, these kids were told that they would be given some questions about the material because "we want to see the kinds of things kids learn from these texts." The idea here was to have this group feel less controlled and personally evaluated.

Now, both groups did pretty well on the "rote" part of the tests. Those who were more autonomous, however, did better on the conceptual part—they *understood* the text better. In addition to this, the experiment had a twist. One week after it was all over, a different person went back to the school and reminded students of the text they had read. He then asked them to write down everything they could remember from it. Remarkably, those who had studied it for the grade had the *most* memory loss. It was as if they said to themselves, "I read it for the test, which is now over, so why keep that knowledge around?" Once I have my hands on the magic treasure chest, what's the point of remembering the square root of 16?

Given results such as this, one clear opportunity for games to become more successful vehicles for learning is to structure deeper experiences of choice and autonomy, thereby enhancing learning outcomes. Let's build games where learners personally value the learning because it *enhances* the experience of the game. Dangling more controlling elements, like evaluations and gated treasure chests, will only tell players that the learning itself really isn't that interesting. When the learning is integrated and meaningful, players engage that learning more autonomously and are much more likely to retain information and skills. The learning becomes its own reward!

And here's the really interesting alignment we mentioned earlier: We've spent a lot of time in previous chapters talking about how autonomy and other intrinsic need satisfactions are core reasons why we love to play video games and stay engaged with them over time. In other words, we've been focused on mapping the underlying genetic code of "fun" in more detail to help explain the appeal of games *as entertainment*. The classroom study described before, along with the many other studies our colleagues have done on motivation and education, have nothing *directly* to do with games. Yet the studies also reveal that these *same* needs—the needs for autonomy, competence, and relatedness at the heart of fun and engagement—are what facilitate deeper learning and retention. In other words, research demonstrates that the ingredients of successful entertainment games are *also* predictors of deeper motivation and learning in education (and many other areas of life as well). Studies consistently show that better satisfaction of intrinsic needs is associated with both greater enjoyment of games, as well as enduring learning, performance, creativity, and the transfer of learning from one setting to others.[2]

As another example of this alignment, let's look at the intrinsic need for competence (or mastery). In chapter 2, we reviewed in detail how games are unparalleled in their capacity to supply competence feedback, both on a moment-to-moment basis and also over extended periods of time as players develop virtual avatars with lasting skills and abilities. This happens at an individual level, with each player having their own personalized experience of mastery as they move through the game.

Now consider a parallel finding in research on motivation in learning that is completely independent of games. There is a large educational literature suggesting that a focus on *mastery goals* (improving your own abilities) rather than *performance goals* (e.g., testing to see if you do better than others) is much more effective at engaging students and getting results.[3] Whereas feedback in so many educational environments is performance focused, and thus often de-motivating, good video games already have a template that is aligned with optimal learning. Game structures are readily engineered around individual mastery goals as you improve your own skills, gain new levels and abilities, and see your personal progress clearly depicted. In fact, the self-directed, on-demand media world we now live in has created an even broader opportunity to enhance each individual's competence using interactive technology—one where each learner could be customizing a personal learning experience using a combination of games, social networking, and other online resources. But this will only happen if we focus on tying these things together in a way that facilitates personal experiences of mastery, rather than replicating traditional, performance-based evaluation—and only when we recognize that this ability to orchestrate one's own experience need not be a distraction from a lesson plan, but the foundation for better learning itself.

What these examples highlight at a broader level is the natural "motivational marriage" or alignment between engaging games and deep and enduring learning. Focusing on experiences of mastery (competence), autonomy, and relatedness is the key to *both*. Motivationally, there is no need to wrestle with different strategies that "balance" fun with learning, or to craftily contemplate how best to hide the learning pill within "sugary" gameplay. When viewed through the lens of PENS and self-determination, fun and learning happen in the same psychological space.

PUTTING THIS MOTIVATIONAL SYNERGY TO WORK

More and more, educators are beginning to intuitively see this marriage, using the learning power of successful entertainment games. Some schools now make games a formal focal point of learning. *Quest to Learn*, a joint venture of Parsons, The New School, and The Institute of Play in New York City, puts games and interactive technology at the core of their entire curriculum. In this way they are hoping to not only engage students, but to simultaneously advance the information technology skills that learners need in today's marketplace.

We recognize that in such initiatives there are plenty of knotty issues to resolve. How do evaluations of learners fit in? How can they be held accountable to required work and objectives? Resolving these things means navigating tricky motivational waters, because concepts like "incentives" and "grades" naturally come to mind as part of the program. This leads to gatekeeping, reward strategies, and other external structures that may feel necessary to ensure that learners reach designated goals and milestones. Usually this also leads to things we all hate—like tests. It can be a vicious cycle.

But goals and milestones can also be embedded in ways that are more intrinsic, while still being clear and measurable. In traditional education, for example, one shuffles into science class and begrudgingly memorizes the laws of Newtonian physics by applying them to abstract problems, with nothing remotely rewarding or relevant about the experience except the extrinsic reward of passing an exam. Beyond the test, there is no other reason to remember this information, and we can see no real benefit to anything that intrinsically interests us. No wonder we can't remember these things even a week later.

Now let's take a page from gaming's motivational playbook and envision a virtualized learning environment. Here we trade in our desk for a medieval battlefield where we must learn Newton's principles to successfully siege a castle with a trebuchet. If we don't understand how to adjust force and compensate for gravity, our projectiles are flung haplessly into the air and thud harmlessly to the ground. But if we learn and apply the principles correctly, there is immediate and gratifying feedback—the walls come tumbling down, trumpets herald our victory, and we feel intrinsic satisfaction of the same need for mastery that is directly related to both more enjoyment *and* deeper learning. The reward is not some abstract system of evaluation (the perennial gold star), but a natural extension of our actions. More simply put, the reward is integrated *into* the activity, rather than dangled outside it. And instead of being imposed by a stern teacher, the goals and milestones that demonstrate mastery are instead sought after by the learner, who autonomously *chooses* to learn in order to achieve game goals. Reaching these goals also clearly demonstrates mastery of the learning objective without the need for a dry external test.

The castle siege described before illustrates that old adage "learning by doing." That saying's always had positive appeal because it suggests in some way that the learning is "real." On the other hand, "book learning" has the connotation of being somewhat hollow or lacking in real-world value. Along these lines, those who have long advocated for games and simulations as learning tools have often noted that games often result in deeper and more lasting learning than traditional textbook approaches.[4] We believe that when students are immersed in a virtual learning environment that is well-designed for need satisfaction, the quality of learning improves because it presents them with opportunities to take *direct* action in satisfying their needs, rather than simply learning in the abstract.

This motivational "principle of direct experience" holds that interactive contexts deepen learning because they involve highly active experiences with an increased potential for *agency* and *impact* (i.e., satisfaction of autonomy and competence). This creates a fertile field for learning to take deeper root—interactivity unlocks greater opportunity for need satisfaction, resulting in a deeper connection and motivation for learning. As with entertainment games, it's important to keep in mind that it's not simply the interactivity alone, but a design that is successful at meeting intrinsic needs.

Let's look at yet another strategy from immersive gaming and see why it works for learning. One principle in gaming, in particular highly engaging RPG games, is *leveling* (discussed in chapter 2). As players advance in experience and accomplishments, they periodically reach milestones that offer them greater powers, privileges, or options. The system works in games because it provides clear goals (i.e., thresholds for advancement) and subsequently rewards players in ways that further enable activity, growth, and satisfaction. Contrast this way of advancing to the typical grading approach used in schools: No matter how much you learn, you will repeatedly be compared to your same-age peers on a bell curve, and not in relationship to where you were before. Thus, a lot more learning doesn't necessarily lead to a greater feeling of growth and competence in the way schools are usually structured.

Recently, however, I observed a "leveling up" structure in mathematics that seemed to make sense. And it was, amazingly, in a school! As part of an innovative urban school reform approach called *First Things First*, ninth-grade students enter a math sequence that is not based on homework, test grades, or the constant threat of a red pen. Instead, all the math skills for the year are broken down into about 110 or so "I can" statements. They are arranged in a sequence so that if you need one skill to master another, you get the simpler one first. For each individual student, math consists of mastering the next skill in his or her line. When it is mastered, you level up. If you miss it on the first test, you can go to a "math café," intended as a supportive tutoring resource, to figure it out and try again. Just like in the video games, you try the quest again. It is a pure mastery system, and not surprisingly, kids like this feeling of leveling up. They see progress and feel a stronger sense of competence satisfaction than that afforded by receiving repeated "As, Bs, and Cs," at the same time learning more and more.[5]

What's important to emphasize is that it's the autonomy and mastery satisfactions in these scenarios that enrich both enjoyment and learning in a synergistic way. The mistake is to believe that the ingredients of enjoyment and learning were ever different in the first place! In reality, within a well-designed game, fun and learning are motivationally aligned from the start.[6] This is also true in a well-crafted school. It is just that too many test-crazy adults keep forgetting that fact. This is also why best-selling entertainment games such as *Sim City* and *Civilization* have made their way into the classroom—they implicitly capture this synergy, and as a result teach more effectively.

NEED SATISFACTION AND BEHAVIOR CHANGE

In addition to learning, virtual worlds and games are increasingly used in health care to provide support and assist people with behavior change. Millions of people—and perhaps all of us in one way or another—aspire to eat better, quit smoking, or in some other way shift our lives to become what we believe is a "better me." Health care spends billions of dollars each year on programs to move our behavior in healthier directions, and such change is seen by most as necessary to avert crises such as obesity, diabetes, and other costly and painful problems.

Into this fray steps non-leisure games focused on healthy lifestyles and behavior. Even commercial entertainment products such as Wii have invested in healthy gaming with the launch of products such as the *Wii Fit*—a balance board that can assist players with activities ranging from step aerobics to yoga to Hula-hooping. Other games are also on the market with the goal of helping us relax, meditate, and reduce the ever-present stress in our lives.

As in learning, motivation in health care is a pivotal issue. How many pieces of exercise equipment are gathering cobwebs, repurposed as bulky clothing racks? How many of us write that monthly check to a health club, but would be hard pressed to remember the last time we actually went? It is in our attitudes about our personal well-being and the health care system that we see some of the starkest distortions of motivation and support. Hit television shows such as *The Biggest Loser* dangle monetary prizes as the incentive to lose weight, because the glamour of winning a million bucks is more fun for the audience than actually improving the contestants' long-term health. But as in other areas where we and our colleagues have studied rewards and motivation, there is little evidence that such external rewards change health behaviors over the long term.

We fear that some of the new fitness games suffer from the reward complex themselves. They are replete with negative feedback and subtle humiliations, as well as ribbons and prizes the player is supposed to desire. The motivation systems "built in" to many such games do not engage people and sometimes are undermining of sustained motivation. Soon people discover they can get points without the effort or exertion, and suddenly that becomes the goal. After a few evenings of family fun, the balance board languishes in the corner next to the exercise bike with the clothes on it. The little we know of persistence in many of the new fitness games suggests that people have not found a path as interesting as the ones in *Warcraft* that would lead players to want to stay for many months and years.

What is known about exercise in the molecular world is that people rarely persist unless they are autonomously motivated and optimally challenged so that they experience mastery.[7] That is, what predicts exercise over time is that a person feels willing, even happy to do it, and feels mastery at the task. Criticism, controlling instruction, and other similar satisfaction killers lead away from exercise and perhaps back to more video games.

But maybe, paradoxically, video games can get some people back to exercise. Given the inherent and well-tuned ability to provide mastery-oriented feedback and optimal challenges, if properly designed, video games could well be a real partner to health. As we often see in education however, this new area of health gaming has yet to hit its motivational stride.

IS THERE A VIRTUAL DOCTOR IN THE HOUSE?

We have become increasingly interested in the transfer between molecular world applications and virtual worlds, as well as the reverse. In this regard, we've discussed the motivational overlap between good gaming and good learning and how learning structures in games can be brought over into the classroom.

In health care this is an equally pressing interest. One of the big challenges to engaging people in changes related to health is *time*. People don't have it, and certainly their doctors don't have it. Practitioners often have less than 10 minutes to meet with a patient, hear their concerns, formulate a diagnosis, and discuss a plan for care. That's not much time to listen to the patient's description of their needs and concerns and to engage in a meaningful conversation, let alone foster feelings of autonomy and competence for change.

This is particularly unfortunate when you consider that there has never been a better time in history for patients to be more informed and involved with their care, given the wealth of information that is now available to them at the press of a button. What a frustrating shame that they can't engage with their doctors in a more empowered way, just as the information age enables them to do so for the very first time! In the end, everyone is dissatisfied and patients are left feeling incompetent and unsupported in their care, with less energy to take care of themselves. In our terms, their intrinsic needs are simply not being met.

The negative results of this motivational problem are measurable. Non-adherence to prescribed medical care is just one of the major crises within the system, each year costing tens of billions of dollars and contributing to declining health in patients.[8] In many cases, the majority of patients who are prescribed medications deemed important for their health will simply discontinue them against medical advice. Perhaps this happens because if they can't feel self-determined in the decision to take their medicine, the most autonomous thing they can do is to *stop* taking it.

About a year ago, a good friend and neighbor, Steve, had a massive heart attack that is affectionately called a "widow maker" because of its severity and high chance of death. Thanks to some quick thinking and skillful emergency doctors, he survived. In the weeks afterward, Steve really seemed to be none the worse for his experience as he continued his high-energy schedule of work as a CEO and daily exercise. One of his biggest complaints was about the medication prescribed to him, which like many medications had undesirable side effects. But despite being a very intelligent guy, Steve really couldn't articulate in detail the pros and cons of his meds. Although it turns out his life depended on them, no one had explained to him *why* they were important. What were these drugs doing exactly to keep him alive, and what concerns and questions did Steve have about them? Having this conversation and getting some answers would have given him a more personally meaningful reason to tolerate the annoying side effects. But Steve simply didn't know, and he took his meds only because the doctor told him to. Like exhausted parents trying to manage their children, the reason we're often given by the health care system is "do it because I said so."

Recently we had dinner with Steve and his wife and learned that he was on the verge of stopping his medications. The side effects were intrusive and they had heard stories of other heart attack patients who had stopped their meds without problems. The shallow motivation Steve had from his doctor's "because I said so" rationale was losing out to his daily (and more meaningful) experiences of side effect discomfort. And he was collecting stories and information from others to make his own decision (i.e., the intrinsic needs for autonomy and mastery spontaneously at work.) In reality, despite having a life-threatening condition, my friend was making a decision without further medical advice largely because our current health care system makes a meaningful conversation with our doctors somewhere between difficult to impossible.

It is here that "virtualized" solutions that borrow from games and implement mechanisms for intrinsic need satisfaction can provide increased support for patients' learning and behavior change. Teaching, answering questions, and coaching patients through engaging simulations designed to support intrinsic needs is one promising avenue to better care for more patients, one that can empower patients and strengthen their motivation to sustain healthier behaviors. We have already reviewed how good games engage and entertain players by giving them clear goals and compelling reasons for taking a course of action. In real-life health care, the motivational dynamics are the same. So when a real doctor or health care professional may be constrained by time to provide this for a patient, why not put a virtual care provider on the team to assist in answering patient questions, walking them through the pros and cons of their care options, and collaborating with them to build a plan they feel more ownership of? Just as a good video game can make every player feel like they are the hero, a virtual care provider can put a patient center stage—giving them all the time, answers, and supports they need.

Working closely with our physician colleague Geof Williams, we have been in development of just such a simulation—one that integrates the principles of PENS not only in its interactive design, but also in the structure of its content. Geof has been on the frontlines of patient motivation for more than 20 years, demonstrating that intrinsic needs are a key component in sustaining motivation for healthier living and compliance with prescribed health care plans.[9] In one clinical study, simply emphasizing support for patient autonomy and competence increased patients' adherence to recommended care by more than 300 percent.

The problem is, these interventions involve significant interaction with care providers and are very time consuming.

Our virtual clinician initiative is a step toward removing constraints of time and resources by making supportive interventions available through simulations that implement the kinds of need support seen in games. The virtual clinician allows a patient to interact with a highly responsive avatar that can answer questions, explain the rationale for interventions or behavior changes, supply or highlight educational materials, and generally collaborate with the patient in developing a customized medical plan that can be reviewed with doctors and other providers. Specifically, it's being developed using techniques for need satisfaction we've observed in successful video games and simulations.

Essentially, the virtual clinician is a "health care NPC" (non-player character) who (1) provides clear options and opportunities to the patient from which they can choose to develop a personal care plan (autonomy support), (2) helps the patient set clear goals and supports them in reaching objectives (competence support), and (3) simulates emotionally "real" interactions with the patient, building a sense of relatedness in the same way that we've seen virtual characters meet relatedness needs in games. In other words, the virtual clinician is not lecturing the patient or acting simply as a glorified search engine for health information, but inviting open and empathic conversation to build a health care plan for which the patient feels personal ownership and empowerment. Just like the virtual characters in entertainment games that support players' intrinsic needs and help them feel meaningful, the virtual clinician leverages these same principles to deepen motivation for behavior change. And if patients have a question or need support, the virtual clinician is always there—(Is there a computer in the house!?) to provide resources that meet their specific needs or point to available resources.

As for Steve, he was fortunate enough to get time with a doctor who explained to him clearly that discontinuing his medication could be life threatening. Steve now feels more competent and volitional in his own care because he had the chance to explore information and medical expertise in depth. Simulations such as the virtual clinician will hopefully bring these opportunities to a wider group of patients who can similarly benefit, for a low price of entry. More importantly, video games have shown us that these "virtual actors" can meaningfully support intrinsic needs for mastery, autonomy, and relatedness—all key factors in deepening motivation for healthy behavior change.

In summary, throughout each of the areas of non-leisure gaming we've discussed, there is a common thread: All evidence suggests that virtual experiences can engage us, teach us, and provide support most effectively when they facilitate the satisfaction of intrinsic needs. Research outside of gaming consistently shows that learning is improved and healthy behaviors sustained when we feel competent, autonomous, and connected. Remarkably, this aligns perfectly with what we see as the heart of fun experiences in entertainment games.

While some attempts at harnessing games for serious purposes forget this alignment, this area of gaming is still finding its footing. We expect that the industry will move toward this natural symmetry in building non-leisure games as the motivational power of need satisfaction is better understood and applied. We have already seen some promising examples. We know of projects recreating historical sites virtually, so one can not only inspect them but "live" in them. We have seen 3-D programs in which one can navigate the body or alter the chemical structure of a compound and see the substance change before them. We have seen developmental programs not far from *The Sims* where kids make life choices (saving money for college, changing careers, etc.) and see the possibilities play out. Educators have always seen the value in "hands-on learning" because of its intrinsic motivational value and the depth of learning that follows. In virtual worlds, we can have some of these same value-added properties of hands-on learning, but using interactive environments instead of traditional methods.

Going further, at a time when it is increasingly difficult to compete for attention in an on-demand world, a focus on intrinsic needs significantly contributes to building the sustained engagement necessary to reach important non-leisure goals. In our next and final chapter, we look at some recommendations that the intrinsic need satisfaction perspective has for all of us around video games and virtual worlds, regardless of whether we play them for fun, build them, or simply feel a need to understand them better as they become a regular part of our culture and our lives.

NOTES

1. Schank, Roger, and Cleary, C. (1995). *Engines for Education*. Hillsdale, NJ: Lawrence Erlbaum, pp. 95–105 (incidental learning chapter).

2. Vansteenkiste, M., Simons, J., Lens, W., Sheldon, K. M., and Deci, E. L. (2004). "Motivating Learning, Performance, and Persistence: The Synergistic Role of Intrinsic Goals and Autonomy-Support." *Journal of Personality and Social Psychology, 87,* 246–260.

3. Cury, F., Elliot, A. J., Da Fonseca, D., and Moller, A. (2006). "The Social-Cognitive Model of Achievement Motivation and the 2 x 2 Achievement Goal Framework." *Journal of Personality and Social Psychology, 90,* 666–679.

4. Gee, James Paul. (2004). *Good Video Games + Good Learning: Collected Essays on Video Games, Learning, and Literacy*. New York: Peter Lang Publishing.

5. Connell, J. P., and Broom, J. (2004). "The Toughest Nut to Crack: First Things First's (FTF) Approach to Improving Teaching and Learning." Report prepared for the U.S. Department of Education. Philadelphia: Institute for Research and Reform in Education. Available at http://irre.org/publications/.

6. Rigby, C. S., and Przybylski, A. (2009). "Virtual Worlds and the Learner Hero: How Today's Video Games Can Inform Tomorrow's Digital Learning Environments." *Theory and Research in Education, 7*(2), 214–223.

7. Hagger, M. S., Chatzisarantis, N. L., Hein, V., Pihu, M., Soós, I., Karsai, I., Lintunen, T., and Leemans, S. (2009). "Teacher, Peer, and Parent Autonomy Support

in Physical Education and Leisure-Time Physical Activity: A Trans-Contextual Model of Motivation in Four Cultures." *Psychology and Health, 24*, 689–711.

8. Abelson, Reed, and Singer, Natasha. "Pharmacists Take Larger Role on Health Team." *New York Times*, August 13, 2010.

9. Williams, G. C., McGregor, H. A., Sharp, D., Levesque, C. S., Kouides, R. W., Ryan, R. M., and Deci, E. L. (2006). "Testing a Self-Determination Theory Intervention for Motivating Tobacco Cessation: Supporting Autonomy and Competence in a Clinical Trial." *Health Psychology, 25*, 91–101.

Chapter 9

RELATING TO GAMES: A PRACTICAL ROAD MAP

Our goal for this book was to provide a new framework for understanding the psychology of video games that would be both empirically grounded as well as practical and accessible to anyone needing to better understand the draw of virtual worlds. In this final chapter, we'd like to address where we see the possibilities in pursuing a positive relationship with virtual worlds and video games. We've referenced many groups that are trying to understand games for various reasons, including developers, parents, politicians, and of course the gamers themselves. Each group has different perspectives and goals, and we'd like to talk to each about the role a need satisfaction approach plays in understanding games better, and how to navigate the pros and cons of games both today and in the future. Let's briefly introduce the groups we like to address directly in the pages ahead.

Game Developers

More than 80,000 game developers in the United States alone get up each day with the singular goal to make something fun for you to play. But as any game developer will tell you, creating fun is actually quite hard work. Theories about what feature or content will work best with players are hotly debated in game development companies on a daily basis. In such discussions, it's important to have a clear way of understanding why specific features and content connect with the psychological needs of players, and exactly how they build value and enthusiasm. When you don't have these specifics, even making a great game can be a golden cage; in your hope to repeat your success, you simply rehash everything, carrying forward the good and the bad rather than knowing what works and building on it. We'll talk a bit about our work with development teams and how we apply our psychological tool kit to bring better insight and empower innovation instead of repetition.

Parents

A primary purchaser of video games is not the players themselves, but the parents of players. They are relentlessly lobbied by their kids to buy expensive games and gaming equipment even though parents themselves are often ambivalent about gaming's impact. Of the hundreds of parents with whom we've spoken about video games, rarely is the topic a neutral one. We see the exasperation and stress of feeling caught between wanting to do the right thing and wanting to make their kids happy. We are most often met with one of two expressions when we tell parents that we work with video games: (1) the narrowed eye glare of disapproval one might expect in response to announcing, "I'm a drug dealer," or (2) the beleaguered look of someone who is worriedly fighting a losing battle. We hope to address a few questions that come from the parental point of view, particularly about understanding and regulating (i.e., setting limits on) gameplay.

Players

Players typically know both the pleasures and perils of gaming. Often players silently experience guilt about their gaming even as they defend it to others. Among those who are not over-involved in games, many gamers we know are reluctant to talk about the extent they play and enjoy games (particularly the many millions of gamers over the age of 30). The stigma of games being a juvenile and unproductive use of time still prevails. Alongside this, because of the dense need satisfactions games provide, self-regulating time spent playing can be hard. We therefore discuss some ideas and guidance for gamers to ensure they are balancing their lives both in and out of virtual worlds.

Policy Makers

Teaming up with millions of concerned parents are politicians and other policy makers who have identified gaming as a significant social issue—one that needs to be appropriately managed and regulated. People often look to government to help regulate or at least advise on issues like game overuse or risks for aggression. This is a challenging task given that gaming has grown so quickly as a mainstream activity, while research on its impact is still developing. Complicating this issue are the strong and disparate feelings gaming evokes across constituents, which pressure policy decisions. Appropriately parsing questions about game psychology can hopefully contribute to more informed and appropriate policy.

Researchers

Research on gaming is accelerating. Much of it has focused on the dangers of video games and has adopted a polarized and strident tone. We come to gaming with a different interest, which is what motivates gameplay at a fundamental level. Since our first publications in 2006, we have received dozens of inquiries from researchers around the world wanting to explore topics ranging from how need satisfaction in games predicts sustained play, to how our model can be used to improve patient health and education through "serious" games. Every month we see applications to an ever-broadening spectrum of ideas, and will speak to some of the more interesting directions we see emerging.

Each of these groups sees gaming from a different perspective and is focused on a unique set of questions. Let's take a closer look at some of these questions and explore some directions for the future.

DEVELOPERS: SOLVING THE ALIEN MACHINE PROBLEM

In the initial chapters of the book describing how games satisfy specific intrinsic needs, we touched upon research work we do with game developers within most of the major genres, including FPS, MMO, action, RPG, and others. We have the opportunity to regularly work with many development teams who are "in the trenches" trying to understand how specific features and design decisions will impact the player experience. Consider that developers live in a world of specific details and decision making and need to make trade-off decisions regularly between different ideas and options. Making the right decisions—meaning the ones that will increase the player's enjoyment and value—is critical at each step along the way. Will the player prefer Feature A or Feature B? Should I make that object red or blue? These decisions are best made with objective data about how they affect the player experience. Even if your instincts allow you to succeed at making a game players love without any formal research, you still have to figure out what you did right if you want the best chance of repeating your success. Otherwise you are left only with your best guess at exactly what happened in players' heads that made them love your cosmic thingamabob or made your super ray gun so "cool!"

Sometimes we call this the "alien machine problem." Imagine for a moment that one day, while out hiking through the forest, you came across a strange alien machine. It's an amazing apparatus made from a luminous extraterrestrial metal that hums gently as you drag it back to your car. You don't know what it does, but it is obviously ingenious and attractive. It's pretty bulky, too, but you manage to get it into the trunk and drive back to town.

As you are wondering what to do with the thing, you realize that you can't stop grinning; you feel remarkably happier, more energetic, and more positive than you have in years. In fact, that annoying shoulder injury that's been nagging you since the company softball game last month is suddenly gone. It's not long before you realize that the purring glow from your trunk is the cause of your euphoria. Whatever its intended function, the alien device is for all intents and purposes a smile-inducing, pain-reducing happy machine.

Being the benevolent type, your mind begins to reel with the potential implications of the device. If society can decipher and duplicate this technology, billions of people around the world would benefit. You poke, prod, and analyze. The good news is that you can figure out how to replicate the machine precisely.

The bad news: you are still not quite sure why it works. Although you can see all the parts, it's not clear how each plays a role in creating the machine's magical effect. As a result, the only reliable way to get the benefits of the machine is to completely replicate all five feet, 214 pounds of it. Oh sure, you can paint it different colors and hang some fuzzy dice off of it if you'd like, but that's about the extent of your ability to customize.

Herein lies the problem: While it's now possible to get some more happiness in your life, you must lug E.T.'s refrigerator behind you wherever you go. The charms of this wear off quickly, and after just a couple of days, you start thinking big thoughts again. If only we could figure out what really made this thing tick, its potential applications would greatly expand. Is the part of the machine that makes us happy the same as the part that reduces pain? If we could just isolate the pain reduction mechanism, we could innovate all kinds of new health care applications for patients. Or if we could discover the underlying processes within the machine that lighten our mood, perhaps we could plug those same ideas into a smaller package that could be carried around more easily. The point is that until we really understand how it works—not just generally but *specifically*—our ability to innovate and maximize its potential is crippled.

Video games are often just like this alien machine: They are built over many years and include thousands of decisions and "moving parts." When they are finished, we can see whether or not they work (i.e., do players like them?) and we can identify the general things players like and dislike. But knowing exactly how and why each part works to build enjoyment with players (when they work at all) is often a mystery even to those that built the games in the first place.

This hinders innovation. Not knowing what works makes it harder to choose the right direction and make the right trade-off decisions on your current project. And it also means you can't accurately carry specific knowledge from one project to the next. The team is in the trenches each day trying to decide exactly what game features and content will make the game a winner with players and turn a profit. But without a means of testing how each big idea actually impacts player motivation, trade-off decisions are usually made on a "best guess" basis, limiting the success rate. With increasing competition and player expectations, the stakes are already too high for this trial-and-error approach. And as the industry grows, the size of investment in game projects (and thus the risk) will only grow larger.

Once you as the developer have survived the current project, it's then time to do it all over again. Even though you wowed them the last time, players want you to constantly improve their experience of immersion and fun through innovative new ideas. Unless you successfully understand how each piece of your prior game contributed to its success, the next time around you'll naturally feel the pressure to simply imitate yourself. You'll feel compelled to replicate the machine, finding yourself in the golden cage we mentioned earlier. And no matter how you dress up a rehash, players aren't easily fooled by a fresh coat of paint and fuzzy dice.

The need-satisfaction approach we've outlined solves these practical problems because it is a more precise tool for understanding the relationship between game elements and psychological outcomes. Let's say that you are developing an RPG game and are deep in the throes of trade-off decisions (budgets, after all, are not unlimited). You have to narrow down what kinds of quests you are going to build, what features to include in your combat mechanics, how deep to develop your story content, and so forth. But more than just wanting to be sure your game is fun, your vision for the game is to instill in players a deep sense of personal freedom and connection to the game's characters. How can you test different design features against these specific experience goals so that you can make the choices that best achieve your vision?

Applied research on what satisfies players can assist on several different levels. For example, during design, the constructs of basic psychological needs and immersion we have outlined provide a motivational framework on which to hang new creative ideas. Instead of simply thinking about what will be "fun," satisfaction of specific needs can serve as more precise "experience targets" in the design plan alongside features that target those needs. In the case of our RPG example, the designer may decide that player needs for autonomy and related-ness are the cornerstone experiences and major objectives for the design vision, providing clear guidance for strategy and testing. As versions of the game are built out, each feature and core mechanic can then be tested to see how well it is achieving these goals and integrating the satisfaction of multiple needs. As our data show time and again, games that balance different needs and create multiple satisfactions simultaneously are the hits. Detailed models of player psychology allow designers to precisely penetrate the mysteries of the "alien machine" in their own creations.

REACHING NEW AUDIENCES

Game developers are increasingly looking to how games can broaden their reach, providing experiences that appeal to different audiences. Although I personally get satisfaction of competence needs from *Call of Duty: Modern Warfare*, my wife is never, *ever* going to play that game. She is not interested in the violent content, nor is she swayed by my wonky speeches about underlying need satisfaction. To her credit, she doesn't like shooting people, or being shot.

Although gaming is expanding, many developers we talk to feel constrained in their freedom to reach out to new audiences. There is that Hollywood-esque pressure to wash, rinse, and repeat whatever works, compounded by the alien machine problem. There is a desire to innovate, but also a fear of sticking one's neck out too far. This slows the pace of creativity and makes it more difficult to jump the gap between games' current audiences and new ones. Simply put, building a game my wife likes is a much harder task than building a game I like—not because she is pickier (she married me after all), but because what

I like is familiar territory for developers. The game industry and I grew up together, from the Atari of my teen years to the Xbox and PlayStation of today. Knowing what I want to play next is a no-brainer compared to the new trails that must be traveled to bring the same enjoyment value to my wife, or to my parents, or to the millions of people who currently have no interest in video games.

In order to make the leap into these new markets, it helps to know the fundamental principles of motivation and engagement that apply to populations outside any given core demographic. The motivating dynamics of mastery, autonomy, and relatedness are important to all of us whether or not we are currently gamers, and can be a link to reaching audiences through innovative new themes (i.e., minus the guns and aliens) built around these core satisfactions. The need-satisfaction approach is therefore a broad platform that allows developers to untether themselves from old content habits and explore new kinds of games that connect with new audiences.

As a final point, there is a growing trend to give players the tools to create their own content and to allow player creations to be added to the virtual world for others to enjoy. The early, text-based games (e.g., MUDs) did this quite well decades ago, drawing in a large audience of dedicated players because of the autonomy and relatedness this freedom afforded. With the rise of more technically complex games and graphics, this freedom was lost. But it's making a comeback in virtual worlds such as *Second Life* and games such as *Spore*. By thinking about what tools will optimally satisfy psychological needs in this act of game creation and design, developers will create even deeper value for players and contribute more strongly to their game's success.

Of course, if these efforts are successful, it means that games will become even *more* compelling and interesting places to be. And consequently, it may be harder for gamers to pull away from them. Since many believe games already chew up too much of our time on this planet, what do we think about the regulation of gaming in our lives and the lives of our kids and loved ones?

PARENTS: SHINING A LIGHT INTO GAMING'S DARK CORNERS

It's a parent's job to protect his or her kids while at the same time providing them with opportunities to learn, grow, and, of course, be happy. So it is not surprising in the least that video games can be a real hand-wringing experience. On the one hand, parents clearly see just how much kids love video games and the great enjoyment they derive from playing them. But as we saw in the chapters on violence and addiction, the intensity with which games leap off the screen and grab hold of kids' attention can cause understandable worry as that protective parental instinct kicks in. With their kids staring wide-eyed at a screen where all hell is breaking loose, who could blame a parent for strong concerns about the healthfulness of video games?

In our conversations with parents, here are some of the more common issues raised and how we like to think about them from a need-satisfaction perspective:

I Worry about All the Shooting and Violence

In the chapter on violence, we demonstrated how the need-satisfaction model provides a clearer window into the appeal of violent games. Beneath the spectacle of violent content is the intrinsic satisfaction of needs such as mastery that are valued more highly than the literal gunfire and mayhem splashed across the screen. This has several interesting implications for how parents can approach the issue of violence and video games with their kids.

First, our data suggest that parents may not need to be as worried that the love of game violence reflects something unhealthy in their kids. While our research indicated that violent content and themes did attract some people to a game when they were deciding what to buy and play, in actuality, the blood and gore was not a significant contributor to their *actual enjoyment*. As long as the satisfaction of basic needs (notably competence and autonomy) was present, we demonstrated that the level of violence could be turned way down and the game would be just as satisfying. In other words, nobody looked up at us and said, "Where's the blood! I need my blood!" If your kids like violent video games, it is quite likely because the themes of war and combat are effective at conveying an experience of challenge and mastery. Certainly, we would also love to see developers continue to find less-violent themes to convey these satisfactions, and the good news is that more and more creative, nonviolent titles are being developed each year. But violent games—like violent movies and stories that have existed for centuries—will always exist. It can be helpful, therefore, to know what is really motivating kids at a deeper level.

Nonetheless, even these facts are likely cold comfort to many parents who simply cannot see any positive reason to allow their kids to engage in the stark aggression of violent video games. While as scientists we have not yet seen definitive evidence that violent gaming has the substantial negative effects that some claim, we are sympathetic to—and share—concerns about the preponderance of violence in games. First, there is concern for young children whose capacity to distinguish fantasy and fiction from real-life societal norms is less established. In addition, we have concerns about vulnerable individuals who may already have propensities toward violence and for whom violent games may catalyze violent actions. And finally, whether our kids actually become violent or not, isn't it possible this exposure to violence ultimately desensitizes us all?

The good news is that parents can make the decision to buy less violent games. As long as those choices are satisfying the core needs we've discussed, chances are even kids who love violent games will also enjoy these less violent, but satisfying alternatives (although they may complain at the moment of purchase). In particular, since violent games are often focused on competence satisfactions and intense challenges, choosing alternative games that also focus on competence with lower levels of blood and gore are likely to be just as enjoyable to your kids once they pick up the game controls and dive in. The point is, as a parent you do have alternative choices if you would like to manage violent video gameplay.

Regarding young children in particular, we recommend that parents monitor and set limits on violent game content. The current ESRB ratings on games provide an imperfect guideline, but they're a starting point. Perhaps even more importantly, we recommend that parents spend a little time watching new gameplay and how your child reacts to games. Play a bit with your kids just to see the game. Then trust your parental instincts to allow or disallow based on what you see. Remember that for most kids, it may simply be a fun mastery experience to blow things up, while others may be affected differently. If you play with them, you'll be in the best position to really know what is going on for your kids as they play.

In addition, it is important for parents to explicitly discuss the difference between fantasy and real-world violence, both in video games and other media.[1] This discussion can help to internalize inhibitions to violence. Overall, attention remains the most important parental ingredient in managing media use and exposure, and we suggest it first and foremost rather than any specific hard and fast rules.

It Bothers Me That My Kids Get So Intense and "Wound Up" When They Play

Another common concern we hear from parents involves the high amplitude of emotion that games evoke, particularly those games that focus on competence satisfactions through intense and sometimes prolonged challenge. We hope that having read to this point, you have a somewhat clearer picture of how deeply games can engage us by connecting with our basic motivational needs, and that this alone has brought you a greater appreciation of the strong emotions games can evoke.

In this regard, we've noted that video games share common ground with sports: Both involve "players" who must face a climate of challenge and competition as they actively, and often intensely, seek victory. The roars of victory and defeat erupting from your kids while playing on their Xbox originate from the same energy that drives us to our feet at a ballgame, cheering or jeering as the situation warrants.

The big difference is that unless you are the one playing the video game, there are often few cues that an epic contest is underway. At the baseball game, there is a charged atmosphere that is shared by all those present. Each crack of the bat is celebrated or cursed by the thousands around you, drawing every spectator into the energy of the contest. Within the stadium, exclamations of victory and moans of defeat are anticipated, expected, and familiar. It's probably part of why you look forward to the games in the first place.

There's an old sitcom bit about the "superfan" husband who, on the Sunday of the big game, is sitting dutifully beside his wife at church while listening to the game through his smuggled headphones. Inevitably, usually during a moment of silence, he leaps out of his seat cheering a touchdown that only he is aware of, jarring those around him. This is not a shared experience, and hence is quite disturbing to those outside of it. It's also a regular occurrence with video game players. A gamer is deeply immersed in an intense experience that is not shared by those around him (often the parents), and the resulting expressions of emotion can be jarring, misunderstood, and worrisome.

We recommend to parents that they consider this in their assessment of their child's enthusiasm (or cries of agony). It can be helpful to keep in mind that the strong emotions that result from gameplay are often a sign of immersion and commitment to overcoming the challenges of the game. These are the same kinds of expressions that in other contexts (e.g., sports) we not only accept, but often encourage and admire as indicating meaningful involvement. While video games may be physically sedentary experiences, they are extremely active mental activities—ones that often evoke passionate responses.

There Are Much Better Things My Kids Could Be Doing with Their Time

We wish we could say that this is something that we only hear from parents. In point of fact, this is a common concern among spouses, siblings, and friends of gamers as well. We do hope that in the preceding chapters, readers have gained some appreciation for the complexity of what games offer players motivationally, as well as a more precise understanding of how games draw such devout love and attention. Kids in particular often feel that there is nothing better that they can be doing with their time than playing a game, while parents simultaneously feel games have little going for them as a meaningful experience.

The debate about the "meaningfulness" of gaming will no doubt continue for a very long time. There is a lot left to learn about the value of time spent in virtual worlds versus time pursuing activities in the molecular one. How do video games compare with time spent watching TV or surfing social networking sites (e.g., Facebook)? What is the comparative value of video games to playing with real kids outdoors? Because we have seen how games satisfy intrinsic needs, it follows that they have the potential to provide meaningful experiences that should not be minimized simply because they are "virtual" or because they seem cartoonish or fake to the outside observer. That said, we saw clearly in chapter 7 that unhealthy patterns of play can easily develop, not just in kids, but in players of any age. Time spent in games can be isolating and can crowd-out relationships, physical and social activities, and "in vivo" experiences of nature. And of course, they pull kids away from homework, real music practice (versus *Guitar Hero*), and other work and home responsibilities as well.

Given this, parents often need to set limits on games. We think this is a good and healthy thing, and we have several recommendations for how parents can approach the issue of limits with respect to both "play time" and the content of games.[2]

First, setting limits starts with understanding and empathizing with the strong desire to play games. The heart of this book has been an explanation of this desire, lending a deeper appreciation for how passionate it can be. We hope this empowers parents to have more productive discussions with their kids about gaming, which is an important step in successfully setting limits. As a parent, you have good reasons for limiting play, so share these reasons directly and clearly with your child while listening to what they have to say.

Just as important, be clear in your own head about your criteria for responsible play. It may be a certain number of hours, or perhaps your child showing that they can accomplish all of their responsibilities (and get a proper amount of sleep) without games interfering. Whatever the criteria that are important to you, be sure that all the parental figures agree and can present a clear and consistent position. Stick with the limit. Then be prepared to sympathize with the resistance: Games are fun, and limiting them is not. Consider too how you can offer, along with empathy, some need satisfying alternatives as well. Go out with your kid. Explore what else there is to do together. Just telling them to go find something better is less likely to be helpful.

We also want to emphasize our earlier recommendation that you play some games with your kids, even if to have just a little taste of what the games are like, and to find out what your kids like about them. Chances are they are better at them then you are, and it can be fun for them to take the lead. Let your child explain to you how to play each game and what the goals and rules are. Try not to demean or scoff at the game, which is easy to do (particularly when you are getting severely beaten by your seven-year-old). Your child, after all, may love this game, and the idea is to share an inside view—your kid's point of view—of what the fascination and temptation is. You'll be better at understanding games and your child will also recognize and appreciate your attempt to engage with his or her interests—and who knows, you might just have fun killing zombies after all!

PLAYERS AND SELF-REGULATION

If you're an avid gamer, we suspect you've had your own internal debates about gaming at one point or another, and perhaps gone a few rounds with a loved one who has wanted you to spend less time gaming. Most gamers we talk to admit to at least some guilt about their love of gaming, particularly as they get older. Gaming, after all, still has the stigma of being a youthful indulgence, even for gamers themselves.

When you are being pressured by others to stop gaming, it's natural to stand up for yourself. Nobody likes to be told what to do or to feel controlled, and when our basic need for autonomy starts to feel threatened, it can lead to being reactive and defensive and zealously protecting your freedom to game. But after the defense, we'd caution you to take some time to consider where these concerns are often coming from. They may reflect the genuine desire of loved ones to enjoy your company and share experiences together, rather than being "shut out" as you leave the molecular world for your virtual one. Gaming can be very isolating to the non-gamers around you who are not sharing the experience. And that can hurt relationships that are important to you. The "nagging" may also reflect the concerns of people who care that you are crowding out other good things as well.

Accordingly, when people wonder why you would abandon the real world for a virtual one, it provides an opportunity to think about that question yourself whenever you play. In general, it's good to be mindful of how much games are bringing you meaningful satisfaction versus how much they may be crowding out relationships and other fulfilling activities. Life, after all, can often be ambiguous, unfair, and overwhelming. If it were a game, we'd try to return it to the store for a refund. Actual games can be a place to feel a breath of freedom and even a place to escape for a while to get reenergized—to find those satisfactions of our competence, autonomy, and even relatedness that we aren't getting in the molecular world. But they shouldn't be the sole well from which one drinks. How, then, can you be mindful about when your gaming may be crossing into an unhealthy place?

First, take a look at your feelings about gaming. Do you enter a game because you are interested in the experience it offers, or because life pushed you there through boredom or frustration? When you leave games, do you feel it's been an energizing experience of interesting challenges or just a place to "kill a few hours?" Most gamers have likely escaped to games in an unhealthy or overindulgent way from time to time, but when this becomes a pattern, it's time to pause and consider what's happening in your life. Feeling a compulsion to play games, or a preoccupation with playing them, can be a signal that need satisfaction in other important areas of life is lacking and needs attention. And games themselves may exacerbate the problem if not regulated.

If you have questions about your gaming, we would also encourage you to ask friends and family how they feel about your gaming. Do they see it as a problem? Listen (as nondefensively as possible) to what they say, as chances are they know you well and can give you some insights. And finally, think about what things you would want to be doing in life if you were not gaming. Are you achieving the other things that are valuable to you? Or is time spent while gaming crowding out those goals? Again, it is all about finding a balance. In our research, we find that gamers who spend more than 20 hours a week gaming are often those that experience less satisfaction in life and more difficulties. To many gamers, that may sound like a low threshold, while to non-gamers, it will surely sound extravagant! Think about it this way: Doesn't any activity that is roughly equal to a part-time job deserve some thought about how and what it's contributing to or detracting from your well-being?

If on reflection you feel concerned about the role of video games in your life or that of a loved one, consulting a mental health professional can be helpful. This may be especially true if you don't have someone close to you who can listen in a nonjudgmental way as you sort through what you think about your situation. Of course, as clinical psychologists ourselves, we believe that therapy and consultation can help with many issues in life. Although most mental health professionals are themselves only beginning to understand what keeps people glued to games, those who are skilled will most likely work to help *you* decide what your goals are, and then help you regulate your own behavior to reach them.

On the positive side of things, consider how you can choose games to reenergize and satisfy basic needs that feel depleted. If you are feeling a bit constrained at work over the past week, a good open-world RPG game or "god game" like *Civilization* might help replenish feelings of autonomy, opportunity, and choice. A multiplayer first-person shooter or MMO might give you the chance to bond with friends who are now far away and perhaps have been missed. A 15-minute puzzle game on your lunch break might stimulate you between deathly boring meetings at the office. Understanding how different games appeal to our needs can help us pick the right games to give us just what we need, when we need it.

SOCIAL POLICY: LAYING A MORE OBJECTIVE FOUNDATION

It is understandable that policy makers are feeling a responsibility to address video games, given all the controversies and questions surrounding gaming. Addressing public concerns is, after all, what they do for a living. And there can be no doubt that many constituents are calling on politicians and other rule makers for immediate action.

We are neither strong opponents nor proponents of specific regulations, but we hope that whatever policies emerge, they will ultimately be informed by the psychological, behavioral, and health-related facts of gaming, rather than fears or hyperbole. Our research suggests that optimal policy decisions on games cannot be made by focusing only on themes and content, such as the level of violence in games (the current hot topic in the regulatory debate). Games' interactive nature creates complex experiences that are highly relevant to their psychological impact above and beyond the images, sounds, and stories that games present. As a society that admires competition at many levels, we also understand that themes of power and mastery (i.e., competence) are at work in many areas of life, and often represent experiences of growth, confidence, and character-building. As such, making extreme policy decisions based on content alone might well be premature. Without testing specific theories of game psychology that further explore motivations and outcomes, there is a risk that policies will be misaligned with gaming's reality.

We certainly agree with current policies limiting game sales based on content, such as sexuality and violence, to adults only. In this realm, we think rating systems can be improved, and sales to those underage can be better managed. But banning games outright (as is happening in some countries) may be going beyond current evidence of serious risk. Although some may see these issues as straightforward, we see complex research issues ahead that warrant more careful attention than they have thus far received. Among these are not just direct impact of content, but also developmental vulnerabilities, individual differences in reactions, and the impacts on health and well-being (both positive and negative).

Beyond violence and the surface issues of content—issues that have involved virtually all forms of media since the invention of the printing press—we see a much broader territory that policy makers will need to cover for the very first time. As we engage in more "real" interactions through virtual representations (such as avatars), should our individual rights extend to these representations? If research continues to show that we derive meaningful satisfactions in virtual worlds, will avatars be seen as true extensions of the self that will need protections, to which future generations may even feel entitled? We are already seeing issues of property rights emerge as the economics of "virtual goods" becomes a reality in our molecular world. We have also seen cases of cyber bullying and hurtful virtual interactions. Can a form of virtual civil rights be far behind? Finally, as we see the strong pull of video games emerging, what are the industry's duty to warn, or parents' duties to control?[3]

These are the new frontiers of policy that we will face in the years to come, and only by continuing to open up serious research into the psychology of identity and experience in virtual worlds will we have the data to make informed decisions. With that in mind, we turn to some thoughts for the game researchers who are pursuing this work.

RESEARCH: MOVING TOWARD MORE THEORY-BASED SCIENCE

The research we've reviewed on need satisfaction in games demonstrates the value of bringing clear psychological theories to game study that can drive real hypothesis testing. By contrast, the vast majority of research we see on the topic of gaming begins with little theory as to the psychological mechanisms of games and instead simply collects data on gaming behaviors in an effort to correlate them with this or that outcome. Detractors focus on collecting negative outcome data while proponents of gaming counter with positive correlations. While sometimes interesting, there are several serious limitations with this kind of research.

First, most research that is not empirically testing specific hypotheses and theory doesn't do much to advance our knowledge on what is *really* going on within the inner mind of players. Correlational studies that collect tons of data that is then combed through to see which variables hang together won't yield the best knowledge. Even if a study finds that gaming behavior A is related to outcome B, without a psychological model that is specifically tested to explain what's happening, we haven't learned much we can put to use. Without true hypothesis testing, we can only guess at what explains the relations between gaming and outcomes of interest, from violent tendencies to well-being. It will be difficult for any of us—whether developers, parents, gamers, or policy makers—to take meaningful action until more theory-driven research is underway.

In addition, not having good theory creates a vacuum, inviting pure speculation about causal connections that might not actually exist. Many studies about games receive a great deal of press simply because they showed a correlation between, say, gaming and grades in school or gaming and depression. Invariably, the news coverage of these studies (and sometimes even the researchers themselves) assumed a causal link between gaming and outcomes even though the data was purely correlational. But as any first-year statistics student learns on day one, "correlation does not prove causation."

A popular contemporary example of this is the staggeringly strong negative relationship between U.S. highway fatalities and the number of fresh lemons imported from Mexico. It turns out that as more lemons are imported from Mexico, U.S. highway fatalities drop. The relationship is amazingly strong, much stronger, in fact, than many of the correlations used to "prove" a causal connection between video games and outcomes.

Now despite the lemon-fatality "connection," it would be absurd to think that we can solve the highway safety problem using Mexican lemons. We were not able to find any headlines out there that read "Mexican Lemons Decrease Driver Deaths." And if the governor propped up this chart and decreed that all drivers will henceforth be required to nail a lemon to their dashboard, we wouldn't bet on his reelection.

Unfortunately, the same kind of data is being used on a regular basis to argue for causal relationships between video games and outcomes,[4] sometimes leading to premature conclusions. For instance, we saw a widely publicized study presumably linking poor school outcomes with video gaming.[5] Indeed, there was a positive correlation between hours of gaming and poor school performance. But in the same study, we saw much stronger associations between parenting factors and poor school outcomes. Were both the video gaming and the poor achievement due to poor parenting? Was video gaming itself a factor at all? We don't know because the research paper did not address these critical questions. Unfortunately, the news coverage on this study was all about the correlation with games, not with parents, leading the reader to believe games played a causal role. It was the Mexican lemon effect, which misinforms and distracts us from a true understanding of games. Researchers have a responsibility to attempt to inform rather than misinform, and that means helping the media interpret properly what is found.

Virtual Worlds as Behavior Test Grounds: *The Sims* as Simulation

Another exciting route for researchers are the possibilities for using virtual worlds as a "next-gen" laboratory for robust social science research, integrating disciplines such as psychology, physiology, sociology, and even neuroscience. Virtual environments allow us to deeply immerse participants in a vast array of circumstances, precisely changing variables of interest while collecting a range of in-depth data difficult to capture in the molecular world. One early example of this is our manipulation of levels of violence, but this is just the beginning. Research on emotion and reaction to situations and circumstances can be virtually simulated while full biometric and psychological data is collected. Environments and interactive objects can be changed in an instant to measure differential effects. In our own labs, we now investigate topics including altruism, violence, cooperation versus competition, and other areas, often cross-pollinating ideas from the virtual world into the real one (and back again). The possibilities for the virtual laboratory are endless, and it's a powerful new tool in the science of human behavior and experience.

SOME CONCLUDING THOUGHTS: THE "REAL" WORLD DISTINCTION

We have looked at many sides of the psychology of gaming, exploring its potential for both positive and negative impact through an understanding of its fundamental ability to connect to our intrinsic motivational needs. In every chapter, this has involved a discussion of where gaming sits in relation to other activities and relationships in life, which we have somewhat playfully referred to as "molecular" life as a way to distinguish it from the virtual worlds of games. Of course, the more common way to draw this distinction is to talk about "real life" (or in gamer shorthand, "RL"), referring to any time spent in non-gaming activities. "Have to get back to RL" or "RL is calling" are common expressions when it's time to log off.

But there is something dismissive in this usage of "real." When video games are distinguished from the "real" world, it's a subtle verbal snicker implying that games are "fake" and thus their experiences fundamentally empty. Society doesn't yet know what to make of virtual experiences, particularly when compared to familiar activities—jobs, sports, a night out with friends, artistic pursuits, and holding hands—that have occupied us for centuries. Only within the last decade have we seen the rise of games that brings people from around the world together in rich graphical environments, allowing them to interact in increasingly complex and personal ways. This is a truly alien concept—and honestly, most people are not yet sure what to make of it or how much to trust it.

For our part, we avoid referring to non-gaming experiences as "real" because we want to remain open to the possibility that games can offer meaningful experiences, just like other activities in life. There is a lot of research to do on this question, but our work so far suggests that games may offer more than mere amusement. In preceding chapters, we explored evidence that games connect with the same psychological needs that motivate us in life generally, often bringing to gamers the deep satisfactions that come from sports, work, and interpersonal interaction. What is it then that makes game experiences less authentic than these other "real" engagements?

It could be argued that game experiences aren't real because their content is *fictional*. You are not really a space knight who has saved the universe. You are a 34-year-old CPA (and you should start acting like one). There is certainly some merit in this argument particularly when people become over-involved in video games. As we've seen, losing oneself in the fictional world of games to the detriment of life's other responsibilities and opportunities is clearly unhealthy. But over-involvement is an issue that is relevant for *any* activity in life, whether fictional or not.

Furthermore, on the train ride home from the office one day, it may be tempting to label your nagging suspicion that the boss is about to give the promotion to your coworker as more "real" than you daydreaming about a video game. But is that daydream really less fictional? Or how about all the pride you have about the softball game this past weekend? Are your impressive feats at beer ball any more real an achievement than our group raid of Slavinkreig Castle last night? Each of us spontaneously creates these personal stories— both positive and negative—on a regular basis. Often we have very genuine emotional reactions to them, even when they turn out to be completely in our heads. In turn, our reactions can sometimes lead to bad decisions and some very "real" trouble. Or alternatively, they can also become the source of great creativity, innovation, and enjoyment.

Simply put, our minds are naturally in the business of storytelling. In every-day life, these can be both fun and useful or a painful waste of time. Video games may be an overt way we immerse our minds in fiction, but let's acknowledge that we'd be cranking out stories no matter what. The advantage to immersing oneself in game fictions may be that they provide clear goals, consistent outcomes, and varied opportunities for interesting activities. In this way, they are actually quite good at providing positive rather than negative grist for our imagination, leading to the many positive emotions and the experiences that gamers love.

But that's also the problem with games. They offer these things to us too readily perhaps, and can feel meaningful even when they are not. We have a healthy skepticism of virtual worlds and video games because they are very good at engaging us in *artificial* "business"—activities that may be satisfying in the moment, but are largely unsubstantial in reality. Video games absorb us for hours of time that could be spent with our families or in dealing with the more difficult challenges and issues that the molecular world presents us all. For the most part, learning a "skill" in a video game has little or no connection to the rest of our lives. I was a healer and herbalist in *World of Warcraft*, but not one skill from that profession has helped me aid a sick family member. This may change, but for the time being there is a danger that we will take our virtual accomplishments for more than they are, perhaps even waking up one day to realize that many opportunities in life were lost because we chose virtual worlds too often. As one gamer told us recently, "I missed the first five years of my kid's childhood because of games, and I don't want that to continue."

The question, therefore, may not be whether game experiences are "real," but whether they are meaningfully contributing to our happiness and well-being. Virtual worlds are part of a remarkable technological revolution that has opened up new channels of experience, where the boundaries between the virtual and the molecular are becoming more permeable. As we explore new ways to interact with others, have fun, learn, and do business together in virtual worlds, we suspect that these experiences will be seen as increasingly "real" and accepted. Once the distinction between "real" and "virtual" begins to drop away, what will ultimately matter is the quality of experience—wherever it occurs—and the choices we make about what we pursue.

One area that interests us greatly is how the principles of motivation and engagement in game design will increasingly cross back over into the "real" world. We've looked at some remarkably clear and powerful mechanisms for sustaining motivation through things such as providing clear goals, rich and timely informational feedback, and rewards that offer meaningful opportunities to enhance our competence, autonomy, and relatedness to others. There's no reason why these same kinds of systems can't exist outside of games as well. What if your day-to-day experience at work was organized into "quests" that, once completed, allowed you to choose between meaningful rewards such as taking on a new challenge or leading a team on a project? What if, as in games, you could clearly see these paths rather than simply hoping one day you'll be acknowledged? The motivational power of game principles can be put to use in such ways to make many areas of life more rewarding and engaging. The more we understand their motivational value and their power to engage, the more we can learn from games that may be beneficially applied. Good game designers may, in fact, find themselves increasingly in demand in many areas as we try to more broadly leverage the power of games' motivational pull.

In the end, our focus on basic psychological needs for competence, autonomy, and relatedness remains a touchstone for a meaningful life both in and out of virtual worlds. Regardless of where one is spending time, we believe that true well-being is a function of pursuing a life that emphasizes personal growth, a sense of purpose and volition, and developing meaningful connections with others (both interpersonally and within the larger community).[6] It's the process of living moment-to-moment, mindful of our intrinsic needs, that our research both inside and outside of gaming has linked to more meaningful and fulfilling experiences.

Thus, when games are pursued for the intrinsically satisfying experiences they provide—such as opportunities to overcome challenges, to explore interesting new contents, and to connect meaningfully with others—they hold promise as very real contributors to well-being. This effect is reflected in some of our early research on need satisfaction in games. Alternatively, when they are interfering with these same fulfillments in other areas of life, they most certainly detract from our lives, as we see in those who are over involved with games.

When we think about our own experiences with gaming, there is a rich tapestry to them. There is a favorite spice in my pantry that I only learned about because of playing video games (a player I met recommended it during a quest). There is an adventure I took with my brother-in-law, travelling together on a safari across a verdant virtual landscape, even though we were physically separated by 10,000 miles. There is the joy of having conquered an awesome battleship in the far reaches of space, but also the clear memory that while doing so I missed seeing the fireworks that were lighting up the night sky outside my house, and my wife's disappointment that, in the moment, I had chosen a virtual world instead of sharing the real one with her. Hundreds of such memories, burning in the minds of players worldwide, bear testimony to the power of games to engage us, often with implications that are both positive and negative. These virtual opportunities recall the final words of Roy Batty, the synthesized, nonhuman, but very psychologically real "replicant" in the movie *Blade Runner*, who says poignantly at the moment of his death: "I've seen things . . . you people wouldn't believe. Attack ships on fire off the shoulder of Orion. I watched C-beams glitter in the dark near the Tannhauser Gate. All those moments will be lost . . . in time, like tears in the rain". The promise of video games is that they can provide similarly compelling experiences through rich virtual worlds. The peril is that, like Batty, our time on this Earth is limited, and time spent in games may distract us from pursuing authentic and meaningful experiences in our molecular world, both rich and mundane.

As gaming continues to develop and deepen its place in our society and our lives, so too will the stories we bring back from them deepen. We anticipate that virtual worlds will continue to evoke very real emotional responses and strong motivational pulls for many of us. The significance and value of time spent there is a question that will certainly be debated for years to come. But there is no doubt that there are robust psychological reasons that will continue to keep millions of people glued to games.

NOTES

1. Walkerdine, V. (2007). *Children, Gender, Video Games*. New York: Palgrave Macmillan.

2. We would also recommend the following for further discussion on limit setting: Grolnick, W. S. and Seal, K. (2008). *Pressured Parents, Stressed-Out Kids*. Amherst, NY: Prometheus Books.

3. See, for example, David Kravets, Addicted Gamer Sues Game-Maker, Says He Is 'Unable to Function,' *Wired*, August 19, 2010, http://www.wired.com/threatlevel/2010/08/lineage11-addiction/.

4. A subset of this problem is the increased focus on "data mining" among game developers. Because games implicitly generate a lot of data on player behavior that can be logged and sifted, developers are more rigorously spreading this data out on the table in the form of correlations, charts, and tables hoping to learn something from the patterns that emerge. While there is certainly value in exploring such patterns, it is also true that no matter how plentiful this data, it is entirely correlational and thus unreliable in ultimately determining the causal "value components" of the game experience. Like lemons and highway fatalities, the data can lead you down incorrect and potentially costly paths if you are not including theory-driven hypothesis testing as part of the research effort.

5. Cummings, H. M., and Vandewater, E. A. (2007). "Relation of Adolescent Video Game Play to Time Spent in Other Activities." *Archives of Pediatric Adolescent Medicine, 161*(7), 684–689.

6. Ryan, R. M., Huta, V., and Deci, E. L. (2008). "Living Well: A Self-Determination Theory Perspective on Eudaimonia." *Journal of Happiness Studies, 9*, 139–170.

Index

About the Authors

SCOTT RIGBY, PhD, is founder and president of Immersyve, Inc. (http://www
.immersyve.com) and a veteran of both the ivory tower and interactive media
development. After earning his doctorate in clinical psychology with a research
emphasis on motivation, Rigby spent eight years building Internet games and
interactive content for Sony, Time Warner, and Viacom, as well as online games
based on major feature films such as *AI: Artificial Intelligence*, *Red Planet*, and
Frequency before founding Immersyve in 2003. He was the host of several
television shows in the New York region, including *Your Internet Show* and Metro
Channel's *Plugged in with Scott Rigby*. His interactive work can also be seen as
part of the "Explore the Universe" exhibit at the Smithsonian Institution in
Washington, DC.

In addition, Rigby is the principal investigator on several grants awarded
by the National Institutes of Health looking at innovative ways to enhance
learning and deepen motivation for healthy lifestyle change through virtual
environments. He has served on the faculty of the Game Developers Conference, the New York New Media Association, and has been a contributing feature
author on *Gamasutra*. His work on measuring the player experience has been
featured by *Wired*, *Gamepro*, and *Electronic Gaming Monthly*, as well as by *ABC
News* and *Scientific American*.

RICHARD M. RYAN, PhD, is professor of psychology, psychiatry, and education at the University of Rochester and the director of the Clinical Psychology Training Program. He is a widely published researcher and theorist in the
areas of human motivation, development, and psychological well-being, having
published more than 250 articles and chapters and two books. He is the code-
veloper (with Edward L. Deci) of *Self-Determination Theory*, an internationally
researched theory of human motivation that has been applied in hundreds of
studies within areas such as education, work, relationships, medicine, psychotherapy, and cross-cultural psychology. Ryan is also an award-winning educator
and researcher and has given addresses at more than 60 universities around the
world. In addition to his work on virtual environments with Immersyve and
his basic research on the psychology of interactive media, his recent interests

include the effects of materialism and other life goals on well-being and health; mindfulness and self-regulation; sources of vitality and life satisfaction; and cross-cultural studies of motivation and values.

Ryan is a fellow of the American Psychological Association and the American Educational Research Association and an honorary member of the German Psychological Society (DGP). He has been a visiting scientist at the Max Planck Institute for Human Development, a James McKeen Cattell Fellow, and a recipient of numerous national and international grants and awards.